'Dr Wilkie has produced a long overdue challenge to the orthodoxy of relationship therapy. This groundbreaking book offers a new way to look at the complexity of human relationships and provide a roadmap that offers clarity, potential and ultimately transformation for couples facing the challenges of modern living. Having wrestled with couples therapy over the years this work is quite simply a breath of fresh air. I have much pleasure in fully endorsing this endeavour.'

Keith Jones, *DProf, psychotherapist and organisational development consultant*

'Reinvent challenges the conventional same old thinking and provides a powerful alternative that's proven to make a sustainable difference in couples relationships. A must have resource for anyone working in this field.'

Nikki Owen, *author and transformationalist*

'*Reinventing Relationship Therapy through the Duo Coaching Framework* has emerged from doctoral research by the author and rigorously peer reviewed by a doctoral examining panel who commended the thesis and the author's thoughtful research and development of a new concept and practice in relationship coaching. It is an excellent addition to his current and popular publications *Reset* and *Recover*.

Compared to other modalities in the arena of psychological interventions, from counselling to coaching, relationship therapy has been slow to evolve to meet the challenges of contemporary times. There are a number of highlights in Reinvent but three standouts are first, how generous this work is in its attention to inviting a range of practitioners in diverse modalities to expand their practices to collaborate in duo coaching. Second is the link between appropriate interventions which duo coaching offers and the collateral benefits of reparative relationships and their role in social cohesion, health and well being. Third, and very importantly is the practical hope Reinvent extends to coaches and clients with its respectful approach, its optimism and its humanity informed by the author's way of being in the world.'

Kate Maguire, *professor, social anthropologist, trauma psychotherapist, Head of Transdisciplinary Research Programmes, Middlesex University*

Reinventing Relationship Therapy through the Duo Coaching Framework

Reinventing Relationship Therapy through the Duo Coaching Framework introduces a revolutionary approach that replaces outdated single-therapist models with innovative dual-therapist collaboration, transforming how we understand and practice relationship therapy in the modern world.

This book systematically examines four key areas: robust theoretical foundations integrating systems theory, attachment theory, and neuroscience; a critical analysis of conventional therapy limitations, including the restrictive "therapeutic hour" and single-therapist models; the innovative Duo Coaching framework featuring two therapists working collaboratively with couples in extended 3.5-hour sessions across a structured six-session framework; and practical implementation guidance for integrating multiple therapeutic modalities. Wilkie addresses how digital technology and evolving social norms reshape contemporary relationships, demanding new therapeutic responses that bridge individual healing with broader societal wellbeing. This framework demonstrates measurable success in helping couples achieve lasting transformation through innovative session structures, blending of multiple modalities, dual-therapist collaboration, and comprehensive between-session support, providing immediately applicable tools for enhancing therapeutic effectiveness.

This transdisciplinary approach offers relationship therapists, academics, and students an evidence-informed alternative to conventional practice.

Dr. Neil Wilkie, is a relationship therapist, founder of Duo Coaching, and creator of the Relationship Paradigm. Recently he was awarded his doctorate in "The Phenomenology of Relationships." He is a visiting fellow in relationships at Middlesex University.

Reinventing Relationship Therapy Through the Duo Coaching Framework

Neil Wilkie

LONDON AND NEW YORK

Designed cover image: David Malan © Getty Images

First published 2026
by Routledge
4 Park Square, Milton Park, Abingdon, Oxon OX14 4RN

and by Routledge
605 Third Avenue, New York, NY 10158

Routledge is an imprint of the Taylor & Francis Group, an informa business

© 2026 Neil Wilkie

The right of Neil Wilkie to be identified as author of this work has been asserted in accordance with sections 77 and 78 of the Copyright, Designs and Patents Act 1988.

All rights reserved. No part of this book may be reprinted or reproduced or utilised in any form or by any electronic, mechanical, or other means, now known or hereafter invented, including photocopying and recording, or in any information storage or retrieval system, without permission in writing from the publishers.

For Product Safety Concerns and Information please contact our EU representative GPSR@taylorandfrancis.com. Taylor & Francis Verlag GmbH, Kaufingerstraße 24, 80331 München, Germany.

Trademark notice: Product or corporate names may be trademarks or registered trademarks, and are used only for identification and explanation without intent to infringe.

British Library Cataloguing-in-Publication Data
A catalogue record for this book is available from the British Library

ISBN: 978-1-041-20182-3 (hbk)
ISBN: 978-1-041-20181-6 (pbk)
ISBN: 978-1-003-71546-7 (ebk)

DOI: 10.4324/9781003715467

Typeset in Times New Roman
by codeMantra

Contents

Acknowledgements ix
About the Author xi

PART 1
A Landscape of Approaches to Relationship Therapy 1

1 Introduction 3

2 The World of Relationships 15

3 Psychotherapeutic Landscape 23

4 The World of Relationship Therapy 55

5 Transdisciplinarity in the Context of Relationships 63

PART 2
Discovering New Frameworks 75

6 The Creation of Duo Coaching 77

7 A Transformative Space—What Comes into the Room? 90

8 Duo Coaching—A New Framework for Relationship Therapy 112

9 The Relationship Paradigm 124

PART 3
Guidance for Coaches, Counsellors, and
Psychoanalysts on Extending Your Practice 133

10 Guidance for Coaches 135

11 Guidance for Counsellors 144

12 Guidance for Psychoanalysts 157

13 The View from the Co-Therapist's Chair:
    A Practitioner's Perspective 171

PART 4
The Essential Needs We Are Supporting 179

14 The Importance of Relationships 181

15 Conclusions: Charting New Waters 186

Case Studies *192*
Bibliography *204*
Index *211*

Acknowledgements

Writing a book about reinvention is, in itself, an act of vulnerability and transformation. This work exists because of the many remarkable people who have shaped my understanding of life, relationships, and the profound courage it takes to change.

First, I want to acknowledge the wonderful people I've worked with over the years, from whom I've learned about life in countless ways. Through various therapeutic approaches and professional collaborations, these individuals have broadened my perspective and deepened my appreciation for the complexity of human experience.

I am deeply grateful to the amazing transdisciplinary team at Middlesex University and my cohort, who have challenged, supported, and inspired me to look at the intricate world of relationships through fresh eyes. They encouraged me not only to examine the dynamics between people but also to look deep within myself, to explore my own experiences and learn from every facet of my journey.

Thanks go to Cathy; without her partnership and collaboration, Duo Coaching might never have come to fruition. Her insights and shared vision laid the foundation for everything that followed. I'm particularly grateful to Maria, my co-pilot, whose calmness, energy, and profound insights continue to support both me and our clients. Her presence has been invaluable in refining and expanding our work.

I feel immensely privileged to acknowledge the hundreds of clients we have worked with over the years. Their bravery, openness, and vulnerability in sharing their stories have been extraordinary. Being welcomed into the inner sanctums of their lives has been both humbling and inspiring. The work we've done together to transform their worlds has been deeply fulfilling and has taught me as much as I hope I've been able to offer them.

I must also acknowledge the women with whom I've shared serious relationships throughout my life. From each of these connections, I learned valuable lessons—some joyful, others challenging, but all contributing to a much deeper understanding of what relationships truly mean. These experiences, both the triumphs and the struggles, have been essential to my growth and to the insights I share in this book.

To my readers, thank you for opening these pages. I hope the words and ideas within will plant seeds of change in your work and in the lives of those you touch. Your willingness to engage with these concepts gives them life beyond these pages.

Finally, and most importantly, I want to thank my wonderful wife, Gwen. It took 63 years before I found you, and it was worth every minute of that journey because only now do I fully understand what true love really feels like. None of this—the book, the insights, the person I've become—would have been possible without you. *Mo Anam Cara*

Thank you all

About the Author

Neil Wilkie is a pioneering relationship therapist and the founder of Duo Coaching, a revolutionary approach to couple therapy that has transformed hundreds of relationships over 15 years of clinical practice. He holds a doctorate in "The Phenomenology of Relationships." This was rigorously peer reviewed by a doctoral examining panel who commended the thesis and the author's thoughtful research and development of a new concept and practice in relationship therapy.

Dr. Wilkie is the creator of The Relationship Paradigm framework, a comprehensive tool for understanding and assessing relationship health across six essential dimensions. His groundbreaking Duo Coaching methodology challenges traditional therapeutic constraints through extended sessions, co-therapy partnerships, and integrative approaches that consistently achieve transformation where conventional methods fall short.

As an accomplished author, Dr. Wilkie has written "Reset" (2020) and "Recover" (2021), alongside more than 370 published articles that have reached 4.8 million readers in print and generated 2.4 billion online impressions. His expertise has earned media recognition, with newspapers describing him as "the relationship guru."

Dr. Wilkie maintains a strong online presence through The Relationship Paradigm platform, where he continues to share insights and tools for relationship health. He is currently completing the Duo Coaching trilogy with Routledge, further expanding his contribution to relationship therapy literature.

Driven by an ambitious mission to "impact and improve ten million relationships worldwide," Dr. Wilkie combines the depth of psychotherapeutic understanding with the practical effectiveness of outcome-focused therapy. His work represents a fundamental reimagining of what becomes possible when relationship therapy is designed around couples' actual needs rather than professional convenience.

Through his clinical practice, writing, and teaching, Dr. Wilkie continues to challenge the field to move beyond traditional constraints, creating new possibilities for couples seeking not just repair but genuine transformation in their relationships.

Part 1

A Landscape of Approaches to Relationship Therapy

Chapter 1
Introduction

The sailing metaphors that navigate through these pages aren't mere literary decoration—they emerge from lived experience of both literal and metaphorical waters, serving as bridges between conscious understanding and deeper, intuitive knowing. As a young adult, I discovered the intoxicating freedom of setting off westward from familiar shores, the boat responding to wind and current as we headed towards horizons that promised adventure and uncertainty in equal measure.

These nautical metaphors serve multiple purposes throughout this exploration of relationship therapy. At their most practical level, they provide familiar imagery for complex therapeutic concepts—the idea of navigating challenging waters, reading invisible currents, or finding safe harbour resonates immediately with anyone who has faced relationship difficulties. But metaphors operate at deeper levels than mere illustration. They bypass our analytical defences, speaking directly to the pattern-recognition systems that process experience holistically rather than sequentially.

When we describe relationship challenges as "storms to weather" or therapeutic breakthrough as "finding new horizons," we activate embodied understanding that purely clinical language cannot reach. The unconscious mind, which processes information through imagery, emotion, and sensation rather than linear logic, responds to these metaphorical landscapes in ways that facilitate insight and change. A couple struggling with communication might intellectually understand the need for "better listening skills," but they intuitively grasp what it means to "read the wind and adjust their sails together."

Moreover, the sailing metaphor captures essential truths about relationship work that more conventional therapeutic language often misses. Successful navigation requires both individual competence and collaborative coordination. It demands respect for forces beyond your control while taking full responsibility for your responses to changing conditions. It recognises that the journey matters as much as the destination and that the most profound discoveries often happen when you venture beyond familiar coastal waters into deeper, more challenging seas.

Throughout this book, these metaphors serve as both compass and chart—guiding our exploration while honouring the truth that in relationships, as in sailing,

DOI: 10.4324/9781003715467-2

the most rewarding passages require courage, skill, and the wisdom to read conditions that are constantly changing.

Every skilled navigator knows that the most dangerous waters are not the ones marked on the charts but those that appear calm on the surface whilst hiding treacherous currents beneath. In my years of sailing both literal seas and the metaphorical waters of human relationships, I've learned that reaching beautiful harbours often requires abandoning familiar shipping lanes and trusting instruments that conventional wisdom dismisses.

When Love Becomes a Ghost Ship

> Carrie and Keith sat in our therapy room like polite strangers at a dinner party—courteous, composed, and utterly disconnected. After 27 years of marriage, they had perfected the art of efficient coexistence. Their conversations rarely strayed beyond logistics: who would collect the dry cleaning, whether the boiler needed servicing, what time their youngest daughter's university graduation ceremony began.
>
> "We're like flatmates who happen to share a bed," Keith admitted with characteristic understatement, though the pain in his voice suggested depths his measured words couldn't reach.
>
> Carrie, ever precise, added: "We function beautifully. Our children are thriving, our home runs smoothly, our finances are stable. We just don't… connect anymore."
>
> What they didn't say—couldn't yet say—was that three years earlier their physical relationship had vanished entirely. The discovery of Keith using pornography had become the final confirmation of what both had feared: they were no longer lovers, barely friends, just two competent people managing a household with ruthless efficiency.
>
> Four months later, the same couple sat in the same chairs, and everything had changed. They leaned towards each other rather than away. When Keith spoke about rediscovering Carrie's "beautiful mind," she blushed like a teenager. When Carrie described feeling "desired again after thinking that part of my life was over," Keith reached for her hand with unconscious tenderness.
>
> "We talk about everything now," Carrie marvelled. "Things we never discussed in twenty-seven years of marriage. Our needs, our fears, even our sexual desires. I had no idea how lonely I'd been for genuine conversation."
>
> Keith added, "I thought passion was something that belonged to young people. I was wrong. We're more intimate now than we were as newlyweds because now we actually know each other."

The transformation you witnessed with Carrie and Keith wasn't achieved through conventional weekly 50-minute sessions. It emerged through a reimagined approach to relationship therapy:

- Two therapists (male and female) working together, creating natural balance, and preventing the triangulation that often occurs in single-therapist models
- Extended sessions (3.5 hours initially, 2.5 hours subsequently) that allow couples to work through complete emotional cycles rather than being cut off mid-breakthrough
- Finite timeline (typically six sessions over 3–4 months) with clear outcomes, creating momentum rather than open-ended drift
- Integrative approach drawing from 15+ therapeutic modalities, selecting whatever tools best serve each unique couple
- "Me, You, Us" focus addressing individual growth alongside relationship dynamics
- 24/7 support between sessions, helping couples navigate challenges as they emerge rather than dealing with aftermath weeks later

This book is the story of that approach. But more importantly, it's about what becomes possible when we stop accepting that relationship decline is inevitable, that passion has an expiration date, or that "good enough" is actually good enough.

Carrie and Keith's story is not unique. In the pages that follow, you'll meet couples who have navigated back from the brink of divorce, rediscovered intimacy after betrayal, and learned to build relationships stronger than the ones they started with. You'll discover why traditional therapeutic approaches—however well-intentioned—often leave couples drifting in calm but lifeless waters, and how a different framework can help them find their way to harbours they never imagined possible.

The method I'm about to share with you didn't emerge from academic theory or therapeutic tradition. It was born from wreckage—from my own relationship failures and the inadequacy of conventional therapy when I needed it most. It evolved through years of working with hundreds of couples who, like Carrie and Keith, had been told that settling for "functional" was wisdom, that dramatic positive change was unrealistic, and that the best they could hope for was managing their differences more effectively.

They deserved better. So do the couples who will seek your help.

Navigation Overview: Charting Your Course through These Waters

Every skilled navigator studies the charts before setting sail, understanding not just the destination but the waters they'll traverse, the currents they'll encounter, and the safe harbours where they can rest and resupply. This overview provides your navigational chart for the journey ahead—a clear sense of where we're heading and what you'll discover at each waypoint.

Part 1: A Landscape of Approaches to Relationship Therapy (Chapters 2–5)

Navigation Note: These chapters establish the foundation for everything that follows. Even experienced practitioners often find surprising insights in this comprehensive mapping of familiar territory.

Waypoint: Understanding Why Traditional Vessels Struggle

Before designing new approaches, we must understand why existing ones often fall short. These opening chapters provide essential reconnaissance:

Chapter 2: The World of Relationships reveals why relationships matter so profoundly to human flourishing and what contemporary forces—social media, pornography, changing commitment patterns—make them increasingly challenging to navigate.

Chapter 3: Psychotherapeutic Landscape offers a comprehensive survey of the major therapeutic modalities currently used in relationship work. Like examining different types of sailing vessels, you'll discover how each tradition offers valuable capabilities while having inherent constraints when applied to couple dynamics.

Chapter 4: The World of Relationship Therapy moves from theory to practice, examining what options couples actually encounter when seeking help and whether these approaches effectively guide relationships to safer harbours.

Chapter 5: Transdisciplinarity in the Context of Relationships fundamentally shifts how you understand relationship complexity, introducing thinking that recognises relationships as phenomena existing across multiple interconnected dimensions requiring diverse ways of knowing.

Part 2: Discovering New Frameworks (Chapters 6–8)

Navigation Note: These chapters represent the book's practical heart. Even if you implement nothing else, the Relationship Paradigm alone will enhance your effectiveness with couples.

Waypoint: Revolutionary Vessel Design and Navigation Tools

Having surveyed existing approaches, we turn to innovation born from necessity:

Chapter 6: The Creation of Duo Coaching follows my intimate journey from relationship therapy client to innovative practitioner, witnessing how personal frustration with inadequate support sparked revolutionary innovation. This isn't academic theory but lived experience of what didn't work and intuitive design of what might.

Chapter 7: A Transformative Space—What Comes into the Room examines the complex, multidimensional reality couples bring beyond their presenting concerns. The chapter demonstrates how practitioners can work with multiple dimensions simultaneously to create truly transformative therapeutic spaces.

Chapter 8: Duo Coaching—A New Framework for Relationship Therapy provides the concrete methodology that emerges from this foundation—the systematic approach that consistently creates transformation for couples in distress. Like a detailed blueprint for a new type of vessel, you'll discover the specific elements that make this approach uniquely effective.

Chapter 9: The Relationship Paradigm introduces your practical compass—a framework for understanding and assessing relationship health across six essential dimensions: Communication, Connection, Commitment, Fun, Growth, and Trust. This tool serves you throughout the remaining journey.

Part 3: Guidance for Coaches, Counsellors, and Psychoanalysts on Extending Your Practice (Chapters 9–12)

Navigation Note: Focus primarily on the chapter relevant to your background, but don't skip the others entirely. Understanding how different practitioners can adapt their approaches enriches your perspective on integration.

Waypoint: Retrofitting Your Current Craft

Recognising that practitioners sail different types of vessels, these chapters provide specific guidance for enhancing your existing approach:

Chapter 10: Guidance for Coaches addresses those ready to venture beyond traditional performance-focused work into deeper emotional territories, showing how your strengths provide valuable foundations while identifying where expansion is needed.

Chapter 11: Guidance for Counsellors helps you expand beyond single-modality constraints while honouring your therapeutic foundations, demonstrating how integration enhances rather than compromises effectiveness.

Chapter 12: Guidance for Psychoanalysts shows how your sophisticated understanding of unconscious processes can be extended into intersubjective territory, adapting profound capabilities for couple work while addressing traditional limitations.

Chapter 13: The View from the Co-Therapist's Chair: A Practitioner's Perspective provides Maria's firsthand account of transitioning from traditional counselling to the Duo Coaching framework—the irreplaceable perspective of someone who has actually navigated these waters.

Part 4: The Essential Needs We Are Supporting (Chapters 14 and 15)

Navigation Note: These chapters transform individual practice into contribution to larger social change—essential reading for understanding your work's broader significance.

Waypoint: Beyond Individual Voyages

The final section expands perspective beyond individual couple work:

Chapter 14: The Importance of Relationships explores the profound societal implications of relationship health, recognising that individual therapeutic intervention, however effective, cannot address systemic challenges requiring broader transformation.

Chapter 15: Conclusions: Charting New Waters serves as both ending and beginning, celebrating the distance travelled while inspiring continued exploration towards possibilities we're only beginning to imagine.

Safe Harbours: Case Studies

Three Detailed Anchorages for Rest and Reflection

Between the theoretical sailing, three detailed case studies provide safe harbours where you can drop anchor and observe transformation in action:

- **John and Sarah**: From efficient co-managers to passionate lovers
- **Carrie and Keith**: When 27 years of politeness nearly killed love
- **Michael and Olivia**: Rebuilding after devastating betrayal

Navigation Note: These cases illustrate theory in practice. Read them when you need concrete examples of abstract principles.

Essential Navigation Equipment

Throughout your journey, you'll acquire essential tools:

- **Clean Language questioning techniques**
- **The Relationship Paradigm assessment framework**
- **Extended session protocols**
- **Outcome-focused contracting methods**
- **Integration strategies across modalities**
- **Co-therapy principles and practices**

Anticipated Weather Conditions

This journey requires venturing beyond familiar coastal waters into deeper, sometimes choppy seas. Expect:

- **Intellectual challenges** to established assumptions
- **Practical obstacles** in implementation
- **Professional growth opportunities** through expanded capabilities
- **Increased effectiveness** with the couples you serve

Introduction 9

Your Role as Navigator

You're not a passive passenger on this voyage but an active navigator. The frameworks and approaches presented here are not finished products but works in progress, offered in the spirit of ongoing exploration and refinement. Your engagement, questions, adaptations, and innovations will advance the field more than adherence to any prescribed formula.

Destination

Our ultimate destination isn't a fixed point but an expanded horizon of possibilities—for the couples you serve, for your own professional satisfaction, and for the broader transformation of how society approaches relationships. The journey itself is the destination, as each chapter equips you for more effective navigation of relationship challenges.

Bon voyage. The waters ahead hold both challenges and rewards for those willing to venture beyond familiar shores in service of healthier, more fulfilling relationships.

Ready to set sail? Our first waypoint awaits in Chapter 2, where we'll explore why relationships matter so profoundly to human flourishing and what contemporary forces are making these waters increasingly treacherous to navigate.

Welcome Aboard

In the world of relationship therapy, practitioners often find themselves navigating unfamiliar waters with only partial maps. We have been taught to use specific tools and techniques—to approach relationships through particular lenses that limit our vision and, consequently, our effectiveness. I was once such a practitioner, faithfully following the coordinates I had been given, yet increasingly aware that the map did not fully represent the territory I was exploring with my clients.

Before any captain sets sail into uncharted waters, they ensure their navigation instruments are properly calibrated. The frameworks you'll encounter in this book didn't emerge from academic theory but from practical necessity—from repeatedly encountering the same navigational challenges in traditional relationship therapy.

Reinvent emerges from my journey beyond these familiar shores. It introduces two frameworks—not merely as theoretical constructs, but as practical methodologies born from years of clinical work with hundreds of couples. These approaches have evolved through my own relationship experiences, intensive study across multiple disciplines, and a willingness to question established practices when they proved inadequate for the complex challenges my clients faced.

Why the Sea Calls to Those Who Navigate Relationships

My early voyages taught me lessons that would prove invaluable decades later when I began guiding couples through the turbulent waters of relationship distress. I learned that the sea rewards those who respect its power while punishing those who underestimate its complexity. I experienced the profound beauty of perfect sailing conditions—wind and boat and crew working in harmony—alongside the humbling reality of storms that test every skill and piece of equipment you possess.

In calms that stretch for days, I discovered the patience required when progress feels impossible, yet the wind always returns for those who maintain their course. In moments of isolation, miles from any shore, I understood the absolute necessity of having reliable navigation tools and the courage to trust them when visibility disappears.

These youthful experiences with the sea would later find their fullest expression in my doctoral thesis, "The Phenomenology of Relationships," which I presented as an auto-ethnographic journey across the oceans. Just as those early sailing adventures had taught me about navigation, courage, and the delicate balance between preparation and adaptability, my academic exploration revealed how relationships themselves are voyages across uncharted emotional territories.

Through this oceanic lens, I examined how couples set sail together with hopes and dreams, how they weather storms of conflict and betrayal, how they navigate the doldrums of routine and disconnection, and how they might chart courses towards renewal and deeper connection. The thesis revealed that relationships, like sea voyages, require not just love and good intentions but practical skills, reliable instruments, and the wisdom to read changing conditions.

The metaphor proved so powerful that it became the organising principle for both my academic work and my therapeutic practice. Whether navigating treacherous coastal waters or the complex emotional currents between two people who've lost their way to each other, the principles remain remarkably similar: careful preparation, flexible responsiveness, unwavering commitment to reaching safe harbour, and the wisdom to know when to adjust course rather than fight conditions beyond your control.

The metaphor of sailing speaks to anyone who has ever ventured beyond safe, familiar shores—whether in a boat or in love. Both journeys require courage, skill, and the understanding that the most rewarding destinations often lie beyond waters marked on conventional charts.

The Trilogy

This book is the first in the comprehensive Duo Coaching framework trilogy:

1 *"Reinvent: Reinventing Relationship Therapy through the Duo Coaching Framework"* establishes the *"why"*—the theoretical foundation and rationale for the approach
2 *"Reframe: A Practitioner's Guide to the Duo Coaching Framework"* provides the *"how"* and *"what"*—practical implementation and techniques

3 *"Relationships: Demystifying Relationship Therapy, a View from the Therapists' Chair"* demonstrates the *"who"*—real clients experiencing transformation through the framework

The Duo Coaching Framework: A Different Kind of Vessel

The transformation you witnessed with Carrie and Keith wasn't achieved through conventional weekly 50-minute sessions. It emerged through a reimagined approach to relationship therapy:

- **Two therapists** (typically male and female) working together, creating natural balance, and preventing the triangulation that often occurs in single-therapist models
- **Extended sessions** (3.5 hours initially, 2.5 hours subsequently) that allow couples to work through complete emotional cycles rather than being cut off mid-breakthrough
- **Finite timeline** (typically six sessions over 3–4 months) with clear outcomes, creating momentum rather than open-ended drift
- **Integrative approach** drawing from 15+ therapeutic modalities, selecting whatever tools best serve each unique couple
- **"Me, You, Us" focus** addressing individual growth alongside relationship dynamics
- **24/7 support** between sessions, helping couples navigate challenges as they emerge rather than dealing with aftermath weeks later

The Relationship Paradigm: Your Compass for Relationship Health

Figure 1.1 Setting sail: a yacht catches the wind and charts its course across open water, evoking the courage and skill required when couples navigate beyond familiar shores towards new horizons in their relationship.

The second framework provides a practical assessment tool—six essential elements that distinguish thriving relationships from those merely surviving (Figure 1.1):

- **Communication**: Not just exchanging information, but truly being heard and understood
- **Connection**: The daily moments and rituals that maintain emotional and physical intimacy
- **Commitment**: Aligned vision and shared investment in the relationship's future
- **Fun**: The playfulness and joy that creates resilience against life's inevitable stresses
- **Growth**: Continued development both individually and as a partnership
- **Trust**: The foundation that supports all other elements

Why Another Approach to Relationship Therapy Is Needed

The field of relationship therapy has developed significantly since its formal inception, with numerous modalities emerging to address the complexities of human connection. Yet despite this theoretical abundance, relationship distress remains pervasive. I will explore why traditional approaches to relationship therapy often fall short for several reasons:

- The standard "50-minute hour" creates artificial time constraints that compress emotions and limit depth
- Single-therapist models can create perceived imbalances in the therapeutic relationship
- Many approaches lack clear outcome measures and timelines
- Most focus exclusively on the "us" without adequately addressing the "me" and "you" dimensions
- Conventional methods often remain at the conscious, conversational level without addressing deeper patterns

The Duo Coaching framework addresses these limitations directly. This approach utilises two therapists working with a couple in significantly longer sessions, providing balanced energy, clear outcomes, and a finite timeline for change. The framework integrates techniques from across the spectrum of psychotherapeutic modalities, selecting the most appropriate tools for each unique situation.

Your Navigation Advantage

As we explore traditional psychotherapeutic approaches in the coming chapters, you'll have these frameworks as reference points. You'll see not just what each approach offers, but what it typically misses—and how that relates to what couples actually need for transformation.

Rather than dismissing established therapeutic traditions, these frameworks integrate their strengths while addressing their structural limitations. They represent evolution, not revolution—building upon decades of therapeutic wisdom while adapting it for the complex realities of modern relationship challenges.

The stories of clients that you will read here are composites of real couples. This protects their confidentiality whilst telling stories of authentic pain, joy, and reset.

The Need for a Transdisciplinary Lens

In Chapter 5, I discuss how relationships exist across multiple interconnected contexts. Transdisciplinarity—the focus on theoretical unity of knowledge that transcends disciplinary boundaries—provides a crucial framework for understanding the complexity of relationship dynamics.

As Nora Bateson suggests, we need to perceive the "warm data"—the transcontextual information produced through communication forms both direct and indirect. A couple is not merely two individuals interacting in isolation; they are complex systems influenced by their histories, cultures, family patterns, and numerous other factors that conventional approaches often fail to fully address.

The Relationship Paradigm framework, introduced in this book, emerges from this transdisciplinary perspective. It considers six key elements—Communication, Connection, Commitment, Fun, Growth, and Trust—as essential dimensions that must be understood within the full complexity of each couple's unique system.

A Journey through Uncharted Waters

In writing this book, I am reminded of Tim Ingold's concept of wayfaring—the idea that we learn by following paths drawn by others until we develop the intuitive knowledge to chart our own course. The Duo Coaching framework invites practitioners to become skilled wayfarers, "feeling their way" towards solutions rather than rigidly applying predetermined techniques.

For Whom This Book Is Written

Reinvent is for experienced counsellors, coaches, therapists, and clinical educators who recognise both the value and limitations of current approaches to relationship therapy. It speaks to practitioners who:

- Seek a more effective, integrative approach to relationship work
- Are willing to question established paradigms when they prove inadequate
- Want to understand the deeper patterns that shape relationship dynamics
- Aim to create transformative change rather than incremental improvements

For masters-level students and academics, this book provides both theoretical innovation and practical applications, bridging theory and clinical practice with case studies and empirical observations.

The Invitation

My intention is not to present these frameworks as definitive solutions but as valuable additions to your professional repertoire—approaches that have transformed my own practice and the relational lives of countless clients.

The invitation of *Reinvent* is to expand rather than replace, to integrate rather than discard, and ultimately to engage in a collaborative evolution of how we conceptualise and facilitate relationship therapy. The pages that follow offer not only new methodologies but a renewed vision of what's possible when we truly reframe both our therapeutic approach and the relationship possibilities available to our clients.

Welcome to the voyage (Figure 1.2).

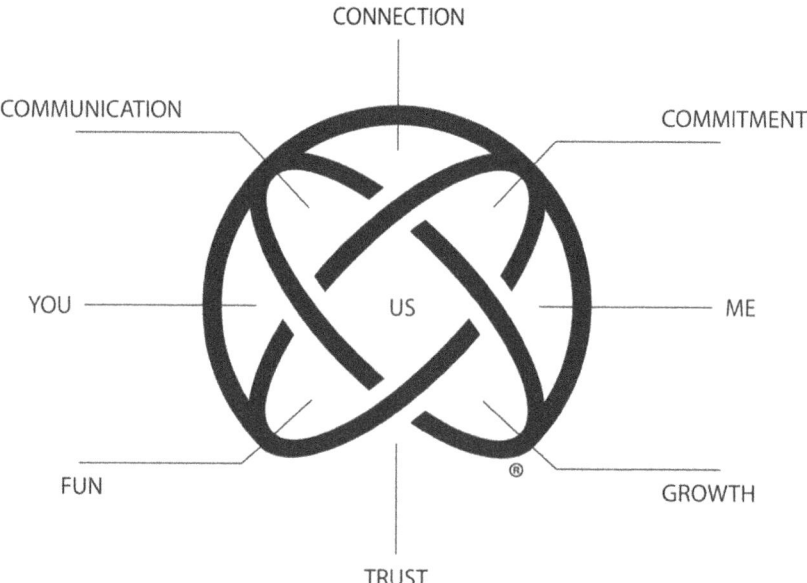

Figure 1.2 The gathering wave: powerful currents converge and crest, reflecting the forces—both visible and hidden—that shape every relationship and the transformative energy released when couples dare to engage with them.

Chapter 2
The World of Relationships

Figure 2.1 Cupid's arrows trace the undulating path of love: hearts emerge along the journey, reminding us that connection is not a straight line but a voyage of discovery through calm and turbulence alike.

Like wise captains studying waters before setting sail, readers must first understand why relationships matter profoundly to individual wellbeing and what contemporary forces—social media distraction, pornography availability, online dating patterns, and evolving commitment definitions—make them increasingly challenging to navigate (Figure 2.1).

This foundational chapter examines relationships' essential role in child development and personal fulfilment, revealing what makes partnerships work or fail at the personal level. Understanding these dynamics as responses to genuine contemporary pressures rather than personal failures provides crucial context for the therapeutic approaches that follow, preparing readers to guide others through relationship storms towards safer harbours.

Why Do We Have Relationships?

We exist in relationship with everything we encounter—not just people, but places, ideas, memories, and experiences. Some of these relationships operate at a conscious level, where we're aware of our connections and responses. Others function unconsciously, shaping our reactions and choices in ways we don't fully recognise. These relationships—both seen and unseen—fuel, strengthen, and sometimes weaken our daily experience. Most significantly, every person we encounter creates some form of relationship with us, however brief or seemingly insignificant. There is no such thing as "no relationship"—only relationships we're conscious of and those operating below our awareness.

Why Do We Need Relationships?

Humans are social creatures, and relationships are essential for our wellbeing in a number of ways (Kansky & Diener, 2017; Pietromonaco & Collins, 2017):

- Strong relationships provide a sense of belonging and acceptance. They can help us feel less alone and give us a support system to lean on during difficult times.
- Studies have shown that healthy relationships can boost our physical and mental health (Huntington et al., 2022). Social connection can lower stress hormones, improve our mood, and even help us live longer.
- Sharing our lives with others can bring great joy and happiness. Relationships can provide us with companionship, shared experiences, and a sense of purpose.
- Healthy relationships can challenge us to grow and become better people. Through our interactions with others, we can learn new things, develop new skills, and gain different perspectives.

Overall, relationships are essential for a happy and fulfilling life. They provide us with love, support, and a sense of connection that is necessary for us to thrive.

What Is a Normal Relationship?

Western society's definition of "normal" for couple relationships is broad and constantly evolving. Rather than a single template, healthy relationships tend to share certain essential qualities:

- **Communication**: Partners can express thoughts, feelings and needs and feel heard and understood
- **Connection**: There are regular moments where partners are fully present and emotionally available to each other
- **Commitment**: Both partners are clear about what they want from the relationship and from each other, investing time and energy accordingly
- **Fun**: Playfulness and joy are fundamental to keeping a relationship alive and vibrant

- **Growth**: Relationships cannot remain static. Thriving partnerships require two fulfilled individuals creating a fulfilled "us"
- **Trust**: This forms the foundation. When trust erodes, the entire relationship begins to weaken

The context and structure of relationships can vary considerably:

- **Living Situation**: Sharing a home is common but not required. Some couples cohabitate, live separately, or practice alternative arrangements
- **Monogamy**: While monogamy remains the prevalent norm in Western societies, polyamorous individuals who practice consensual non-monogamy increasingly challenge this assumption, though they may still face prejudice and marginalisation (Sandbakken et al., 2022)
- **Family Structure**: Nuclear families with children are common, but same-sex couples, blended families, and child-free couples are increasingly recognised and accepted

The key is that the relationship is healthy, supportive, and fulfilling for both partners, regardless of the specific structure.

Religion and Relationships

Many religious faiths believe that a committed couple relationship is fundamentally important (David & Stafford, 2015; Wolfinger & Wilcox, 2008). Religions often emphasise commitment, fidelity, and shared values. A strong couple can be seen as embodying these ideals and providing a stable foundation for raising children within the faith (D'Antonio, 1980). These elements include:

Reflection of the Divine: Many religions view marriage as a sacred union mirroring a divine relationship. In Christianity, for instance, marriage reflects the union of Christ and the Church.

Stronger Moral Framework: Religions often emphasise commitment, fidelity, and shared values. A strong couple can be seen as embodying these ideals and providing a stable foundation for raising children within the faith.

Community and Support: Religious communities often centre around families. Couples provide a foundation for these communities and can rely on the support system for guidance and encouragement in their relationship.

Research indicates that couples with shared religious beliefs are more likely to have a strong relationship (Olson et al., 2015; Skellern et al., 2022). They are part of a supportive community that places high importance on strong sustained relationships, and they are likely to have shared values (Mahoney, 2010).

Contemporary Challenges to Relationships

Impact of Pornography

Pornography is now widely available for immediate consumption. The impact of pornography on relationships can be complex, but research suggests it can have negative consequences (Manning, 2006; Newstrom & Harris, 2016):

- **Unrealistic expectations**: Porn often portrays sex that is far more physically demanding and exciting than real-life relationships. This can lead to dissatisfaction with your partner's sexual performance or your own body image
- **Communication and trust issues**: Porn use can be secretive, creating a wedge between partners. A partner who discovers porn use might feel betrayed or rejected
- **Addiction**: Compulsive porn use can become an addiction, taking time and energy away from the relationship
- **Altered views of intimacy**: Porn can focus on physical aspects of sex rather than emotional connection, potentially hindering intimacy in real life

However, some research suggests the effects may be more nuanced, with perceived rather than actual effects being more significant (Kohut et al., 2017).

Impact of Social Media

My experience with clients is that social media and electronic devices have had a growing and negative impact on relationships (Farrugia, 2013; Yacoub et al., 2018):

- It makes it much easier to start a relationship via dating apps
- Relationships can be much more transitory as swiping left is easy, and there are many more fish in the sea
- They fuel and expose affairs. They are normally the way a partner discovers betrayals through emails or text messages
- They are a diversion from connection as many couples spend evenings together connected in a virtual world rather than with their partners (Procentese et al., 2019)
- They intrude into life in the bedroom and are a passion killer

Used wisely they are a wonderful way of staying in touch with friends and family, especially those far away. Research shows that this can become a source of dissonance in a relationship (Hand et al., 2013; Joo & Teng, 2017).

The Relevance of Sex

Sex can be an important part of a couple relationship. The level of importance will vary by the individuals, context, and time. My experience is this is a frequent source of unresolved frustration, mismatching, assumptions, and dissonance. Couples often find it difficult and embarrassing to talk openly about their sexual desires and what they would like their partner to do (Anderson et al., 2011; Montemurro et al., 2015). Resentment tends to build up until breaking point is reached.

The benefits of sex in a relationship include creating intimacy and closeness between partners, serving as a way to express love and care, boosting self-esteem and confidence, helping reduce stress and anxiety, and taking the couple to a different emotional and psychological space (Metz & McCarthy, 2007; Yoo et al., 2014).

How Do People Find Their Partners?

In Western society, finding a partner used to depend on luck, who you bumped into at work or a social occasion. Internet dating and social media have opened the door to an almost infinite choice (Ali & Wibowo, 2011). Research shows that this can also change the quality and "stickiness" of relationships. With so much choice it is easy to avoid relationship problems by swiping left and finding a nice, new, shiny relationship.

As a counterpoint, online dating offers a wonderful opportunity to meet the right person to create a long-term, loving, and fulfilling relationship when embraced with honesty, authenticity, and a clear purpose (Beasley & Holmes, 2021).

What Is the Life Cycle of Relationships?

Marriage and Cohabitation Trends over Time

Declining Marriage, Rising Cohabitation: Both the US and UK show similar patterns of declining marriage rates and increasing cohabitation. In the US, marriage rates fell from 58% in 1995 to 53% today, while cohabitation rose from 3% to 7% (Pew Research Center, 2019). The UK shows more dramatic change, with married/civil partnered adults dropping from 58.4% in 1991 to 46.9% in 2021, while never-married adults rose from 26.3% to 37.9% (ONS, 2023b). UK cohabiting couples increased by 144% from 1.5 million in 1996 to 3.6 million in 2021 (House of Commons Library, 2024).

Cohabitation as the New Norm: Pre-marital cohabitation has become standard practice—70% of US couples (Lamidi et al., 2019) and over 90% of UK couples now live together before marriage (ONS, 2024b). However, relationship duration patterns differ significantly: US cohabiting relationships average 12–18 months (Lamidi et al., 2019), while UK first cohabitations average 46 months (ONS, 2013). Most US cohabiting relationships either end or transition to marriage within 3–5 years, whereas UK couples increasingly remain in long-term cohabitation rather than marrying. Both countries maintain similar divorce rates of approximately 42%, with marriages lasting an average of 12–13 years before divorce (ONS, 2024a), though most marriages end with death rather than divorce.

Relationship Satisfaction and Wellbeing

Marriage Advantage Varies by Context: US research consistently shows married individuals report higher relationship satisfaction, stability, and commitment than cohabiting couples—with married adults 12 percentage points more likely to report high satisfaction, and 26 percentage points more likely to report high stability (Wilcox et al., 2019). However, UK research reveals a more nuanced picture: while cohabiting individuals report lower relationship happiness than married couples, these differences largely disappear when relationship quality and satisfaction are taken into account (Perelli-Harris et al., 2019).

Quality Trumps Status: The most significant finding across both countries is that relationship satisfaction matters more than legal status. High-quality cohabiting relationships can be as fulfilling as marriages, while low-quality marriages offer little advantage over cohabitation. Marriage benefits appear stronger for women than men in both countries (Perelli-Harris et al., 2019), and the "marriage premium" in happiness is most pronounced among individuals with lower propensity to marry. This suggests that for couples with strong, committed relationships, the legal distinction between marriage and cohabitation may be less important for wellbeing than previously thought.

Knapp's model of a relationship shows ten stages moving from Coming Together (Initiating, Experimenting, Intensifying, Integrating, Bonding) to Coming Apart (Differentiating, Circumscribing, Stagnating, Avoiding, Terminating) (Knapp & Vangelisti, 2005).

The stagnating phase is almost inevitable and gives an opportunity for the relationship to be reviewed and reset. Growth could then follow.

Why Do So Many Relationships Fail?

Failure of a relationship comes at a huge emotional and often financial cost. My experience with clients is that relationships fail for the following reasons:

- The couple had no real understanding of how to have a great relationship. They weren't taught and didn't have a good model from their parents
- They had unrealistic expectations—this is becoming an increasing problem with idealised online portrayals
- They expected the magical period of love to transport them through the rest of their lives
- Reality mismatched with expectations
- Communication became superficial and focused on blaming
- Sexual desires and feedback were not expressed, so frustration grew
- Connection diminished as work, life, and being busy took priority
- Focus on bringing up children to the detriment of the couple's relationship
- One felt that the other was not as committed to the relationship
- Fun faded away
- Growth of the relationship stalled and it withered
- Distrust crept in, often because their partner was behaving unusually

I believe that the failure rate of relationships could be radically reduced if there was education in secondary school and beyond on how to start a great relationship, grow it and deal with dissonance, understanding of the benefits of therapy, and better-quality provision of relationship therapy.

Symmathesy

Nora Bateson used the word Symmathesy to describe living systems which emerge from communications and interactions (Bateson, 2023b). This highlights the expression and communication of interdependency and particularly mutual learning.

The roots are the Greek words Sym, together, and Mathesi, to learn, to create. Symmathesy is learning together. She goes on to describe that:

> Symmathesy operates across diverse domains; it is the concept of a human relationship, which is a social system operating at multiple scales.

In intimate relationships, Symmathesy operates through mutual learning and adaptation between individuals. Each person's thoughts, emotions, and behaviours are influenced by their interactions with the other, leading to the emergence of shared experiences, norms, and patterns of communication. These micro-level interactions shape the dynamics of the relationship and contribute to its evolution.

In family systems, Symmathesy extends beyond individual relationships to encompass the interactions between family members and the emergent patterns that arise from these interactions. Family systems theory highlights how family dynamics are shaped by complex patterns of communication, power dynamics, and intergenerational influences. Symmathesy in the context of family systems emphasises the co-evolution of family members as they navigate shared experiences, roles, and responsibilities.

In community and society, Symmathesy operates within larger social systems. Here, the interactions between individuals and groups give rise to emergent social structures, cultural norms, and collective identities. These macro-level patterns influence and are influenced by the micro-level interactions between individuals and smaller social units. Symmathesy within social systems underscores the interconnectedness of individuals and the reciprocal nature of social influence, where collective learning and adaptation occur through the ongoing exchange of ideas, values, and behaviours.

We need to be aware that relationships operate in multiple contexts simultaneously, with conflicting perspectives, and are ever shifting. As humans needing a level of security, what can we do to anchor our needs while being responsive to those of others?

What Is Love?

It is hard to talk about a couple relationship without the word love appearing. I am only going to touch on this here as it deserves the space of a whole book. In summary, love is possibly the most important thing in the world and the most difficult to understand.

I believe that:

- We are looking for the answer in the stars when the real answer lies deep within
- Love is a journey; it is not a destination
- In any relationship there is no reality; there is only perception
- Love is a fundamental part of relationships, so with love there is no reality; there is only perception, and those perceptions shift over time and context
- Every single artist, every singer, every playwright, every actor, every author, and every poet may have found the answer for themselves but not for us. We can only use others' expressed experiences as a starting point for our own exploration
- There is no universal answer to this life-changing question. What is love to one person is very different from what is love to another. What is love to one person will vary significantly from context to context, and even in the same context will vary from time to time

The Future of Relationships

The purpose of my work is to significantly improve the future of relationships. I want to equip couples to become the experts in their own relationships.

Understanding these individual-level challenges provides crucial context for the therapeutic approaches explored in subsequent chapters. Yet addressing relationship distress at scale requires looking beyond any single couple to the broader systems that shape relationship possibilities—a perspective we'll explore in our concluding chapter (Figure 2.2).

Understanding why relationships matter and the challenges they face is essential, but it raises an urgent question: what tools do we currently have to help couples navigate these increasingly complex waters? The therapeutic world has developed numerous approaches over the past century, each promising to guide relationships to safer harbours. But do these traditional vessels actually serve the couples who board them?

Figure 2.2 Intertwined hearts carried on crossed arrows: the complexity of human attachment, where individual desires must find alignment and where love's trajectory depends on the direction both partners choose together.

Chapter 3
Psychotherapeutic Landscape

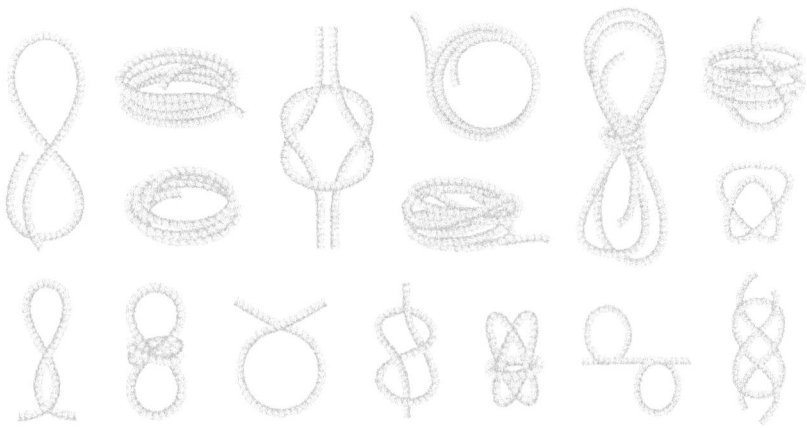

Figure 3.1 A collection of nautical knots: each configuration represents a different therapeutic modality—distinct in structure, purpose, and strength—reflecting the diverse approaches practitioners use to hold relationships secure.

The maritime world offers many types of vessels—from nimble dinghies to mighty galleons—each designed for specific conditions and purposes. Similarly, the therapeutic world has developed numerous approaches, each with distinct advantages and limitations. But what happens when the vessel, however well-built, simply isn't designed for the particular waters you need to navigate? (Figure 3.1)

The Vessels Currently Sailing These Waters

There are many different approaches used in psychotherapy. Most therapists are strong adherents to the one modality that they were trained in and use this in all their client interactions.

There are well over fifty different types of psychotherapy, and the number is growing as people continue to develop new approaches. It is an unregulated world where the quality of therapists can vary enormously. The efficacy of an approach is subjective to each client, each context, and each temporality so is difficult to compare.

I summarise here the two main progenitors of psychotherapy and discuss the approaches most often used in relationship work.

Before exploring contemporary approaches, it's worth acknowledging the foundational figures whose work still influences relationship therapy today.

The Historical Foundation

Sigmund Freud (1856–1939) was an Austrian neurologist and the founder of psychoanalysis.

In founding psychoanalysis, Freud developed therapeutic techniques such as the use of free association and discovered transference, establishing its central role in the analytic process. He formulated the Oedipus complex as the central tenet of psychoanalytical theory. His analysis of dreams as wish fulfilments provided models for the clinical analysis of symptom formation and the underlying mechanisms of repression.

Freud elaborated his theory of the unconscious and went on to develop a model of psychic structure comprising id, ego, and superego. He defined libido as sexualised energy with which mental processes and structures are invested and which generates erotic attachments and a death drive, the source of compulsive repetition, hate, aggression, and neurotic guilt (Freud, 2012).

Arguably, Freud was the father of psychotherapy, providing the conceptual foundation upon which all subsequent modalities have built. This historical context helps us understand why most therapeutic approaches focus heavily on individual psychology, even when applied to couple relationships—a limitation that becomes apparent when we examine each modality's application to relationship work.

Carl Gustav Jung (1875–1961) was a Swiss psychiatrist and psychoanalyst. He became friends with Freud and created a joint vision of human psychology. His thinking started to divert from that of Freud particularly on the nature of libido. Their differences widened and they last met in 1913.

He expanded psychoanalytic thinking by developing concepts like individuation, the collective unconscious, and psychological types. Jung's work on introversion and extraversion directly influences modern assessment tools such as Myers-Briggs, DISC, and Insights Discovery that many relationship therapists use today (Jung, 1921, 1953–1979).

While psychoanalysis as a technique is now in decline with ongoing debate about its efficacy, Freud's core insight—that unconscious patterns from early relationships influence adult partnerships—remains fundamental to most approaches to relationship therapy.

Person-Centred Counselling—Beautiful Empathy, Missing Lifeboat

Carl Rogers revolutionised therapy in the 1940s with a radical idea: people have everything they need to heal within themselves. His person-centred approach offered three gifts that couples desperately need—empathy, authenticity, and unconditional positive regard (Rogers, 1951, 1961).

The Promise

Imagine walking into a therapy room where you're met with complete acceptance. No judgement about your relationship failures, no criticism of your choices, just deep listening and genuine care. For individuals carrying shame about their relationship struggles, this can feel like coming home.

Rogers believed that "the curious paradox is that when I accept myself just as I am, then I change." In this non-directive approach, clients lead the conversation while therapists provide a safe container for self-discovery.

The Reality with Couples

Here's what this can look like in practice:

> *Session 8: Mark and Janet sit across from their person-centred counsellor, both emotionally raw from another week of silent meals and separate bedrooms. Mark shares his frustration; the counsellor reflects it beautifully. Janet expresses her loneliness; the counsellor mirrors her pain with perfect empathy. They leave feeling heard and understood.*
>
> *Session 20: Mark and Janet still sit across from the same counsellor. They understand their feelings more clearly now, can articulate their pain more eloquently—but they're still eating in silence and sleeping apart.*

The Gap: When Understanding Isn't Enough

Person-centred therapy excels at helping people feel seen and validated. But couples drowning in destructive patterns need more than a witness to their pain—they need someone to throw them a lifeline.

The approach's strength—its refusal to be directive—becomes its limitation with couples. When two people are locked in toxic cycles that they can't see clearly, non-directive listening can inadvertently enable those cycles to continue.

The Bottom Line

Rogers' gifts of empathy and acceptance form the essential foundation for all relationship work. But couples need both the safety of unconditional regard *and* the guidance to navigate towards healthier shores.

Enhancing Person-Centred Practice for Relationship Work

Your empathic foundation provides the essential safety couples need for vulnerable work. To enhance your effectiveness:

- **Add gentle structure** while maintaining your non-directive core—create containers for difficult conversations without controlling their content

26 Reinventing Relationship Therapy

- **Develop pattern interruption skills** to prevent harmful cycles from reinforcing during sessions
- **Practice outcome clarification** helping couples articulate specific hopes without imposing your agenda
- **Learn to balance individual and systemic awareness** extending your empathy to include the relationship as an entity needing understanding
- **Experiment with experiential exercises** that allow couples to feel different ways of connecting, not just talk about them

Psychodynamic Therapy: Deep-Sea Exploration in Individual Submarines

Psychodynamic therapists are the deep-sea explorers of the therapeutic world. Where others skim the surface of conscious thoughts and behaviours, they dive into the profound depths of the unconscious mind, armed with Freud's original charts and a century of refined navigation techniques.

The Treasure They Uncover

Psychodynamic work reveals the hidden cargo that every person carries from their past—the unconscious patterns forged in childhood that still steer their adult relationships. Through techniques like dream analysis, free association, and careful interpretation, these therapeutic archaeologists help clients understand why they keep running aground on the same emotional reefs.

A Session in the Depths

> *Emma sits across from her psychodynamic therapist, exploring why she feels "suffocated" whenever her partner David becomes affectionate. Through careful exploration, they uncover how her critical, controlling mother created an unconscious equation: love equals loss of autonomy. This insight transforms Emma's understanding of her relationship patterns.*

The Gift: X-Ray Vision for Relationships

Psychodynamic therapists bring profound insights to relationship work:

- They see how partners unconsciously recreate familiar childhood dynamics
- They recognise when someone is relating to their "internal parent" rather than their actual partner
- They understand that defensive patterns often protect against vulnerabilities too painful to face directly
- They appreciate that lasting change requires understanding the emotional logic behind "irrational" behaviours

The Navigation Challenge: Individual Submarines Can't Dock Together

Here's where traditional psychodynamic work hits the relationship reef: it was designed for solo voyages. The classic analytic setup—one therapist, one client, careful attention to transference—creates an intensive individual journey that doesn't easily accommodate a travelling companion.

What This Looks Like in Practice

- Emma gains profound insight about her fear of engulfment, but David isn't part of the discovery process
- When Emma tries to share her insights, David feels analysed rather than understood
- The deep work happens in isolation from the relationship system it's meant to heal
- Progress can feel frustratingly slow for couples in crisis who need immediate course corrections

The Evolution: Bringing Deep-Sea Discoveries to the Surface

Innovative approaches have emerged that preserve psychodynamic wisdom while adapting it for couple work:

Emotionally focused therapy uses attachment theory (psychodynamic offspring) to help couples understand their emotional cycles and create corrective experiences together.

Psychodynamic couple therapy brings unconscious patterns into the shared therapeutic space where both partners can witness and understand them.

Object relations approaches help couples see how their early relationship templates affect their current partnership

The Bottom Line

Psychodynamic insights are like precious pearls from the ocean depths—incredibly valuable but needing to be brought to the surface where couples can examine them together in the light. The depth remains essential; the challenge is making those discoveries accessible to the relationship system that needs healing.

Enhancing Psychodynamic Practice for Relationship Work

Your depth insight into unconscious patterns is invaluable. To extend your effectiveness:

- **Include both partners in insight work** helping each understand their contribution to co-created patterns
- **Balance historical exploration with present-moment intervention** using your understanding of origins to inform immediate change strategies

- **Develop communication coaching skills** translating unconscious awareness into conscious interaction abilities
- **Practice systems thinking** seeing how individual dynamics create relationship-level phenomena
- **Create time-limited frameworks** maintaining depth while providing clearer therapeutic direction

Classical Psychoanalysis: The Deep-Sea Archaeological Expedition

Classical psychoanalysts are the archaeological deep-sea divers of therapy—equipped with sophisticated tools for excavating the buried treasures and sunken vessels of the unconscious mind. Where others might skim across surface waters, analysts descend to profound depths, following ancient currents that still shape the emotional geography of adult relationships.

The Foundational Discovery

Freud's revolutionary insight—that unconscious forces from childhood continue to steer adult relationships—remains one of the most profound discoveries in understanding human connection. Classical analysis, with its careful attention to free association, dreams, slips of the tongue, and the intricate dance of transference and countertransference, provides unparalleled access to these hidden depths.

The Archaeological Treasure

A Session in Action

> *Individual analysis with Robert reveals a recurring dream about being trapped in a small room with his demanding mother. Through careful exploration of associations, Robert discovers how this early claustrophobic experience creates his pattern of emotional withdrawal whenever his wife Sarah expresses needs. The insight is profound—but Sarah isn't present to witness this discovery or understand its implications for their relationship.*

What Classical Analysts Excel At

- **Unconscious pattern recognition**: Seeing how early object relations create templates for adult partnership
- **Transference analysis**: Understanding how partners unconsciously relate to each other as early significant figures
- **Dream work**: Accessing symbolic material that reveals unconscious relationship dynamics

- **Free association**: Allowing unconscious material to emerge without conscious censorship
- **Long-term depth work**: Patient exploration that reveals layers of meaning over time
- **Neutrality and containment**: Providing a consistent, boundaried space for unconscious exploration

The Archaeological Method

Classical analysis offers extraordinary depth—like having access to geological surveys that reveal how current landscape was shaped by ancient forces. The patient, careful excavation of unconscious material can illuminate relationship patterns that seem mysterious or irrational from the surface.

The Excavation Challenge: Individual Submarines in Relationship Waters

Here's where classical analysis encounters its greatest limitation for relationship work: it was designed for solo expeditions into individual unconscious depths, not for navigating the shared waters where relationships actually exist.

What This Looks Like in Practice

- Robert gains profound insight about his withdrawal patterns during individual sessions
- Sarah experiences his continued withdrawal at home without understanding its unconscious roots
- The analysis reveals Robert's internal dynamics but doesn't address the interactive patterns between them
- Sarah may begin to feel excluded from Robert's therapeutic process, potentially increasing relationship tension
- Progress happens in individual sessions but doesn't necessarily translate to relationship change

The Structural Limitations

- **Individual focus**: Cannot accommodate the systemic nature of relationship dynamics
- **The analytic frame**: Couch, individual sessions, and neutrality don't suit couple work
- **Pace and timing**: Relationships in crisis often need more immediate intervention than classical analysis provides
- **Practical skills**: Deep insight doesn't automatically create communication abilities or conflict resolution skills
- **Partner exclusion**: The non-analysed partner may feel mystified or threatened by the process

Classical Analysis in a Relationship Context

While extraordinary for individual depth work, classical analysis faces inherent challenges when applied to couple relationships:

- Robert's insights about his mother's influence are profound but remain isolated from his actual relationship with Sarah
- The analytic process may inadvertently increase distance between partners if only one is engaged
- Unconscious understanding doesn't automatically translate to conscious relationship skills
- The lengthy timeframe may not suit couples needing more immediate relationship repair

The Bottom Line

Classical psychoanalysis provides unmatched depth for understanding the unconscious forces that shape relationship patterns. Your ability to perceive and interpret unconscious material offers insights unavailable through other approaches. When integrated with more immediate, practical, and systemically aware interventions, psychoanalytic understanding becomes the foundation for profound and lasting relationship transformation.

Your archaeological skills are invaluable—when brought to the surface where couples can use them to navigate their shared waters more consciously and skilfully.

Enhancing Classical Analytic Practice for Relationship Work

Your archaeological skills reveal profound unconscious currents. To adapt for couples:

- **Modify the analytic frame** working with both partners present while maintaining your depth orientation
- **Translate unconscious insights into relationship language** helping couples understand how internal dynamics affect their connection
- **Balance neutrality with strategic intervention** maintaining analytic stance while actively supporting the relationship system
- **Integrate practical skill-building** ensuring unconscious awareness translates into conscious relationship capabilities
- **Develop shorter-term intensive approaches** preserving analytic depth within more relationship-appropriate timeframes

Systemic Counselling: Reading the Currents between People

Systemic therapists are the marine biologists of relationship therapy. Rather than studying individual fish, they observe the entire ecosystem—how creatures interact, what patterns emerge when they're together, and what happens when you change one element of the living system.

The Revolutionary Insight

Born from family therapy in the 1950s, systemic thinking made a radical discovery: the problem isn't usually *in* any individual person—it's *between* people, in the invisible currents that flow when they interact. A couple isn't just two separate individuals who happen to live together; they're a dynamic system that creates its own weather patterns.

The Power: Seeing the Dance, Not Just the Dancers

A Session in Action

> *Tom complains that Lisa "never listens." Lisa insists she does listen, but Tom "never shares anything important." The systemic therapist sees something different: whenever Tom starts to share something vulnerable, Lisa immediately offers solutions. This makes Tom feel unheard, so he withdraws. Lisa, seeing his withdrawal, tries harder to help by offering more solutions. The more she helps, the more he retreats. The more he retreats, the harder she tries to help.*
>
> *Instead of asking why Tom won't share or why Lisa can't just listen, the systemic therapist focuses on interrupting this circular dance.*

What Systemic Practitioners Excel At

- **Pattern recognition**: They spot recurring cycles that couples can't see from inside the dance
- **Practical focus**: Less interested in why problems started, more focused on how to change them now
- **Systems thinking**: They understand that changing one person's moves changes the entire dance
- **Present-moment clarity**: Problems are maintained by current interactions, not just past wounds

The Strength: No Archaeological Digs Required

Unlike approaches that require extensive exploration of childhood or unconscious motivations, systemic therapy gets straight to work. It's like having a skilled sailing instructor who says, "Never mind how you learned to sail badly—let's adjust your technique right now so you stop capsizing."

The Limitation: Sometimes the Deeper Currents Matter

While systemic therapy excels at changing patterns, it can sometimes miss the underlying emotional currents that created those patterns in the first place.

In Practice This Looks Like

- Tom and Lisa successfully interrupt their cycle and develop better communication patterns
- But Tom's deep fear of criticism (rooted in a critical father) and Lisa's anxiety about being needed (from caring for a depressed mother) remain unaddressed
- Six months later, different triggers activate the same underlying dynamics, just with new surface patterns

The Missing Piece: Individual Depth Work

The most effective systemic work often benefits from understanding not just *what* patterns exist, but *why* each person is drawn to their particular role in the dance. Sometimes you need to understand what's happening below the waterline as well as on the surface.

The Bottom Line

Systemic thinking is essential for relationship work—you absolutely must see the dance between partners, not just focus on individual dancers. But the most transformative work often combines your systems perspective with deeper exploration of what draws each person to play their particular role in the relationship choreography.

Your skill at seeing patterns that couples miss is invaluable. When enhanced with tools to address the emotional undercurrents that maintain those patterns, systemic approaches become extraordinarily powerful for lasting relationship change.

Enhancing Systemic Practice for Relationship Work

Your pattern recognition provides crucial relationship intelligence. To deepen your impact:

- **Add individual depth work** understanding why people are drawn to particular roles in relationship dances
- **Include historical context** exploring how current patterns developed while maintaining your systems focus
- **Develop emotional processing skills** helping partners express vulnerable feelings, not just change behaviours
- **Practice outcome-focused work** using your systems awareness to create specific, measurable relationship goals
- **Integrate attachment understanding** connecting systems patterns to underlying emotional needs and fears

Transactional Analysis: The Relationship Weather Station

In the 1950s, psychiatrist Eric Berne made a brilliant observation that revolutionised how we understand relationship conflicts. He noticed that adults don't just have one consistent personality—they shift between different "ego states," depending on the situation, like actors playing different roles in the same relationship drama (Berne, 1964).

The Three Players in Every Conversation

Berne identified three distinct ego states that live within each person:
   The parent: The voice of authority, rules, and "shoulds"—often echoing actual parents or authority figures
   The adult: The rational, present-moment problem-solver who deals with facts and reality
   The child: The emotional, spontaneous part that holds feelings, creativity, and vulnerability

The Revelation: It's Not What You Say, It's Who's Talking

A TA Session in Action

> Sarah snaps at her partner Mike: "You never help with the dishes!" (Critical Parent) Mike responds defensively: "I'm really busy with work right now!" (Adapted Child) This triggers Sarah's Parent even more: "That's just an excuse!" (Critical Parent) Mike retreats: "Fine, I can't do anything right." (Sulky Child)
>
> The TA therapist points out, "Notice that two adults just had a Parent-Child argument. What would happen if your Adult spoke to Mike's Adult instead?"
>
> Sarah tries again: "I'm feeling overwhelmed with household tasks. Could we figure out a system that works for both of us?" (Adult to Adult)

The Magic: Instant Relationship X-Ray Vision

TA gives couples immediate insight into their relationship dynamics:

- **Parent-child transactions** create power struggles and resentment
- **Child-child transactions** can be playful but lack problem-solving ability
- **Adult-adult transactions** create equality and effective communication
- **Crossed transactions** (when ego states don't match) cause immediate conflict

"Games" That Couples Play

Berne identified recurring patterns he called "games"—predictable sequences where couples unconsciously recreate familiar dynamics:

- **"Why Don't You... Yes But"**: One partner asks for help, then rejects every suggestion
- **"If It Weren't For You"**: Blaming the partner for everything that's wrong in life
- **"Kick Me"**: Behaving in ways that invite criticism, then feeling victimised

The Strength: Immediate Pattern Recognition

TA provides couples with:

- **Clear language** for understanding relationship roles
- **Instant awareness** of when they're slipping into problematic dynamics
- **Practical tools** for shifting from conflict-generating to problem-solving conversations
- **Insight into** why certain topics always escalate into the same arguments

The Navigation Challenge: Individual Compass, Shared Journey

While TA brilliantly illuminates relationship dynamics, it has some limitations for comprehensive couple work:

What it reveals: *Mark realises he often speaks to his wife Emma from his Critical Parent, just like his father did. Emma recognises she responds from her Adapted Child, just like she did with her controlling mother.*

What It Might Miss

- Why Mark feels compelled to be controlling when anxious
- What Emma actually needs to feel safe enough to stay in her Adult
- How their individual histories created these particular ego state preferences
- The deeper attachment needs underlying their Parent-Child dance

The Missing Pieces: The Whole Relationship Ecosystem

TA excels at moment-to-moment transaction analysis but sometimes needs support with:

- **Deeper emotional work** that addresses why certain ego states feel safer
- **Attachment understanding** that explains the emotional logic behind the "games"

- **Systemic perspective** that sees how their transactions affect the entire relationship system
- **Future visioning** that helps couples create new relationship patterns beyond avoiding problematic ones

The Bottom Line

TA provides couples with invaluable real-time awareness of their relationship dynamics. It's like having a weather station that tells you exactly when storm systems are developing between you. When combined with deeper work that addresses why those storms keep forming in the same places, TA becomes an extraordinarily effective tool for creating lasting relationship change.

Your skill at helping couples recognise and shift their ego state transactions is a gift. Enhanced with tools that address the underlying emotional currents, TA becomes a powerful navigation system for relationship transformation.

Enhancing Transactional Analysis Practice for Relationship Work

Your ego-state awareness provides immediate relationship clarity. To expand your effectiveness:

- Deepen emotional work exploring the attachment needs underlying ego-state preferences
- Add systems perspective seeing how individual ego states create couple-level dynamics
- Include somatic awareness helping people recognise ego-state shifts in their bodies before they become problematic
- Develop trauma-informed approaches understanding how ego states sometimes protect against historical wounds
- Practice future visioning helping couples imagine relationship patterns beyond avoiding problematic transactions

Gestalt Therapy: The Present-Moment Navigators

Gestalt therapists are like skilled sailors who read the wind and waves in real-time, responding to immediate conditions rather than following predetermined routes. Where other approaches might chart courses based on historical patterns or future destinations, Gestalt practitioners excel at navigating the ever-changing present moment where relationships actually live and breathe.

The Revolutionary Insight

Fritz Perls and his colleagues made a radical discovery: the most profound healing happens not through analysing the past or planning the future, but through fully experiencing what's happening right now (Perls et al., 1951, 1994). In relationship work, this translates to extraordinary power—helping couples notice what's actually occurring between them rather than what they think should be happening or what happened last week.

The Gift: Microscopic Awareness of Contact

A Session in Action

> *Tom and Lisa arrive reporting "communication problems." Rather than discussing their communication patterns, the Gestalt therapist invites them to simply look at each other for two minutes. "What do you notice?" she asks. Tom realises he's been avoiding eye contact. Lisa discovers she's holding her breath. In five minutes of present-moment awareness, they learn more about their actual contact patterns than months of discussing communication could reveal.*

What Gestalt Practitioners Excel At

- **Present-moment awareness**: Helping couples notice what's actually happening rather than what they think is happening
- **Body-based information**: Recognising that the body often reveals relationship truths that words conceal
- **Contact and boundaries**: Understanding how couples make and break contact and what interferes with genuine meeting
- **Experiential learning**: Creating opportunities for couples to experience new ways of relating rather than just talking about them
- **Energy and aliveness**: Bringing attention to the vitality (or lack thereof) in the relationship system
- **Integration**: Helping couples integrate thoughts, feelings, and bodily sensations into coherent experience

The Power: Making the Invisible Visible

Gestalt's genius lies in illuminating the micro-processes that create relationship satisfaction or distress. When couples can see how they actually interact—the subtle ways they move towards or away from each other, the moments when contact is made or lost—they gain access to change at the most fundamental level.

The Navigation Challenge: Present-Focused in a Time-Travelling World

Here's where Gestalt's strength becomes its limitation: relationships exist across time, not just in the present moment.

What This Looks Like in Practice

- Tom and Lisa develop exquisite awareness of their present-moment contact patterns
- But Tom's fear of emotional intimacy (rooted in childhood experiences with an alcoholic father) remains unexplored
- Lisa's tendency to over-function (learned from caring for a depressed mother) continues operating outside conscious awareness
- They improve their immediate interactions but don't address the historical patterns that will likely recreate the same dynamics

What Gestalt Practitioners Bring to Enhanced Relationship Work

Your present-moment awareness and contact skills are invaluable when enhanced with:

- **Developmental understanding** that explains why certain contact patterns feel threatening or necessary
- **Communication training** that translates awareness into practical daily skills
- **Historical exploration** that reveals the origins of contact difficulties
- **Future-focused work** that helps couples envision and create desired relationship patterns

The Bottom Line

Gestalt therapy brings irreplaceable gifts to relationship work—the ability to illuminate what's actually happening between partners in real-time and to create experiences of genuine contact that couples may have forgotten were possible. When combined with approaches that address historical patterns and future possibilities, Gestalt awareness becomes extraordinarily powerful for creating lasting relationship transformation.

Your skill at helping couples experience authentic contact in the present moment is a treasure. Enhanced with tools that address the broader context of their relationship journey, Gestalt principles become catalysts for profound and sustainable change.

Enhancing Gestalt Practice for Relationship Work

Your present-moment awareness creates powerful contact experiences. To enhance your approach:

- Include developmental understanding exploring why certain contact patterns feel threatening or necessary
- Add communication skill-building translating contact awareness into daily practical abilities

- Develop historical exploration skills understanding how contact patterns developed while maintaining present-moment focus
- Practice between-session support helping couples maintain contact awareness in their daily lives
- Create future-focused work using present awareness to envision and practice desired relationship patterns

Cognitive Behavioural Therapy: The Skilled Marine Engineer

Cognitive behavioural therapy (CBT) practitioners are the marine engineers of the therapeutic world—highly trained specialists who excel at identifying exactly what's malfunctioning and providing precise, practical solutions to get systems running smoothly again. When relationship machinery is breaking down, they arrive with well-organised toolkits and systematic repair protocols.

Developed from the recognition that thoughts, feelings, and behaviours are interconnected, CBT offers couples something many other approaches struggle to provide: concrete, measurable progress towards specific goals. CBT therapists don't just explore problems—they systematically dismantle them.

The Systematic Approach

- **Identify the problem**: What exactly is going wrong?
- **Map the connections**: How do thoughts, feelings, and behaviours reinforce each other?
- **Challenge distorted thinking**: What assumptions might be incorrect?
- **Practice new behaviours**: What specific actions would create different outcomes?
- **Track progress**: How do we know it's working?

A CBT Session in Action

> *Mark and Sarah arrive reporting "constant arguments." The CBT therapist helps them identify specific triggers: Sarah thinks, "Mark doesn't care about me," when he checks his phone during conversations. This thought creates anger, leading to accusations. Mark thinks, "I can't do anything right," feels defensive, and withdraws. This confirms Sarah's belief that he doesn't care.*
>
> *The therapist provides tools: thought records to catch distorted thinking, communication scripts for expressing needs clearly, and homework assignments to practice new patterns. Within weeks, they're arguing less frequently.*

What CBT Practitioners Excel At

- **Precision engineering**: They identify exactly which thoughts and behaviours need adjustment

- **Practical tools**: Clients leave sessions with specific techniques they can use immediately
- **Measurable progress**: Clear metrics show whether interventions are working
- **Skill building**: Couples develop concrete abilities for managing future challenges
- **Structured approach**: Sessions have clear agendas and logical progression
- **Evidence base**: Strong research support for effectiveness with many issues

The Strength: Fixing What's Broken

CBT shines when couples need immediate relief from destructive patterns:

- Teaching communication skills that reduce conflict frequency
- Providing anxiety management techniques for jealous partners
- Offering depression coping strategies that affect relationship mood
- Building problem-solving frameworks for recurring disagreements
- Creating exposure exercises for relationship fears

The Navigation Challenge: Engine Room vs. Navigation Bridge

While CBT brilliantly repairs relationship machinery, it can sometimes miss the deeper currents that created the problems in the first place.

What CBT addresses well: *Sarah learns to challenge her "Mark doesn't care" thoughts and express needs directly. Mark develops skills for staying present during difficult conversations. Their arguments decrease dramatically.*

What Might Remain Unexplored

- Why Sarah's mind automatically jumps to "he doesn't care" (perhaps childhood experiences of emotional neglect)
- What Mark's phone-checking behaviour actually represents (maybe anxiety about work demands)
- How their individual attachment styles created this particular dynamic
- Whether solving this surface pattern might allow deeper disconnection to continue unaddressed

The Symptom vs. Source Dilemma

CBT's focus on present-moment thoughts and behaviours can be simultaneously its greatest strength and its primary limitation for relationship work:

- **The strength**: Couples get immediate relief from painful patterns
- **The limitation**: The underlying emotional logic that created those patterns may remain untouched

In Practice This Looks Like

- Mark and Sarah stop arguing about phone use but don't address their fundamental disconnection
- They develop excellent communication skills but struggle with emotional intimacy
- Surface symptoms improve while deeper relationship satisfaction remains elusive
- New problems emerge that follow the same underlying emotional patterns

The Missing Piece: The Heart Beneath the Head

Relationships aren't just thinking and behaving systems—they're emotional ecosystems where past wounds, attachment needs, and unconscious patterns create the very thoughts and behaviours that CBT addresses.

> **The enhancement example:** *Instead of just teaching Sarah to challenge "Mark doesn't care" thoughts, explore why her nervous system interpreted phone-checking as abandonment.*
>
> *Instead of just giving Mark communication scripts, understand what makes emotional presence feel threatening to him.*

The Bottom Line

CBT provides invaluable tools for relationship repair—like having a skilled engineer who can quickly fix what's broken and get couples functioning again. These practical skills form essential foundations for relationship health.

However, the most lasting relationship transformations often require understanding not just *what* patterns need changing, but *why* those particular patterns felt necessary in the first place. CBT's systematic approach becomes extraordinarily powerful when enhanced with deeper exploration of the emotional undercurrents that created the surface symptoms.

Your skill at identifying and changing problematic patterns is a gift to couples in distress.

When combined with tools that address the emotional and historical roots of those patterns, CBT becomes part of a comprehensive approach that creates both immediate relief and lasting transformation.

Think of it as providing both engine repair *and* navigation training—fixing what's broken while helping couples understand the deeper currents that brought them off course in the first place.

Enhancing CBT Practice for Relationship Work

Your practical tools provide immediate relief from destructive patterns. To deepen your impact:

- **Add emotional depth work** exploring the feelings and attachment needs underlying thought patterns

- **Include family-of-origin exploration** understanding historical roots of cognitive schemas about relationships
- **Develop systems awareness** seeing how individual thought patterns create couple-level interaction cycles
- **Practice somatic integration** including body-based information alongside cognitive processing
- **Use metaphor and creativity** supplementing logical analysis with more intuitive, experiential approaches

Integrative Therapy: The Master Navigator's Toolkit

Integrative therapists are like master mariners who've studied every navigation technique ever developed—from ancient celestial charts to modern GPS systems. Rather than limiting themselves to one method, they select whatever tools will best guide each unique vessel through its particular waters.

The Philosophy: No Single Map Covers All Waters

Integrative therapy emerged from a practical recognition: human beings are wonderfully complex, and no single therapeutic approach can address every dimension of that complexity. Why force someone into a Freudian framework if cognitive techniques would serve them better? Why stick to CBT if body-based work would unlock what talk therapy cannot reach?

The Integrative Promise: Whole-Person Healing

Integrative practitioners work across multiple dimensions simultaneously:

- **Emotional** (feelings and emotional patterns)
- **Cognitive** (thoughts and belief systems)
- **Behavioural** (actions and habits)
- **Somatic** (body-based experiences and sensations)
- **Spiritual** (meaning, purpose, and transcendent connection)
- **Relational** (patterns of connection with others)

A Session in Action

Claire and David arrive stuck in a recurring conflict about money. An integrative therapist might:

- *Help them identify the emotional triggers beneath their financial arguments (emotional)*
- *Explore the stories they learned about money in childhood (cognitive)*
- *Practice new communication patterns (behavioural)*
- *Notice how their bodies tense when money topics arise (somatic)*
- *Connect their conflict to deeper values about security and freedom (spiritual)*
- *See how their money dance reflects broader relationship patterns (relational)*

The Strength: Adaptive Flexibility

Integrative therapy's greatest asset is its responsiveness. Like skilled sailors who adjust their approach based on wind conditions, integrative therapists adapt their methods to what each couple actually needs:

- **For intellectual couples**: More cognitive and insight-based work
- **For emotionally overwhelmed couples**: Body-based regulation and containment techniques
- **For conflict-avoidant couples**: Direct communication training and structured exercises
- **For trauma-affected couples**: Gentle somatic work combined with safety-building
- **For spiritually oriented couples**: Meaning-making and values-based interventions

The Art: Seamless Integration, Not Random Selection

Effective integrative work isn't about throwing different techniques at couples to see what sticks. It requires:

- **Accurate assessment** of what each couple needs in each moment
- **Seamless blending** of approaches so they support rather than confuse each other
- **Clear rationale** for why particular methods are being used
- **Ongoing attunement** to what's working and what needs adjustment

The Navigation Challenge: Jack of All Trades, Master of None?

The flexibility that makes integrative therapy so valuable can also create challenges:

The competence question: *Can any therapist truly master enough approaches to integrate them effectively? There's a difference between knowing about CBT techniques and being skilled enough to apply them at the right moment with the right couple.*

The coherence challenge: *Without a clear theoretical framework, integrative work can feel scattered. Couples may wonder: "Are we doing therapy or are we just trying everything until something works?"*

The training dilemma: *How does someone train to be integrative? Most therapy programs teach single modalities in depth, not multi-modal integration.*

What Works: Principled Integration vs. Random Eclecticism

The most effective integrative practitioners operate from clear principles:

- **Assessment-driven intervention**: Using thorough assessment to guide technique selection

- **Theoretical coherence**: Understanding how different approaches complement each other
- **Skill depth**: Developing genuine competence in multiple modalities, not just superficial familiarity
- **Client feedback loops**: Constantly checking whether interventions are helpful

The Bottom Line

Integration done well is therapy's equivalent of master craftsmanship—the ability to select and blend the right tools for each unique situation. It requires not just knowledge of multiple approaches, but the wisdom to know when and how to use them together.

Your willingness to draw from multiple traditions serves couples beautifully when guided by clear principles and solid skill foundations. The art lies not in knowing every technique, but in seamlessly weaving together approaches that create more than the sum of their parts.

The future of relationship therapy likely belongs to skilful integrators who can navigate between different therapeutic waters while maintaining a clear sense of direction and destination.

Enhancing Integrative Practice for Relationship Work

Your adaptive flexibility serves couples well. To strengthen your integration:

- **Develop clear assessment frameworks** (like the Relationship Paradigm) to guide your technique selection
- **Create structured progression models** ensuring your flexibility serves therapeutic direction rather than replacing it
- **Build deeper competence in core approaches** rather than surface familiarity with many techniques
- **Practice outcome tracking** measuring whether your integration actually improves results
- **Seek ongoing supervision** in navigating complex multi-modal decisions with couples

Eclectic Therapy: The Pragmatic Captain's Approach

Eclectic therapists are the pragmatic captains of the therapeutic world. When a storm hits, they don't consult theoretical manuals—they grab whatever tools will keep the ship afloat and get everyone safely to harbour. Their guiding principle is beautifully simple: "Whatever works, works."

The Philosophy: Results over Purity

While integrative therapists carefully blend approaches into theoretical harmony, eclectic practitioners take a more utilitarian approach. They're less concerned with whether their techniques come from the same theoretical family and more focused on whether they actually help couples reach their desired outcomes.

The Key Distinction

- **Integrative**: "How can I thoughtfully combine CBT and psychodynamic approaches so they complement each other theoretically?"
- **Eclectic**: "This couple needs CBT communication skills right now, and next session they might need Gestalt awareness exercises—whatever gets them where they want to go."

The Eclectic Advantage: Pure Responsiveness

A Session in Action

> *Session 1 with Rachel and Tom: They're stuck in intellectual discussions about their problems. The eclectic therapist shifts to experiential work—having them stand and physically represent their emotional distance.*
>
> *Session 3: Tom has breakthrough insight about his father's influence. The therapist immediately draws from psychodynamic techniques to explore this further.*
>
> *Session 5: They're ready for practical skills. Out comes structured communication training from behavioural approaches.*
>
> *Session 6: A crisis hits. The therapist pulls from crisis intervention protocols, regardless of theoretical origin.*

What Eclectic Practitioners Excel At

Adaptive precision: Like emergency room doctors, they assess what's needed most urgently and respond accordingly

Outcome focus: Their primary loyalty is to client results, not theoretical consistency

Intuitive flexibility: They can shift approaches mid-session based on what emerges

Surprise factor: Clients never know what tool might appear, preventing therapeutic stagnation

Practical effectiveness: Less time spent justifying theoretical choices, more time creating change

The Liberation: Freedom from Theoretical Constraints

Eclectic therapists enjoy remarkable freedom:

- No need to force couples into predetermined frameworks
- Permission to use whatever technique feels right in the moment

- Ability to surprise clients (and themselves) with unexpected interventions
- Focus on "what works" rather than "what's theoretically pure"

The Navigation Challenges: Freedom's Hidden Costs

The flexibility that makes eclectic therapy so responsive can also create complications:

- **The competence question:** *How many approaches can one therapist truly master? There's a difference between knowing about various techniques and being skilled enough to apply them effectively when the pressure is on.*
- **The rationale challenge:** *"Why did you choose that intervention?" If the answer is just "intuition," clients (and supervisors) might wonder about the professional basis for decisions.*
- **The training dilemma:** *How does someone learn to be effectively eclectic? Most training programs teach specific approaches, not the meta-skill of intelligent technique selection.*
- **The coherence risk:** *Without some underlying framework, sessions can feel scattered: "Are we doing therapy or just trying random techniques until something works?"*

What Makes Eclecticism Work: Informed Intuition

The most effective eclectic practitioners operate from:

- **Broad competence**: Genuine skill in multiple approaches, not just surface familiarity
- **Pattern recognition**: Understanding which techniques tend to work for which types of issues
- **Outcome tracking**: Constantly monitoring whether their choices are actually helping
- **Principled flexibility**: Clear values about what they're trying to achieve, even if methods vary

The Bottom Line

Eclecticism at its best is therapy without artificial constraints—the freedom to use whatever tools serve each unique couple's needs. It requires not theoretical purity but practical wisdom: the ability to read what's needed and respond with the most effective intervention available.

Your willingness to prioritise results over theoretical elegance serves couples beautifully. The art lies in developing sufficiently broad competence that your intuitive choices are informed by genuine skill rather than just hope.

In relationship work, where couples present infinite variations of human complexity, eclectic flexibility may be less a choice than a necessity. The future belongs to practitioners who can navigate fluidly between approaches while maintaining clear sight of their destination: healthier, happier relationships.

Enhancing Eclectic Practice for Relationship Work

Your results-focused flexibility is valuable for couples. To refine your approach:

- **Develop pattern recognition skills** understanding which techniques work best for which types of couple dynamics
- **Create rationale frameworks** helping couples understand why you're selecting particular interventions
- **Build competence depth** ensuring your technique selection comes from genuine skill rather than just intuition
- **Practice systematic assessment** using clear criteria to guide your eclectic choices
- **Maintain theoretical coherence** ensuring your techniques support each other rather than working at cross-purposes

Exploration of Delivery

One on One

The conventional approach is for one therapist to meet with one client. My view is that this is ineffective when working on a couple relationship. The therapist will only hear one perspective; the other part of the couple will not be represented and may feel threatened. Sustained change is only likely if both, the whole system, are involved and working to their agreed outcomes,

The other danger with one on one is that it may become just an echo chamber, and resentments will become even more deeply embedded.

Group Therapy

Group therapy is widely used in contexts of strangers with a shared problem, such as an addiction. It provides a safe, supportive environment where the problem holders feel part of a community with a shared purpose.

It is rarely used with couples and relationship problems. It is very unlikely that a couple would be prepared to bare all of their inner stories to a group of strangers. The problems would also be unique to each couple. It can work in a couples retreat environment where the emotional depth is less and the focus is on improving rather than rescuing a relationship.

Co-Therapy

In co-therapy, two or more therapists treat one or more clients in groups, families, couples, or individual psychotherapy at the same time and in the same place. It is a form of psychotherapy treatment in which the therapists relate not only to a client or clients but also to a peer or peers.

In research done by Roller and Nelson (1991), they found the benefits from co-therapy were:

- A greater opportunity for learning through discussion and collaboration with a therapist
- Widened perspectives for therapists
- Widened transference possibilities for clients
- Greater learning opportunities
- Opportunities for therapists to check and balance their complementary behaviours
- Clients can learn about relationships as they watch two people both equal in power and self-esteem model how to behave as individuals in a relationship
- They can see the co-therapists' different responses to a single stimulus and learn there is probably more than one choice that is right. They can see that there are many pathways to the same goal
- Modelling allows co-therapists to magnify the impact of the therapeutic encounter in a way not possible by solo practice. They are able to model transactional and interpersonal behaviour between peers with their clients
- A co-therapy team coaches and teaches by example the exquisite crafting of human relationships. Modelling by therapists consists largely of non-verbal actions which are often missed by those in treatment

For a co-therapy team to be successful, there were six key factors:

- Complimentary balance of therapist skills
- Compatibility of the therapists' theoretical viewpoints
- Openness and communication
- Quality of participation
- Liking each other as people
- Respect

Co-therapy teams for relationship work are rare but almost exclusively couples in an intimate relationship. There are special problems and vulnerability of lovers and marriage partners who enter a co-therapy relationship:

- Unrecognised competition
- Partners can be jealous of a client's attraction to their spouse and transference
- They can also fall in love with his or her client
- It can suddenly and surprisingly expose the inequality that exists in the marriage relationship
- Some couples enter into co-therapy contracts to treat couples in order to solve their own relationship problems

- The non-therapist spouses may feel excluded from the intimate circle the co-therapy team creates for itself

I also believe that the clients will be seeing an "idealised relationship" and will be looking for micro signs of disconnection or unease. This will potentially destroy the credibility of the relationship "experts."

Virginia Satir said in interviews in 1985 and 1986 (Starr, 1993):

> If we proceed with the idea that what we need in treatment are models for people then the male/female model is a natural one for co-therapy. It models what you want to teach people. In practice it has not succeeded because a lot of co-therapy presents a dominant therapist and submissive therapist.

Does co-therapy benefit the therapist more than the client, or do the clients benefit more? That is the question that can never be answered. In some situations, the therapist may gain the most. For example, co-therapy can be a support to a therapist and stem his or her loneliness. There is a lot of loneliness amongst therapists. When a husband and wife team conduct therapy, many of their own problems surface, and the fate of therapy depends on their own ability to confront this as it happens. It is that simple.

An effective co-therapy team can provide objectivity for each other. For example, let's think about a stream. A stream in which people are boating. When they all feel they are with the current, they can sing and enjoy themselves, but suddenly the boatman may decide to leave the flow of the current and turn against it. The passengers will experience resistance against the flow. If the passengers are responsible and aware of people, they will say, "Hey, we feel we are off course." They would do it lovingly.

We can adapt that to co-therapy. When a person is inside of something, he may not be as aware of the flow going on as a person looking on. A co-therapist can be that person looking on.

My belief is that co-therapy, with two equal therapists working with a couple, is significantly more powerful than one therapist. It produces balance, depth, and insight that one therapist can never have. There is also reduced triangulation.

There are two therapists in the room, so there is less possibility of either of the partners feeling like they are being left out or blamed. This is an experience I had with my previous relationship counselling, where I believed that the therapist was siding with one of them. Typically, males feel marginalised in a female-dominated profession.

Co-therapy in relationships is very rare worldwide and normally involves a couple who live and work together. I believe that Duo Coaching is unique.

Family Therapy

A family is a complex system with many dyads. Family therapy, involving parents, children, and maybe even grandparents, can be helpful if the whole system is dysfunctional. It does require the parents to be well anchored, first as it would be counterproductive to open up their couple problems to their children.

The Therapeutic Hour

How long should a therapeutic session be? The 50-minute session has become deeply embedded in psychotherapeutic practice without any evidence of research into how efficacious and appropriate this is for the client.

It is said that the therapeutic hour was started by Sigmund Freud in the 1890s for the pragmatic reason that he had a weak bladder and 50 minutes was the longest he could go without going to the toilet. "The 50-minute hour emerged from Vienna in triumph and established itself throughout the world in the decades that followed" (Will, 2018).

Herbert Will argues that the clock has a significance as a relational factor in the session with the alienness of the time of day to the unconscious and the consequences of this alienness. He then investigates the phenomenon of the stretching effect of time in analytic sessions. He claims how cleverly the 50-minute hour excises the time needed for unconscious processes from our accelerated present; that it challenges the social convention of time and has a structuring effect in that it "times" psychic processes.

All of this seems to me to be a wonderful post-rationalisation of a structure that suits the therapist without any significant research from the perspective of the most important factor, client success.

In a 1975 interview, Carl Rogers was reported to have said that if he were to go back to individual therapy, he would take a more flexible approach:

> I don't know what I would do, but I would experiment with various things… I think I would try various things depending on the client and try and keep my own time as flexible as possible. I think I would try to have the client share with me the responsibility of determining how much time to spend.
>
> (Francis, 1975)

The French psychoanalyst Jacques Lacan was known to refuse to offer appointments—instead, clients turned up and waited to be summoned by Lacan for a session that may have lasted hours or, if he felt the client was wasting time, was abruptly ended after just a few minutes. Freud meanwhile famously conducted a four-hour session in 1910 with the composer Mahler walking around the city of Leiden. Hopefully there were suitable conveniences on the way.

There is limited research into whether 50 minutes is the most effective duration for therapy or whether clients would do just as well or better with shorter or, conversely, longer sessions. A 1976 study (into brief emotive psychotherapy) compared client outcomes from being seen for either 30 minutes twice a week, 60 minutes once a week, or 120 minutes biweekly. It found there was no relationship between length and frequency of sessions and outcomes, although clients reported preferring having more time to talk (Bierenbaum et al., 1976). Similarly, a study carried out by Turner and colleagues in the 1990s that compared groups who were given eight sessions of either 30- or 50-minute therapy found that session length did not determine client satisfaction or outcome—researchers concluded that "the ability of the therapist to be present and empathic with the client may be more influential than the length of the treatment hour" (Turner et al., 1996).

The positive effect of giving clients autonomy over booking their sessions was also confirmed by a study by Professor Timothy Carey on NHS clients in Scotland. His study aimed to explore what might happen if clients, rather than therapists, took control of appointment scheduling:

> I established systems so that clients could book their own appointments at the clinics where I worked [in the NHS in Scotland]... Essentially, clients made appointments to see me in the same way they would make an appointment to see their GP. We informed clients they could come four times a week if they wanted to, or once a week, or whatever they thought was appropriate. If clients thought that a one-hour appointment was too brief, they could schedule two appointments in a row to give themselves more time. The data indicated that clients appreciate the increased choice and flexibility. One of the fundamental differences with this method of therapy provision is that the number of non-attended appointments reduces dramatically.
>
> (Carey, 2011, 2016)

The reasons why the 50-minute hour has become embedded include:

- Simple and pragmatic reasons. It allows the sessions to start on the hour with a ten-minute break in between clients. This gives them time to have a break, decompress, and prepare for the next
- It sets psychological boundaries for the therapist and client. It allows therapists to offer a fresh perspective and remain objective without getting too immersed in a client's life
- The length of time feels more contained, so it lessens the risk of over-exposure to painful emotions
- Having a clear endpoint after less than an hour can help create a safe space for the client to feel, process, and contain intense emotions, rather than go into it with the sense that there's no end in sight
- Therapy is an ongoing conversation, and the real change happens when the clients practice what they learn in their lives outside the therapist's office. The focus should be on the skills and insights they gain during sessions and how they'll implement them—not the length of the sessions
- Keeping therapy sessions under an hour may also motivate both parties to make the best of the time allotted
- In the US, insurance companies tend to base reimbursement on the type and length of therapy. A common billing code is 90834, which denotes 45 minutes of individual psychotherapy

- It keeps the therapist firmly in control of the relationship. It allows them to say, at 50 minutes in, even if the client is in mid-flow, on the brink of a breakthrough moment, or in tears; "our time is up, we will continue this next week." What does this say about the power dynamic?
- It is financially beneficial to the therapist to keep the client embedded for longer. I believe that progress in 50 minutes is likely to be slower than longer, more intense sessions. There is warm up time and the beginning of the session and wind down time at the end which means that the core, productive time is limited. As a therapist what can you do to achieve great, sustainable outcomes for your clients?

The Therapeutic Relationship

My framework is simple:

The clients have relationship problems, often for many years, and they have reached a point where the pain of remaining as they are now exceeds the pain of dealing with it. The couple are often at different stages of the change curve.

We are the guides and provide a safe space for the clients to be open and vulnerable. We use our skills and experience to discover the outcomes they both want and the root of the problems, often predating the start of the current relationship. We then work with the couples to help them understand their unhelpful patterns of behaviour and give them the skills and knowledge to change these and achieve their outcomes.

We work at both the conscious and subconscious levels and will use whatever tools and techniques will deliver the best results. Sessions are not pre-planned and the ability to flex and work with what is in the room is essential.

In terms of the power dynamic, we are the guides and know more about relationships than the clients. We are there to facilitate and transfer knowledge.

Rivera outlined four stages of the therapeutic relationship (Rivera, 1992):

1 Commitment
   In the initial stage, the client and therapist make an agreement to devote time and energy to achieve specific goals. In this stage, the perception of the therapist, intensity of client motivation, and compatibility of personality/experiences are important factors.
2 Process
   This is the most complex stage and is the body of treatment and the relationship. This is when the therapist searches for patterns, gathers information, and consolidates it.

   The therapist will look for triggers, cycles, and repetitive interactions in the client. This stage is also when the therapist will gain additional information and seek to implement change.

   Various therapeutic tasks, techniques, and approaches may be used in the process stage.

3 Change
   This stage represents a conclusion and success of the treatment plan. The client can accept their mental or emotional state and adopt habits to improve wellbeing.
4 Termination
   During this stage, the client "graduates." The therapist and client can recognise each other as autonomous and independent individuals.

By this stage, positive transference and regressive forms of dependence have been resolved. The client should now have the tools and knowledge to develop their life independently.

What Is the Relevance of Power in the Therapeutic Relationship?

Surely it is very simple. The client comes to see a therapist that he can trust to help them achieve the outcome they want. The client has the power to stop coming and therefore stop paying. The therapist is there to use their expertise to help the client achieve their outcomes and can stop providing their services when the client has achieved their outcomes or feel they unable to help or to work with that client.

The power dynamic becomes much more complex and insidious when the outcomes are not expressed or when working with a couple where the outcomes are not compatible or are not honestly expressed.

Power issues in psychotherapy are often addressed from the perspective of intersectional and societal power, enacted or embodied in the therapy relationship. Following the thinking of Young-Bruehl (1996), who argued for acknowledging the heterogeneity of oppression. There are four areas of power in the therapeutic relationship.

Professional Power

It is an asymmetric relationship. The therapist has extensive information about the client; the client lacks similar data about the therapist. The therapist is paid to see the clients, keeps a record, and in most cases has more extensive psychological knowledge. This kind of power asymmetry involves overt, observable factors.

Transferential Power

A second way, and a common one, of conceptualising power in psychotherapy concerns the implications of the transference and other unconscious parts of the therapeutic relationship. Greenacre suggested that because of the emotional dependency in the client role and the phenomenon of transference, the therapeutic relationship is *tilted*:

> In appreciation of the client's vulnerability in a situation of unequal psychological power, Freud warned against acting out erotic countertransferences. He also

cautioned analysts not to take on the role of prophet or saviour based on this artificially.

Relational theorists have emphasised more mutual, interactive processes. According to Slochower (2013), therapists in the interpersonal tradition were the first to move the paradigm of transference beyond the notion of the regressive client: "They formulated a model in which the client is an adult and the analyst a participant observer." The relational perspective appreciates transference phenomena but construes power as issuing from unconscious shared dynamics and the emotional interdependency of client and therapist.

Socio-Political Power

This includes extensive and heterogeneous phenomena that enter the therapeutic space. It includes how gender, social class, and overall social norms affect the therapeutic relationship.

At Duo Coaching, this is balanced by having a male and female co-therapist. We also present as professional as well as warm and caring.

Bureaucratic Power

The fourth common perspective on power in psychotherapy involves bureaucratic aspects of access to care. Subordinated groups are often at a relative disadvantage in obtaining treatment or social benefits.

In contemporary psychoanalytic writing, there is increasing emphasis on appreciating unconscious power dynamics. Many of these have been conceptualised by earlier philosophers and political theorists. The application of their ideas to psychotherapy, however, is relatively new. Power themes are complex, fluid, various, and heterogeneous. Often, we talk about power issues in psychotherapy only from the perspective of intersectional and societal power issues enacted or embodied in the therapy relationship.

Most theoretical writing on power addresses political or sociological power rather than interpersonal power or the power endemic in treatment relationships. For example, Marx (1867) wrote about the violence and power of capitalism; Bourdieu (1977) addressed power in what he called "habitus," the underlying structure of social life, including the power inherent in embodied cultural capital such as the higher classes' formulation of privilege as "taste"; Machiavelli wrote about power in governance (Machiavelli, 1993)—specifically about how a sovereign ruler can maintain power. Weber addressed questions of the legitimacy of power, arguing that bureaucratic power is preferable to that of a charismatic leader.

Power was also an interest of the liberal philosopher J. S. Mill who worried about the "tyranny of the majority" (Jacobs, 1993). Such preoccupations are ancient: Plato's concern with issues of power led to his suggestion that a good society should be ruled by philosophers (Cooper & Hutchinson, 1997).

Summary: What This Analysis Reveals

Each therapeutic modality offers valuable insights while also having inherent limitations when applied to relationship work. Your understanding of these strengths and limitations guides you towards more effective practice.

Rather than dismissing established therapeutic traditions, I believe we need integration that preserves their strengths while addressing their structural limitations. This represents reinventing, not revolution—building upon decades of therapeutic wisdom while adapting it for the complex realities of modern relationship challenges.

The limitations of current relationship therapy approaches aren't simply about technique—they reflect deeper issues about how we understand relationships themselves. Perhaps the reason so many therapeutic vessels struggle in relationship waters is that we've been navigating with incomplete charts, seeing only fragments of a much more complex reality (Figure 3.2).

Figure 3.2 A single, tightly woven rope: the intertwined strands symbolise how effective integrative practice draws multiple therapeutic threads together into one resilient line, stronger than any single strand alone.

Chapter 4

The World of Relationship Therapy

Figure 4.1 Two sailing vessels share the same waters under an open sky: the parallel journeys of couples seeking help, with birds overhead suggesting the freedom that comes when effective guidance is found.

Assessing Current Navigation Methods

Charts can be misleading. What appears as a safe passage on paper may prove treacherous in reality, while routes marked as dangerous might offer the swiftest path to harbour. In relationship therapy, many accepted practices persist not because they're most effective, but because they're familiar waters where therapists feel confident navigating (Figure 4.1).

Options for Couples Seeking Relationship Help

The important questions for couples wanting to improve their relationships are: What are the options available when love feels lost at sea? Does relationship

DOI: 10.4324/9781003715467-5

therapy actually help guide couples to safer harbours? What are the most effective approaches for navigating relationship storms? And what conditions are needed for therapeutic work to succeed?

When relationship distress reaches a tipping point, couples face a bewildering array of choices. Like mariners in distress, they must decide whether to attempt repairs alone, signal for rescue, or abandon ship entirely.

The Solo Journey Options

Do Nothing and Hope

This is the default option that many couples find themselves trapped in—a kind of relationship purgatory where problems are acknowledged privately but never addressed directly. It's comfortable because it avoids facing reality and being vulnerable while feeding the seductive myth that "if they loved me, they would know what I want without having to tell them."

The Prochaska Model of Change (Prochaska and Norcross, 2001) shows that individuals move through six stages when approaching behavioural change:

- Precontemplation (unaware of need for change)
- Contemplation (considering change)
- Preparation (planning change)
- Action (implementing change)
- Maintenance (sustaining change) and often
- Relapse (returning to old patterns)

For couples, this process becomes exponentially more complex because partners are rarely at the same stage simultaneously. One person may be actively contemplating relationship change while their partner remains in precontemplation, creating dynamics where the "ready" partner grows increasingly frustrated while the "unready" partner feels pressured and resistant.

This explains why "hoping" feels safer than acting—couples must not only navigate their individual readiness for change but also achieve sufficient alignment to take action together, a process that requires communication skills many distressed couples have lost.

Why Couples Choose This Option

The reasons couples avoid direct action are often rooted in childhood experiences and previous relationships:

- Fear of conflict: Many people naturally avoid situations they perceive as potentially confrontational
- Fear of rejection or judgement: Opening up about relationship insecurities can feel devastatingly vulnerable

- Catastrophising: "If I raise my concerns, they will end the relationship"
- Guilt and low self-worth: "This is the best I deserve"
- Lack of communication skills: Not everyone feels equipped for emotionally charged conversations
- Past relationship trauma: Previous experiences create protective patterns
- Power imbalances: When one partner feels unheard, they may retreat into silence

The Change Process Reality

Understanding how people approach relationship change helps explain why "hoping" feels safer than acting.

For couples, this process becomes exponentially more complex because partners are rarely at the same stage simultaneously. One person may be actively contemplating change while their partner remains in precontemplation, creating dynamics where the "ready" partner grows increasingly frustrated while the "unready" partner feels pressured and resistant.

The likely outcome: Without intervention, this approach typically leads to gradual relationship decline until a crisis forces action.

Individual Self-Help: Books, Apps, and Learning

When couples feel stuck but aren't ready for professional help, the self-help route offers appealing middle ground—the promise of transformation without the vulnerability of therapy.

There are significant relationship resources available: Amazon lists over 100,000 relationship books, Google Scholar contains about 9.36 million articles, and YouTube offers countless relationship experts. All the answers are there—or are they? Is it like the Rime of the Ancient Mariner: "Water, water everywhere, and not a drop to drink"?

What Individual Self-Help Can Offer

- New perspectives offering different viewpoints on common issues
- Practical skills including communication techniques and conflict resolution strategies
- Validation showing that relationship struggles are common and normal
- Conversation catalysts providing frameworks for discussing difficult topics

The Fundamental Challenge

The problems include misunderstanding and resentment from the partner ("What have I done wrong?"), solutions that are generic and may be unhelpful, and the fact that complex issues often get simplified in books. Self-blame can result when books put the onus of fixing the relationship solely on the reader.

Individual Therapy for Relationship Issues

In my experience, relationship therapy is a journey for both partners. If only one is having therapy, then the other is left behind. They will often feel disenfranchised and suspicious: "What are they saying about me?"

The other significant problem is that the therapist is only hearing one perspective and does not get a shared context. This means that the one having therapy may remain trapped in a world where they are the victim and their partner is the persecutor.

The Partnership Approaches

Both Reading Books Together

It is very unusual for both of a couple to read a book together or in synchronicity. The benefits and problems include those mentioned above, and the benefits are amplified if a couple can share their thoughts and agree on actions they will both take. In my experience, few couples will finish a book and have a constructive conversation around it—facilitation is needed to break through walls of defensiveness.

Both Doing Online Programs

This can work well if the couple are aligned in their outcomes and prepared to invest the time and energy. This is limited by the fact that programs are generic and lack direct guidance by a therapist.

One American study of the OurRelationship Online Programme (Doss et al., 2016) compared the impact of an online program with a control group of couples on the wait list. It showed positive improvements in relationship functioning (but only measured short-term) but not in relationship quality.

Using a nautical metaphor, online programs are like antifouling a boat—they will protect the relationship against the growth of unhelpful patterns but are unlikely to go deep and find the cause of those patterns.

Professional Therapy Together

This feels like the best form of therapy as it requires investment of time, energy, and money by both partners. It crucially depends on the commitment of each person and the quality of the therapist.

Traditional Couples Therapy: The Relate Model

Relate is the leading relationships charity in the United Kingdom, seeing about 150,000 clients annually from 600 locations. Their approach combines several therapeutic traditions.

Relate's Therapeutic Framework

- Systemic approach: Views relationships as systems, examining interaction patterns
- Person-centred elements: Emphasises empathy and client-led discovery
- Psychodynamic insights: Considers how past experiences influence current dynamics
- Time-limited structure: Typically offers a set number of 50-minute sessions
- Inclusivity: Works with diverse relationship types

Structural Challenges

Like many large-scale counselling services, Relate faces challenges inherent to their delivery model:

- Resource constraints mean many counsellors are trainees working for minimal income
- Online delivery has become primary since COVID-19, limiting emotional connection
- Increasing costs have made services less accessible
- Traditional 50-minute format may not provide sufficient time for complex work
- Single-therapist model can create perceived imbalances

The AI Question: Can Technology Replace Human Connection?

As artificial intelligence (AI) becomes increasingly sophisticated, the possibility of AI-delivered relationship support has captured both imagination and concern.

The AI Promise

- 24/7 availability with no scheduling constraints
- Infinite patience—never tired, frustrated, or judgemental
- Vast knowledge base accessing entire libraries of research
- Personalisation ability to tailor responses to specific dynamics
- Anonymity reducing embarrassment for hesitant couples
- Cost accessibility potentially much less expensive

Current AI Applications

- Sentiment analysis of text communications between couples
- Predictive modelling using communication patterns
- Personalised advice that learns and improves over time
- Educational support providing interactive skill-building

The Fundamental Limitations

When asked about their capabilities in relationship therapy, AI systems themselves acknowledge important constraints: "Critics rightly point out that even the most advanced AI today lacks the true emotional intelligence, psychological depth, and human experiences required to effectively guide couples through profoundly personal issues."

Critical missing elements include warm data that emerges through in-person communication, emotional attunement and genuine empathy, contextual wisdom about cultural and personal nuances, and crisis response capabilities for acute situations.

Does Relationship Therapy Help?

The Research Challenge

Unlike medical interventions that can be tested through randomised controlled trials, relationship therapy faces fundamental methodological problems:

- **Control group impossibility**: How do you create a meaningful control group when the very act of seeking therapy indicates couple readiness for change?
- **Homogeneity assumptions**: Research assumes all therapists are equally skilled and all approaches equally suitable
- **Self-scoring bias**: Relationship satisfaction measures rely on self-reported questionnaires subject to confirmation bias
- **Sample size limitations**: Most studies involve relatively small numbers of couples
- **Dropout rates**: Long-term follow-up studies suffer from significant participant attrition
- **Measurement inconsistency**: Various studies use different assessment tools, making comparison difficult

A 1980 study noted that "there are almost no systematic longitudinal follow-up studies in the field of marital therapy" and concluded that "most marital therapy research has focused on improvement within or at the termination of treatment." Remarkably, this situation has barely improved over four decades.

What Limited Research Suggests

When studies are conducted, they typically show "moderate effect size improvement in relationship satisfaction"—suggesting therapy helps but not dramatically. Most research examines immediate post-therapy outcomes rather than long-term relationship health.

One significant finding emerged from long-term research: couples treated together (conjoint therapy) had significantly better outcomes five years later compared to those treated individually, including lower divorce rates and higher satisfaction. However, most research examines immediate post-therapy outcomes rather than long-term relationship health, and the variety of assessment tools used makes comparison between different approaches difficult.

The Measurement Challenge

Relationship therapy effectiveness is typically measured using self-scored questionnaires such as the Dyadic Adjustment Scale, Couple Satisfaction Index, or Golombok Rust Inventory of Marital State. The variety of different assessment tools used makes comparison between studies difficult, and all rely on subjective self-reporting rather than objective measures. This creates a fundamental challenge: unlike medical interventions with clear biological markers, relationship "health" remains largely subjective, making definitive effectiveness claims nearly impossible to establish scientifically.

The Pragmatic Perspective

Given these research limitations, couples might be better served by pragmatic rather than statistical considerations. If your relationship is significantly distressed, it's genuinely important to both of you, you've tried addressing issues independently without success, you're both prepared to invest time and energy, you're willing to be open and vulnerable, and you find therapists you trust with appropriate skills—then relationship therapy should logically help.

What Are the Best Forms of Relationship Therapy?

The honest answer is that the best form of relationship therapy is the one that works for each unique couple. This creates a practical problem: couples rarely have objective information or ability to comparison-shop different approaches.

In my experience, many Duo Coaching clients have tried traditional relationship counselling years earlier and found it unhelpful—which brought them to seek alternatives. This suggests that "effectiveness" is highly individual and contextual rather than universal.

What Is Needed for Relationship Therapy to Work?

Based on my clinical experience with hundreds of couples, several conditions appear essential for effective relationship therapy.

From Both Partners

- Presence: Both people physically and emotionally engaged
- Commitment: Genuine willingness to invest time, energy, and vulnerability
- Honesty: Complete transparency about issues, history, and feelings
- Responsibility: Moving from blame to understanding their own role
- Outcome clarity: Specific understanding of what they want to achieve
- Growth orientation: Willingness to change personally, not just demand partner change

From Therapists

- Appropriate skills: Match between therapist capabilities and couple needs
- Balanced alliance: Ability to maintain therapeutic relationships with both partners
- Systemic perspective: Understanding couples as systems rather than individuals
- Active intervention: Willingness to interrupt destructive patterns
- Outcome focus: Clear goals and progress tracking
- Flexible approach: Adapting methods to couple needs rather than rigid adherence

From the Process

- Sufficient time: Adequate session length for deep work
- Appropriate pacing: Balance between allowing natural unfolding and maintaining momentum
- Safety creation: Environmental and emotional conditions that allow vulnerability
- Skill building: Practical tools couples can use independently
- Integration support: Help applying insights and skills in real-life situations

When these conditions align, relationship therapy can create remarkable transformation. When they're absent, even well-intentioned therapeutic work may leave couples feeling frustrated and unchanged.

The challenge for couples seeking help is finding approaches and practitioners who can create these conditions consistently. This recognition of what's needed—but often missing—in traditional relationship therapy led to the development of alternative frameworks designed to address these gaps systematically.

The limitations of current relationship therapy approaches aren't simply about technique—they reflect a deeper issue about how we understand relationships themselves. Perhaps the reason so many therapeutic vessels struggle in relationship waters is that we've been navigating with incomplete charts, seeing only fragments of a much more complex reality (Figure 4.2).

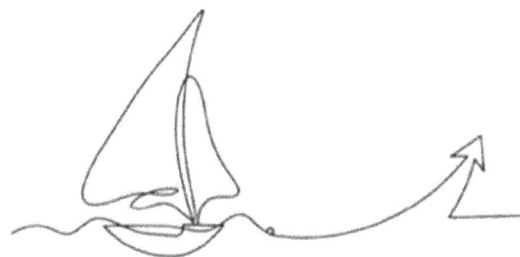

Figure 4.2 A yacht under sail with its wake pointing towards a new heading: the moment of decisive change when couples move from navigating with incomplete charts to charting a purposeful course forward.

Chapter 5

Transdisciplinarity in the Context of Relationships

Figure 5.1 A shoal of fish moving as one: individual creatures forming a collective intelligence, illustrating how transdisciplinary understanding reveals the interconnected dimensions that shape every relationship.

When One Compass Isn't Enough

The most skilled navigators don't rely on a single instrument. They read the stars, feel the wind, watch the birds, and listen to the rhythm of the waves. Relationships, like the sea itself, exist across multiple interconnected dimensions that require diverse ways of knowing to truly understand the forces at work (Figure 5.1).

When One Lens Isn't Enough: Sarah and James's Story

> Sarah and James sat across from me in their first session, both articulate professionals who had already tried traditional couple's therapy. "We understand our communication patterns perfectly," Sarah explained with

DOI: 10.4324/9781003715467-6

frustration. "We've learned all the techniques. We can describe exactly what happens when we fight. But we keep having the same arguments anyway."

From a **communication skills perspective**, they were model students—they used "I" statements, practiced active listening, and could identify their conflict cycles with textbook precision.

From a **psychodynamic viewpoint**, they had insight into their family-of-origin patterns—Sarah's tendency to pursue when anxious (like her mother with her distant father) and James's withdrawal when feeling criticised (echoing his father's response to his critical mother).

From a **cognitive-behavioural angle**, they could recognise their thought distortions and had practiced alternative responses to triggering situations.

Yet none of this intellectual understanding had created lasting change. Why?

The Missing Dimensions

As I watched them interact, I noticed what their previous therapy had missed:

Somatic level: Sarah's breathing became shallow whenever James's voice took on a particular tone, triggering an unconscious stress response that made rational communication impossible.

Energetic level: The space between them felt charged with unspoken grief—they had lost a pregnancy two years earlier but "moved on" without fully processing the loss together.

Systemic level: Their arguments always escalated during the week before James's mother visited, but neither had connected this pattern to their conflicts.

Cultural level: Sarah's Italian family expressed love through passionate engagement, while James's British upbringing equated emotional restraint with respect—they were speaking different emotional languages without realising it.

Temporal level: Their current struggles were amplified by the anniversary of James's father's death, though this connection wasn't conscious for either of them.

No single therapeutic approach could have captured all these dimensions. Each lens revealed important information, but none provided the complete picture needed for genuine transformation.

The Transdisciplinary Recognition

This is transdisciplinarity in action—the recognition that complex human experiences like relationships exist across multiple interconnected dimensions that can't be fully understood through any single disciplinary lens.

Traditional therapy often asks couples to fit into theoretical frameworks rather than allowing frameworks to adapt to couples' unique realities. But relationships are among the most complex systems humans create, involving:

- **Individual psychology**: Each person's internal world of thoughts, feelings, beliefs, and unconscious patterns

- **Interpersonal dynamics**: The unique "chemistry" that emerges when two specific people interact
- **Family systems**: The multi-generational patterns and influences that shape relationship expectations
- **Cultural context**: The spoken and unspoken rules about how relationships "should" work
- **Somatic experience**: The body-based information that often contradicts what people say they feel
- **Spiritual dimensions**: Questions of meaning, purpose, and transcendent connection
- **Historical influences**: How past experiences, both individual and collective, continue to shape present interactions
- **Environmental factors**: The impact of work stress, financial pressure, living conditions, and life transitions

Why Relationships Demand Multiple Ways of Knowing

Instead of forcing couples into predetermined theoretical boxes, transdisciplinary work means asking, "What lenses do we need to understand what's really happening here?"

The Shift from Single-Focus to Multiple-Focus

Traditional approach: "Let's work on your communication patterns" (ignoring body language, family history, cultural differences, timing factors, etc.)

Transdisciplinary approach: "Let's understand your communication patterns within the context of your stress responses, family patterns, cultural backgrounds, current life pressures, and relationship history"

From Problem-Focused to Pattern-Focused

Traditional approach: "You argue about money" (treating the topic as the problem)

Transdisciplinary approach: "Money discussions trigger deeper patterns related to security, control, childhood experiences, gender roles, and life stage pressures" (seeing the topic as one expression of multiple underlying dynamics)

Beyond Academic Theory: Practical Transdisciplinarity

Transdisciplinarity isn't just an academic concept—it's a practical necessity for effective relationship work. The key characteristics that make it effective aren't abstract principles but practical approaches that create breakthrough moments for real couples.

Principle 1: Focus on Connections, Not Just Parts

Traditional therapy often examines relationship elements in isolation: communication skills, conflict patterns, sexual intimacy, and family dynamics.

Transdisciplinary work recognises that these elements interact in ways that create the actual relationship experience.

Principle 2: Include Multiple Perspectives Simultaneously

Rather than choosing one theoretical lens and sticking with it throughout treatment, transdisciplinary work fluidly incorporates whatever perspectives illuminate the couple's reality.

Principle 3: Work with Living Systems, Not Static Problems

Relationships are dynamic systems that change moment by moment. Transdisciplinary work responds to what's emerging rather than following predetermined treatment protocols.

Principle 4: Address Real-World Complexity

Academic therapy often happens in controlled environments, focusing on isolated issues. Transdisciplinary work acknowledges that couples exist within complex webs of influence: extended family, work pressures, health challenges, financial stress, cultural expectations, and life transitions.

The Integration Challenge: Multiple Ways of Knowing

Effective relationship work requires understanding that human connection operates across multiple dimensions simultaneously. This insight emerges from various fields, each offering crucial perspectives.

The Minor Key of Relationships

Anthropologist Tim Ingold (Ingold, 2021) distinguishes between approaching life "in the major key" (logical, systematic, cause-and-effect) vs. "in the minor key" (intuitive, flowing, responsive to subtle variations). Most relationship therapy operates in the major key: "Identify the problem, apply the technique, expect the result."

But relationships exist primarily in the minor key—full of subtle variations, emotional currents, and responses that follow feeling rather than logic. The major key asks, "What communication technique will fix this?" The minor key recognises, "What deeper yearnings are expressing themselves through this conflict?"

Effective relationship work requires fluency in both keys: systematic intervention when needed and intuitive responsiveness to what emerges. The most transformative moments often happen when therapists can move fluidly between structured guidance and sensitive attunement to the emotional undercurrents that logic alone cannot reach.

The Hidden Third

Basarab Nicolescu (Nicolescu, 2016) identified "the Hidden Third"—the invisible dimension that emerges between any two elements in relationship. In couples work, this is revolutionary.

Every relationship contains three elements: Person A, Person B, and the Hidden Third—the unique field that emerges when these specific two people interact. This Hidden Third has its own properties, rhythms, and possibilities that exist neither in individual A nor B alone.

Effective relationship therapy must access this Hidden Third—the living connection between partners rather than just their separate psychologies. As Nicolescu notes, "Love is not a representation but the presence of the Hidden Third." Couples can't think their way into love—they must create conditions where love can emerge as the space between them.

Pattern Recognition

Gregory Bateson spent his career understanding "the pattern that connects"—the underlying relationships that create meaning in living systems. For relationship therapy, this insight is crucial.

Every couple creates unique patterns—ways of greeting, handling conflict, making decisions, and expressing affection. Problems arise not from individual defects but from pattern violations—when natural rhythms become rigid, distorted, or broken.

Effective relationship therapy requires pattern recognition: seeing underlying rhythms and structures, respecting how current patterns once served the relationship, and helping patterns evolve rather than forcing completely new ones. As Bateson (1972) noted, "What couples argue about (territory) isn't as important as the pattern of how they engage with differences (map)." Therapy works with the map—the underlying pattern—rather than getting lost in content.

The Integration Imperative

These insights from multiple disciplines converge into practical guidance: relationships require both analytical understanding and experiential knowing, both historical insight and present-moment awareness, and both individual psychology and systemic perspective. The transdisciplinary approach doesn't choose between these—it integrates them based on what each unique couple needs.

This integration explains why single-approach therapies often struggle with relationship complexity and points towards frameworks that can honour the full richness of human connection while providing clear, effective intervention strategies.

The Practitioner's Journey: Beyond Single-Method Expertise

For relationship therapists trained in specific modalities, embracing transdisciplinary work can feel both exciting and overwhelming. The essential shift is from mastery to curiosity—developing what Tim Ingold (Ingold, 2021) calls "wayfaring" skills: the ability to read the terrain and adapt your navigation accordingly.

The Wayfaring Therapist

- Observes multiple dimensions simultaneously during sessions
- Notices when their primary approach hits limitations and becomes curious about what else might help
- Asks different types of questions to access information their training might miss
- Collaborates with colleagues from different backgrounds when appropriate
- Remains humble about what any single perspective can reveal

Transdisciplinary Integration across All Modalities

The transdisciplinary approach doesn't ask practitioners to abandon their foundations but to expand beyond single-lens limitations. Here's how each therapeutic tradition can integrate multiple ways of knowing while honouring their core strengths.

Person-Centred Counsellors: From Individual Empathy to Systemic Attunement

Your empathic foundation provides the perfect launching point for transdisciplinary expansion:

- **Expand your empathy** to include the relationship itself as an entity deserving of understanding, not just two individuals
- **Include somatic awareness** alongside emotional reflection—noticing what bodies reveal that words don't express
- **Integrate cultural context** understanding how clients' backgrounds shape their relationship expectations and communication styles
- **Add temporal dimensions** connecting present feelings to historical patterns while maintaining your here-and-now focus
- **Include systemic patterns,** seeing how individual experiences reflect larger family and social dynamics

Psychodynamic Therapists: From Individual Archaeology to Relational Excavation

Your depth insight becomes more powerful when expanded across multiple contexts:

- **Apply unconscious understanding systemically** seeing how individual internal dynamics create co-constructed relationship patterns
- **Include present-moment awareness** alongside historical insight—tracking how past patterns manifest in current interactions

- **Integrate cultural and social contexts** understanding how unconscious material is shaped by broader systems
- **Add somatic dimensions** recognising how unconscious patterns manifest in body language and physical presence
- **Include practical application** translating unconscious insight into conscious relationship skills

Classical Psychoanalysts: From Individual Depths to Intersubjective Waters

Your sophisticated unconscious understanding can be extended into shared territory:

- **Adapt analytic insight for couple systems** understanding how individual unconscious processes create relationship-level phenomena
- **Include intersubjective dynamics** seeing how unconscious material is co-created and maintained between partners
- **Integrate multiple timeframes** balancing historical understanding with present-moment intervention needs
- **Add practical skill dimensions** ensuring unconscious insight translates into conscious relationship capabilities
- **Include cultural and social contexts** understanding how unconscious patterns reflect broader systemic influences

Systemic Counsellors: From Pattern Recognition to Multidimensional Understanding

Your systems perspective provides an excellent foundation for transdisciplinary expansion:

- **Add individual depth work** understanding why people are drawn to particular roles in relationship systems
- **Include historical context** exploring how current patterns developed across multiple generations and contexts
- **Integrate emotional processing** helping partners access and express the feelings that drive systemic patterns
- **Add somatic awareness** recognising how systems patterns manifest in body language and physical positioning
- **Include cultural dimensions** understanding how broader social systems influence couple dynamics

Transactional Analysis Practitioners: From Ego States to Multi-Contextual Awareness

Your ego-state clarity can be enhanced with broader contextual understanding:

- **Expand beyond cognitive analysis** including emotional and somatic dimensions of ego-state shifts

- **Add developmental context** understanding how ego-state preferences developed through historical experiences
- **Include cultural perspectives** recognising how different cultures value different ego-state expressions
- **Integrate attachment understanding** seeing how ego states often protect against attachment injuries
- **Add systemic awareness** understanding how individual ego states create couple-level interaction patterns

Gestalt Therapists: From Present Moment to Multi-Temporal Awareness

Your present-moment skills become more comprehensive when expanded across time and context:

- **Include historical context** understanding how present contact patterns developed while maintaining here-and-now focus
- **Add cognitive frameworks** helping couples understand the meaning of their present-moment experiences
- **Integrate cultural awareness** recognising how different backgrounds affect contact styles and comfort levels
- **Include future dimensions** using present awareness to envision and practice desired relationship patterns
- **Add between-session support** extending present-moment awareness into daily life contexts

CBT Practitioners: From Cognitive Focus to Whole-Person Understanding

Your practical tools become more effective when integrated with deeper dimensions:

- **Include emotional depth work** exploring the feelings and attachment needs underlying thought patterns
- **Add somatic awareness** recognising how thoughts and behaviours manifest in physical experience
- **Integrate historical context** understanding how cognitive schemas developed through past experiences
- **Include cultural perspectives** recognising how thought patterns reflect broader social and cultural influences
- **Add relationship system focus** seeing how individual cognitions create couple-level interaction cycles

Integrative Therapists: From Multi-Modal to Truly Transdisciplinary

Your integrative foundation can evolve from technique combination to genuine transdisciplinary practice:

- **Move beyond technique collection** to understanding how different approaches illuminate different dimensions of the same relationship reality
- **Develop assessment frameworks** that guide integration based on what each unique couple actually needs
- **Create coherent theoretical synthesis** rather than random technique selection
- **Include multiple ways of knowing** simultaneously—cognitive, emotional, somatic, cultural, historical, and systemic
- **Practice fluid responsiveness** moving between different perspectives as the therapeutic moment requires

Eclectic Therapists: From Pragmatic Selection to Contextual Responsiveness

Your results-focused flexibility can be enhanced with deeper contextual awareness:

- **Develop pattern recognition** understanding which approaches work best within which cultural, historical, and systemic contexts
- **Include multiple assessment dimensions** ensuring your technique selection considers cognitive, emotional, somatic, and cultural factors
- **Create rationale frameworks** helping couples understand how different interventions address different aspects of their experience
- **Add contextual sensitivity** recognising how timing, culture, and relationship stage affect intervention effectiveness
- **Practice integrated assessment** using multiple perspectives simultaneously to guide your eclectic choices

The Transdisciplinary Shift: From Single Lens to Kaleidoscope Vision

What distinguishes transdisciplinary practice from simple technique integration is the simultaneous consideration of multiple dimensions. Rather than switching between different lenses, transdisciplinary practitioners develop kaleidoscope vision—seeing cognitive, emotional, somatic, historical, cultural, and systemic dimensions as interconnected aspects of the same relationship reality.

This doesn't mean becoming expert in every approach, but rather developing sensitivity to when your primary modality might benefit from complementary perspectives. It means asking not just "What technique should I use?" but "What dimensions of this couple's experience require attention, and how can I address them coherently?"

The goal isn't to abandon your therapeutic identity but to expand it—becoming a person-centred practitioner who includes systemic awareness, a Cognitive Behavioural Therapist (CBT) therapist who incorporates emotional depth, a Gestalt therapist who includes historical context, or a psychodynamic practitioner who integrates present-moment intervention.

Practical Steps Towards Transdisciplinary Practice

For all modalities, begin your transdisciplinary journey by:

1 **Identifying your primary strengths** and the dimensions they naturally address
2 **Recognising consistent limitations** in your current approach when working with complex couples
3 **Selecting one complementary perspective** to explore and integrate gradually
4 **Seeking supervision or consultation** with practitioners from different traditions
5 **Experimenting with small expansions** rather than attempting dramatic practice overhauls
6 **Tracking outcomes** to see whether expanded approaches actually improve your effectiveness

The transdisciplinary path requires humility about what any single approach can achieve and curiosity about what becomes possible when multiple ways of knowing inform each other. It's not about becoming everything to everyone but about developing the flexibility to respond to relationship complexity with approaches that match its multidimensional nature.

From Understanding to Innovation

The transdisciplinary understanding developed in this chapter sets the stage for exploring how these insights translate into practical therapeutic frameworks. The journey from philosophical recognition to effective intervention requires both courage and creativity—the willingness to venture beyond familiar theoretical territories while maintaining clear sight of the destination: healthier, more fulfilling relationships.

This recognition—that relationships demand transdisciplinary approaches—naturally leads to the question: What would such an approach actually look like in practice? This question, born from both personal necessity and professional curiosity, became the catalyst for developing new therapeutic frameworks that could honour relationship complexity while providing clear, effective pathways to transformation.

The journey from theoretical understanding to practical innovation begins with a simple but radical recognition: sometimes the most profound discoveries happen when you're genuinely lost at sea and must design a new vessel to reach safe harbour. It was in my own relationship shipwreck—and later, as a frustrated passenger on someone else's poorly equipped therapeutic vessel—that I began sketching the design for a different kind of craft altogether.

Reflection on Part 1: A Landscape of Approaches to Relationship Therapy

We have completed our reconnaissance of familiar waters, mapping both the treasures and treacherous currents that define the current landscape of relationship work. Our journey through the world of relationships revealed why these connections matter so profoundly to human flourishing, while acknowledging the unprecedented challenges couples face in our digital age. We've surveyed the major therapeutic vessels currently sailing these waters—from person-centred empathy to classical psychoanalytic depth, from CBT's practical tools to Gestalt's present-moment awareness—discovering both their valuable capabilities and inherent limitations when navigating couple dynamics.

Our exploration of current relationship therapy options revealed significant gaps between what couples need and what's typically available, while our dive into transdisciplinary thinking illuminated why single-approach frameworks inevitably miss crucial information about relationship complexity.

This comprehensive mapping provides essential context for what comes next: the discovery of new frameworks specifically designed to address the limitations we've identified. Having charted existing territories, we're now ready to explore innovative approaches that integrate multiple ways of knowing while maintaining clear direction towards relationship transformation.

Part 2

Discovering New Frameworks

Chapter 6

The Creation of Duo Coaching

Figure 6.1 A yacht approaching a tropical island: the promise of safe harbour after an ocean crossing, capturing the genesis of Duo Coaching—a new destination discovered through the lived experience of navigating relationship waters.

Designing a New Vessel from Personal Necessity

Sometimes the most profound discoveries happen when you're genuinely lost at sea. It was in my own relationship shipwreck—and later, as a frustrated passenger on someone else's poorly equipped therapeutic vessel—that I began sketching the design for a different kind of craft altogether (Figure 6.1).

This chapter is the story of the genesis of Duo Coaching: what caused it and what was within the vessel when it was launched. It is a story of intuitive enquiry, impulse, and innovation.

The Desire to Explore Uncharted Waters

This had been sown in me by my experience with relationship counselling and also experiencing the pain of relationships which had gone wrong over many years. I recognised that those years of unsuitable relationships had been a wonderful learning experience for me. I wanted to be able to use these experiences to help others maximise their years of good relationships.

My Need for a Destination

This was uncertain, but I needed forward movement, and it involved helping people on the way.

A Boat to Get Me and My Fellow Travellers to a New Destination

I had the rough sketches of a design, but there was a lot of work required to produce the detailed drawings and convert these into an attractive and seaworthy craft.

A Crew, as I Did Not Want to Do It on My Own

I was conscious that, having experienced one counsellor with two people, there was a power imbalance as I felt marginalised and ganged up on. I wanted the dynamics to be of a male and a female working jointly with the couples that wanted relationship help.

A Method of Operation

We needed to determine our therapeutic approach: would we rely on the steady, methodical progress of traditional weekly sessions or harness the powerful momentum of intensive, extended work? What range of therapeutic tools would we need for different couples facing different challenges at various stages of their relationship journey?

Just as skilled mariners select different sailing configurations based on weather conditions, crew experience, and destination urgency, we had to develop a flexible methodology that could adapt to each couple's unique circumstances. Some relationships needed gentle, consistent progress through calm waters; others required immediate, intensive intervention to navigate crisis storms. Our therapeutic toolkit would need the versatility to shift from one approach to another within the same session, responding to what emerged rather than rigidly following predetermined courses.

This operational flexibility became central to our developing framework—the ability to read the conditions in the room and adjust our approach accordingly, ensuring we could guide any couple towards their desired destination regardless of the complexity of waters they were navigating.

All those went into the melting pot alongside my transition from my previous career of running businesses and being an entrepreneur to becoming a full-time psychotherapist. During that transition I was working with business leaders who were successful but unhappy. A big part of that unhappiness was fundamentally about their relationships because they had devoted so much time and effort into having the trophy house, wife and children that they did not have the time to build and maintain great relationships. This normally created unhappiness and resentment. The unspoken thoughts were often revealed to me as *I work really hard so they have a nice house, school, holidays, life and yet I get no thanks, they just don't appreciate me.* Our society often drives people to be "successful," and the measure of that success is often those material trophies which are cries for external validation.

The Crew

I found Cathy who was in a psychotherapeutic practice group with me. I looked at her from afar and heard she was an Olympic sailor. I loved sailing but felt she was a level above me. She was quiet, and it took a few months before I summoned up the courage to talk to her in any depth. We got talking and found we both wanted to explore new avenues. I talked to her about my thoughts about relationship counselling and the need to have two therapists working together intensively. We grew in alignment and very quickly started to sketch out how we would work together and what would be different about our approach.

We decided we would sharpen our skills and trained with John and Julie Gottman (Gottman & Gottman, 2008) in America. They were probably the most famous relationship therapists at the time. For branding and language, we decided to use nautical analogies. Our logo was a boat in a rough sea; our language was very much about sailing and talking about rough seas and drifting apart. We designed what could be the style and format of our sessions. It was wonderful to reflect on how effortlessly this flowed. The agreement was that we were fundamentally going to do several things which are very different from established practice.

The Revolutionary Framework

What emerged wasn't born from strategic planning or academic research, but from something far more organic—intuitive enquiry guided by a simple yet radical question: "What do couples actually need?" Rather than starting with existing therapeutic conventions and trying to make them work better, we began with a blank canvas, allowing creativity and openness to reimagine relationship therapy entirely. This wasn't systematic design but intuitive responsiveness—part inspiration, part desperation, part happy accident.

We questioned everything: Why 50 minutes? Why one therapist? Why open-ended processes? Why separate individual issues from relationship dynamics? Each assumption became an invitation to explore alternatives, each limitation a doorway to possibility. The framework that emerged felt less like invention than discovery—as if we were uncovering something that had always been waiting to be found, something that honoured both the complexity of human connection and the practical realities of creating lasting change.

We designed what could be the style and format of our sessions. It was wonderful to reflect on how effortlessly this flowed. The agreement was that we were fundamentally going to do several things which are very different from established practice:

- **Two of us working with a couple** to create balance and prevent triangulation
- **Working intensively**—normally with six sessions spread over a few months because we wanted the therapy to be focused and brief. It emerged that the first session would be about three and a half hours, and subsequent sessions would be about two and a half hours
- **Outcome focused** with these agreed up front with the clients. Without this we would be wrestling with uncertainty and lack of coherence between the couple as to the purpose. The outcome also moves from the "problem" or "remedy" frame and creates ownership across the dyad
- **Integrated mix of approaches** and techniques from our wide range that would get the best result for each couple
- **Working on the triad** of the "You," "Me," and "Us." The normal relationship counselling approach is to look at the couple, their dynamics, and the present state. My view is that a couple cannot have strong foundations unless the individuals do too. It is important to understand the two separate individuals and the unhelpful patterns of behaviour that they have brought with them from their childhood, upbringing, and previous relationships
- **Comprehensive consultation forms** to be completed before they started, giving their background, timeline of their life, perspective on the relationship problems, and what they would like to have happen
- **Unlimited telephone and email support** between sessions 24/7 as we felt it would be better dealing with problems as they were emerging rather than dealing with the aftermath

We decided that it was important to triage clients before they came and, after an investigatory telephone conversation with both, to get them to complete a Consultation Form. Many clients commented that this made them really think and get in touch with their own experiences. It also set a tone for the first meeting that it will be an adult-to-adult relationship where they have agency and power.

Launch and First Voyage

We put all the ingredients together and produced a website because that was the way to find clients. We signed up to Google Pay per Click and sat there waiting for the phone to ring. From thoughts to launch was only a few weeks. We had no idea what would happen when the clients arrived, if, indeed, they would. The first contact was in 2009, and clients came in through the door in my house to a professionally set up counselling room, depersonalised and a very safe spacious environment.

I wanted clients to feel like welcome and valued guests. Water was available freely, and tea, coffee, and herbal tinctures were offered when they first arrived. Healthy snacks were even available for those losing energy during a long session. I also wanted to create a timeless space where there was no visible clock. This avoided them monitoring their progress through the dimension of time and allowed them to relax knowing the approximate length of the session. They also knew that we would try and end the session in a good place rather than on the stroke of twelve. Comfort breaks were also encouraged.

We positioned ourselves as the guides rather than the "experts" and made it clear in the introductions that we were there to understand how they had got to where they were now. We were not there to judge so that their openness and honesty would help us to understand and to plot together the course forward.

The First Breakthrough

Our first couple, let's call them William and Mandy, were not particularly well off. He liked to participate in sexual activities that she was not keen on. The first session unfolded, and we sat there as the so-called "newly appointed experts" hearing their stories and helping them understand each other's perspectives. It was interesting that their response was that we were the experts and seasoned veterans at this game.

One of my first realisations was in a relationship there is no reality, there is only perception, and those perceptions can be very different but equally correct. With a superficial layer of calmness and a *We have done this for ages,* we got through the first session and breathed a sigh of relief and thought *Wow, we are onto something, this feels like it is working.* Other sessions continued, and progress was being made. Our confidence grew as we were in tune and could see the enormous shifts that were happening in their relationship. By the end of six sessions, William and Mandy were launched on their own boat, crewing together with new energy and a changed destination. Since then, clients continued to flow. It seemed to be relatively effortless to find clients, who came through the website.

The essence of what we started off doing has remained the same. The approaches we used broadened out, and no doubt our insights, intuition, and skills got sharper. The feedback we got was hugely positive. I realised that what we had created was very different from traditional methods; it was also life-changing and hugely important. We had many clients who had followed the traditional route and, in their words, had spent a lot of time getting nowhere until they found us.

My Own Journey through Therapeutic Modalities

My quest began with a simple yet profound desire: to understand myself and help others on their paths to transformation. Like an explorer of ancient seas, each therapeutic modality became an island to visit, each offering unique treasures in the form of seeds of wisdom to collect and nurture.

The first port of call was clinical hypnotherapy, an enchanting island that offered the first glimpse of the power of the unconscious mind. Here lay tools both elegant and effective, providing direct access to the deeper layers of human experience. Yet while hypnotherapy offered profound insights, it felt somewhat one-directional, like reading a script without the richness of dialogue.

This realisation led to the twin islands of counselling—person-centred and psychodynamic approaches standing side by side. These shores offered new skills in empathic listening and understanding, yet they too felt incomplete. While they excelled at helping people unburden themselves and explore their past, they seemed to lack the tools for crafting lasting change and future direction.

The journey continued to the shores of coaching, both personal and business. Here was a welcome structure and future focus, starting firmly in the present moment. Yet questions arose: How had people arrived at their current situation? What unconscious patterns held them in place? Were their stated future desires truly their own, or merely conscious-mind constructs?

Then came the transformative discovery of Neuro Linguistic Programming (NLP)—a vibrant community that felt like finding my tribe. Here was a fresh approach to understanding and changing human patterns, dealing with the unconscious mind while avoiding the trap of being stuck in past trauma. It offered quick, elegant changes and an ever-growing toolkit of techniques. This island felt different—more alive, more dynamic.

But the journey wasn't over. Clean Language appeared on the horizon, offering a way to purify therapeutic questions, stripping away unintended influence. This led to Clean Space, using physical environment to facilitate change, and Symbolic Modelling, providing new ways to understand and work with internal experiences.

Perhaps most magical was the island of Constellations, where rooms full of strangers could become living maps of another's psyche, channelling insights and solutions from the collective field. This magic extended to work with pebbles— each one carefully collected from around the world, carrying its own energy and story. These simple stones, when arranged by clients to represent their current reality and desired future, became powerful tools for insight, revealing deep patterns and possibilities in mere minutes. The alchemy of watching seventy or more transform through this work or witnessing a single client discover profound truths through the constellation of carefully chosen pebbles revealed new dimensions of human connection and healing.

The expedition continued through various psychotherapeutic territories— Gestalt, transactional analysis, and beyond. Each new shore offered its own unique gifts, its own seeds of wisdom to be collected and carried forward.

Now, these collected seeds have been planted on a new island—one of transformation. Here, they grow together in a garden of possibility, each tool and technique available to be used at the perfect moment. This is not about being bound to a single approach but about having the freedom to draw from a rich repertoire, creating unique symphonies of change with each client.

This transdisciplinary approach represents the culmination of the journey—not as an endpoint, but as an ever-evolving practice. Like a master musician with access to many instruments, the art lies in knowing which tool to use, when to use it, and how to blend different approaches into harmonious and effective interventions for each unique individual's journey of transformation.

Some of these modalities are used within the 121 sessions, and some are used in the joint sessions. It is often helpful for the partner to see what is being uncovered within their partner and the tools used to unlock and create positive change.

New Crew Comes on Board

About eight years ago Cathy became unwell and was unable to devote the focused time that was needed in our sessions. It came to the point where I had to decide whether to stop completely or whether I should carry on. I went out and searched for who might be suitable. The brief was simple: female, experienced relationship counsellor, open to expanding her skills and someone I could trust and enjoy working with.

I met with two and intuitively chose Maria. She was a very experienced relationship counsellor and supervisor. She loved our approach, and what was different about it she found refreshing. Maria and I have been working together for over eight years. It is a different relationship from the one I had with Cathy, as Maria's skills and background are very different from mine. It is a partnership that works effortlessly creating the space for each other to contribute, hearing the insights the other one has on what is happening with a client. The sessions feel like two experienced musicians sometimes playing together, sometimes soloing and producing harmonious music for the clients. I feel incredibly fortunate to have found Maria and work with her. Together we can do so much more than we could do individually.

There is nothing more rewarding in a session than working with a couple that have been together for many years and have drifted apart and fallen out of love with each other and helping them reconnect and experience that moment in the room where they fall in love once again. The feelings, the emotions, and the energy are visceral. I often end a session and reflect on the difference that our interventions have made. They can have had a magical effect on the couple as well as changing their future. This can also have a huge benefit to their families and future generations.

I wanted to use my experiences, bad and occasionally good, in relationships to help others avoid the pain I had suffered and to experience the joy of great and sustainable relationships. I felt I had the skills, knowledge, and desire to make it happen.

The creation of Duo Coaching was different, unique, and broke the mould of relationship counselling in the UK and maybe beyond. I felt proud to break away from the normal ways of doing things, to be a disruptor.

Fifteen Years of Organic Evolution

The fundamental architecture we intuited in those early days has remained remarkably stable—two therapists, extended sessions, finite timelines, integrative approaches, outcome focus. What has evolved over fifteen years is the sophistication, confidence, and artistry with which we navigate within this framework.

Our therapeutic palette has expanded significantly. Where we once drew from perhaps six or seven modalities, we now fluidly integrate fifteen or more approaches—not because we collect techniques like trophies, but because each new tool we've mastered has revealed itself as essential for particular moments with specific couples. Constellation work, timeline therapy, parts negotiation, Clean Language, somatic approaches—each addition emerged from encountering couples whose needs exceeded our existing capabilities.

More importantly, we've developed what can only be described as seamless weaving. In early sessions, the shifts between modalities felt somewhat mechanical—we'd complete one intervention, pause, then consciously choose another approach. Now the integration flows like a conversation between old friends, with techniques blending so naturally that couples rarely notice the transitions. A constellation might evolve into timeline work, which flows into communication practice, which opens space for parts negotiation—all within the same therapeutic movement.

Perhaps most significantly, we've learned to trust silence and space. Early enthusiasm led us to fill every moment with intervention, afraid that unused time meant missed opportunities. Experience has taught us that some of the most profound transformations happen in the spaces between our words—when couples process, integrate, or simply breathe together in the safety we've created. We've become comfortable with not knowing, with allowing the session's organic rhythm to guide us rather than forcing predetermined agendas.

Our confidence has deepened into what feels like unconscious competence. Where we once consciously selected from our toolkit, we now find ourselves responding intuitively to subtle shifts in energy, emotion, or connection. This isn't abandoning a systematic approach but transcending it—the framework has become so internalised that we can focus entirely on what's emerging between the couple rather than on what we should do next.

The core design remains unchanged because it was right from the beginning. What's evolved is our artistry within that design—like master musicians who've moved beyond reading sheet music to creating spontaneous symphonies that serve whatever the moment requires.

Couples That We Welcome

We work with couples where they have a significant relationship problem and want help to get to a better place. The problems are typically that they have drifted apart over a number of years and need to reset their relationship, or there has been a betrayal, normally a physical or emotional affair and need help in recovering from this.

Our standard framework is six sessions spread over a few months. The sessions are long to give enough space for the clients to relax and make progress. The first is normally 3½ hours and subsequent ones 2½ hours. There is flexibility built in so that we can end each session in a good place rather than on the tick of the clock.

Some couples achieve their outcomes in less than six sessions. It is important that couples are fully committed to the process and are able to devote time and energy to making changes and seeing significant payback.

Our structure is that the sessions are spread out over time, depending on what the client's development is, what other priorities there are in their lives (but typically three to four months from start to finish). I want to make sure there is enough space between sessions for them to apply the learning in real life, to test out the ideas, get feedback, and embed the learning. The standard model of coming week after week at the same time and on the same day just doesn't give that space and could become a regular chore with not much having changed.

My view is that I do not want to spend the rest of my life working with a couple. It may be good financially, but am I really helping the client if after years they have not made a significant step forward? I feel that either they are wrong for me or I am wrong for them. When I hear stories of well-known and well-regarded therapists or psychoanalysts talking about seeing people for several years every week, I wonder if that is meeting the needs of the client or whether an alternative approach may be more appropriate.

Experience has shown that the first session needs to be about three and a half hours to explore how the couple have got to where they are right now. To understand them as a couple and the dynamics but also to understand them as individuals, previous relationships, and upbringing. In that first session we clarify the outcomes that they both want because we are driven very much by outcomes that are wanted. That way we can make sure they are coherent and compatible and can calibrate the progress that is being made.

It feels like the traditional approach is just drifting along and seeing if anything happens. Or, ending, as was my experience, with an abrupt and inelegant ending with one of the couple being dissatisfied. Our way is to clarify that *this is our destination, you are on board now, let's get there as quickly as possible but also in a way in which you will enjoy the journey, learn from us and learn from each other.*

Subsequent sessions are typically about two and a half hours long and are a mixture of the two of us working with the two of them on the "us" issues of them as a couple. Where relevant, we do one-on-one work on individual issues including unhelpful patterns of behaviour which are causing problems within the relationship.

We give unlimited telephone and email support between sessions, 24/7, because it is much better dealing with the problem in the moment rather than having to deal with the aftermath weeks later. That is something which everyone is impressed with and makes them feel safe and supported. From our side there is a professional boundary that this will not be misused. We have not yet had a four in the morning phone call, but this is a clear demonstration of our commitment to a healing process that does not engender dependency but trusts them as adults, over time, to take responsibility for their own choices and behaviours.

As to what happens within the session, we have a wide range of tools and techniques and will use whatever is going to get the best results for each couple and each individual. We can choose intuitively within the session focusing on the core areas such as communication and connection and pulling from our repertoire of over one hundred different exercises.

I liken this to the continually growing collection of tools that I have on my boat to keep her afloat, safe, and sailing well. There are a range of sails: main, genoa, storm jib, gennaker to deal with different wind strengths and directions. There are bungs and special glue to fill holes and stop her sinking; powerful cutters to cut through the rigging if the mast falls down; hammers to make things flatter or better joined; screwdrivers of different heads, angles, and sizes to tighten up the relationship between fittings; socket sets and spanners to improve the connections; magnets to pick up important items that have been dropped; tape to provide temporary repairs; sailmakers thread, needle, and palms to fix tears; torches to light the darkest horizon and crevices; meters to measure flow and energy; screws, washers, bolts, pins, and rings of varying sizes to replace ones that have fallen out under pressure or neglect; oil, lubricant, and sealant to keep moving parts working smoothly and antifouling to prevent other organisms getting attached and slowing down or destroying the integrity of the boat.

In terms of style, there is some empathetic listening and some directive work and some *would you like to try x?* There is also frequently the need to deal with what is happening in the unconscious (out of full awareness), what are the embedded patterns of behaviour which need to be changed. We are also flexible and aware enough to be able to make, in the moment, changes of direction and re-contracting.

The room in which we operate is in a very different environment from the counselling rooms that I have experienced. We get frequent positive feedback about our premises, that it feels safe, confidential, spacious, and professional and helps couples to open up, be vulnerable, and express facts and feelings that have been hidden for many years.

Our psychotherapeutic modality is truly integrative using a wide range of psychotherapeutic techniques. I have trained in a wide variety of modalities as I believe that there is no one "best" approach. What is most efficacious will depend on the client, the context, the problems, and their timing. We need to work on what is consciously presented, the unconscious and unsaid, the interplay and energy between the couple and all the warm data (Bateson, 2023) that is being picked up. Our clients are often surprised at the self-awareness that is created.

The Experiences Given

We try and give our clients a seamless journey to their desired outcomes through drawing on our training. Maria is trained in integrative counselling, and mine encompasses an eclectic range of modalities that are woven into our work. In the field of human understanding there is no limit on learning. For me it is about striking a balance between what is interesting, useful, and feels right to apply in our context. It is about both breadth and depth and what will, collectively, have the most positive impact. The modalities that we use encompass:

- Psychodynamic counselling: informed by the works of Freud (1949), Klein (1975), Bowlby (1988), Jacobs (2017), Erikson (1950), and Malan (1979)

- Client-centred therapy: informed by the works of Rogers (1951, 1961)
- Coaching: informed by the works of Passmore (2010), Day (2012), Dunbar (2016), Scott (2004), and Whitmore (2017)
- NLP: informed by my trainings with Pegasus NLP and the works of Bandler and Grinder (1975, 1976, 1979, 1982), Dilts (1980, 1990), O'Connor (1990, 2000, 2001), Andreas and Faulkner (1994), Hall (2011), and Seymour (1990),
- Gestalt: informed by the work of Perls (1951, 1994)
- Clean Language: informed by the works of Lawley (2000), Rees (2008), Owen (2004), and May (2013)
- Clean Space: informed by the works of Lawley (2017)
- Symbolic Modelling: informed by the works of Lawley (2017), Hodgson (2010), and Sullivan (2008)
- Time Line Therapy: informed by the work of Hall, M (1997), Hall, L (2005), and James (1988, 1989, 2009, 2017)
- Transactional analysis: informed by the works of Berne (1964) and Stewart (2012)
- Drama triangle: informed by the works of Karpman (2014), Stewart (2012), and Whitfield (1991)
- Clinical hypnotherapy: informed by the works of Erickson (1991), Allen (2004), Aravind (2002), Yapko (2012), Gafner (2000), Hammond (1990), and Hudson (2000)
- Parts negotiation: informed by the works of Satir (1988)
- Systemic Constellations: informed by the works of Hellinger (1998) and Whittington (2016)
- Human Constellations: informed by the works of Hellinger (1998, 2001, 2003), Franke (2003), Cohen (2006), and Payne (2005)
- Personality profiling: tools that we use include:
  - Jungian archetypes (Jung, 1921, 1953–1979)
  - Emotional command systems
  - Bowlby's attachment styles (Bowlby, 1979)
  - Seligman's character strengths (Seligman & Peterson, 2004)
  - Kahler's drivers (Kahler, 1975)

Inspiration and Reflection

Clarity often only comes after a passage of time to allow yourself to look back with interest. Being open-minded about what happened and intrigued about why you did what you did then and what the consequences of that were. My experiences with traditional relationship counselling led me to launch across a very uncertain sea. Duo Coaching was an intuitive leap and maybe at the time I didn't really know why I shaped it as it was. Looking back there were some very clear intentions.

I had learned what didn't work for me, so the key elements that I had created were:

- The space needed to be liminal, to be a place where people felt safe, where they felt there was room physically and emotionally for them to occupy

- Time—which also needed to be spacious. To walk into a session knowing that you have only got 49 minutes to go compresses feelings and creates a sense of urgency and anxiety
- Balanced energy—my experience was that one counsellor with two clients created an imbalance, a feeling of preference, taking sides even if that didn't exist. It was also really important for there to be two different perspectives, male and female, and different experiences
- Destination—it must have a clear destination; otherwise, as I had experienced, there is just a sense of drifting with no idea of how many months or years it would take to get to a better place
- Length of intervention—it was pre-framed as six sessions, and I would say 95% of clients achieved their outcomes within six sessions, and some quicker than that. This is really important in galvanising the couples to maximise their efforts in a short journey
- Flexibility—we were all on a journey and had no idea what the wind and sea state would be. We had to be able to respond to what was happening in that moment, what was emerging between one session and the next
- Engagement—both of the couple have to be engaged in the process and working on it as if not we can't help. We have sacked couples because they weren't committed
- A wide range of tools—if there is only one modality being used, then that might fit a few but is unlikely to be flexible and dynamic enough to cope with all situations
- Commitment—we are there to provide support between session 24/7. This keeps clients engaged and shows our commitment to them. It increases their feelings of power and is a demonstration of our faith in their ability to behave as adults
- Costs—counsellors typically charge an hourly rate with uncertainty over the number of sessions. We pre-frame the number of sessions that most people need and the total cost so that the cost of cure is clear
- Scheduling appointments—we are flexible and space out sessions, and it typically takes three to four months from start to finish because what is really important is to create that space, to apply the learning in real life and to test out new ideas to see what is happening

What has changed between day one and now, fifteen years later? Very little. To see the evidence that it works is incredibly fulfilling. The Duo Coaching framework emerged organically from necessity and intuition, but sustainable change requires more than innovative practice—it demands clear principles that can guide others. What essential conditions must be present for relationship therapy to create genuine transformation, and how can practitioners ensure these conditions exist regardless of their theoretical background?

Sometimes the most seaworthy vessels emerge not from careful naval architecture but from the urgent necessity of mariners who found themselves adrift in inadequate craft. The Duo Coaching framework wasn't designed in theoretical shipyards but forged in the practical crucible of real couples seeking safe passage through relationship storms. What began as an intuitive response to the limitations of conventional therapeutic vessels has evolved through fifteen years of voyages into a craft that consistently guides couples to harbours they never imagined possible. Like all innovations born from necessity rather than convention, its true test wasn't whether it matched established blueprints but whether it could navigate the actual waters where relationships struggle and thrive. The vessel has proven itself not through theoretical elegance but through the transformed lives of hundreds who have sailed aboard it—each voyage refining the design, each successful passage validating the courage to venture beyond familiar shores in service of more effective navigation.

Chapter 7

A Transformative Space—What Comes into the Room?

When experienced mariners prepare for a challenging voyage, they understand that success depends not just on the vessel and crew they can see but on reading the invisible forces at work—the deep currents running beneath the surface, the pressure systems moving across distant horizons, the gravitational pull of unseen celestial bodies that influence tides. Similarly, when couples enter the therapeutic space, they bring far more than their presenting concerns. They carry the invisible cargo of generational patterns, cultural currents, and unspoken histories that shape their relationship in ways neither partner may fully recognise.

Who Is This Not For?

The Deception Dilemma

The first category of couples we cannot effectively help involves fundamental dishonesty about the relationship's current reality. Most commonly, this manifests when an affair has been discovered but continues covertly while the couple attends therapy. The unfaithful partner engages with the therapeutic process not to rebuild the relationship but to create a narrative that allows them to leave with their conscience intact: "Well, I tried therapy, but you didn't try hard enough."

This dynamic creates an impossible situation. The betrayed partner attempts to heal and rebuild trust based on incomplete or false information while unknowingly competing with an ongoing outside relationship. They blame themselves for being unable to "get past" what they believe happened, unaware that the betrayal is actually continuing and often deepening.

The presence of two therapists with different perspectives allows us to identify these patterns relatively quickly. We may ask direct questions about the affair's status, but even when met with dishonesty, our combined observations and experience typically reveal the truth within a few sessions. We approach these situations with compassion, understanding the complex motivations involved, but we cannot facilitate healing built on a foundation of ongoing deception.

The Emotional Departure

The second category involves couples where one partner has already emotionally exited the relationship while maintaining the appearance of engagement. This individual has moved through their own internal process—often including grief, anger, and acceptance—and reached a decision to leave but hasn't yet communicated this clearly to their partner or to themselves.

They attend therapy to satisfy external expectations or to ease guilt about ending the relationship, but their heart and mind are already elsewhere. Unlike the engaged partner who brings genuine hope and energy for change, this person goes through the motions without authentic investment in the outcome.

This emotional departure creates a profound imbalance that makes meaningful therapeutic work impossible. One partner is fighting for the relationship while the other has already surrendered. We recognise this pattern with understanding—sometimes people need time to reach difficult decisions, and the therapeutic process can provide valuable closure even when reconciliation isn't the outcome. However, we cannot create genuine transformation when only half of the couple is genuinely present for the journey.

The Secondary Gain of Staying Stuck

There is a third category of couples we cannot effectively help: those who derive secondary gain from maintaining their relationship problems. These are individuals who find it more comfortable to remain in the victim role, using their partner's behaviour as the primary explanation for their own unhappiness, unfulfillment, or life circumstances.

In 15 years of practice, I have yet to encounter a relationship problem that was entirely one person's creation. Whether the dynamic is 99% one partner's patterns and 1% the other's, or a more equal 50/50 co-creation, there is always some element of mutual construction in relationship difficulties. The partner who "doesn't cause problems" may contribute through withdrawal, enabling, conflict avoidance, or simply choosing to remain in a situation they find unacceptable.

For some individuals, acknowledging their role in co-creating relationship patterns feels too threatening. It's safer to maintain the narrative that "if only my partner would change, everything would be fine." This position provides several unconscious benefits:

- It absolves them of responsibility for their own happiness and life choices
- It allows them to avoid the vulnerability required for genuine intimacy
- It provides a ready explanation for any personal dissatisfaction or unfulfillment
- It eliminates the need to examine their own patterns, triggers, or contributions

These individuals often express interest in relationship improvement while simultaneously resisting any exploration of their own role in maintaining problematic dynamics. They seek validation for their victim narrative rather than tools for transformation.

We cannot help someone who is more invested in being right about their partner's wrongness than in creating positive change. Effective relationship work requires both partners to move from blame to curiosity, from righteousness to vulnerability, from "fixing them" to "growing together."

Unless both people can visualise a better relationship and are willing to invest the energy and vulnerability required to create it, our approach will feel threatening rather than helpful. The comfort of familiar dysfunction often feels safer than the uncertainty of genuine change.

We recognise this pattern with compassion—sometimes staying stuck serves important psychological functions. But we also acknowledge our limitations: we cannot want change more than our clients do, nor can we create transformation for those who prefer the secondary benefits of remaining in their current patterns.

Who Is This All For?

Our clients are couples that have been together for some time and who are not in a good place in their relationship. They come from a wide range of cultures, religions, and backgrounds. They may be married or in a long-term, committed relationship. They are generally reasonably well off and heterosexual, although we are open to all preferences. The problems in the relationship have often been simmering for some time, with one being more consciously aware of the other.

There is often embarrassment about how two intelligent capable people who once loved each other have failed in something so important. There is also fear, both of remaining stuck in an unhappy place and of splitting up and all those years "gone to waste."

Diversity and Universality

The Duo Coaching framework is entirely agnostic regarding race, culture, creed, religion, and sexual orientation. Maria and I are both heterosexual individuals in separate committed relationships, yet we work effectively with couples across the full spectrum of sexual preferences and relationship structures. While same-sex couples bring different energetic dynamics to the therapeutic space, the fundamental principles of healthy relationships—communication, connection, commitment, fun, growth, and trust—remain universally applicable.

Statistically, the vast majority of our clients are heterosexual couples, reflecting the broader population demographics. However, we have worked successfully with same-sex couples, polyamorous individuals, and partners from vastly different cultural and religious backgrounds. The beauty of focusing on underlying relationship dynamics rather than surface characteristics is that the work transcends these differences.

Our clients have included couples from different continents, opposing political viewpoints, contrasting religious traditions, and widely varying cultural expectations about partnership roles. What we consistently discover is that beneath these surface differences lie remarkably similar human needs: to be seen, understood, valued, and loved authentically.

The framework's effectiveness doesn't depend on couples sharing our backgrounds, beliefs, or lifestyle choices. It depends on their willingness to engage honestly with the process of understanding themselves, each other, and the relationship they're creating together. Love, after all, is a universal human experience that transcends the boundaries we often imagine separate us.

Whether working with a Christian-Muslim couple navigating interfaith challenges, partners from different socioeconomic backgrounds, or same-sex couples facing family acceptance issues, the core work remains the same: helping two people create a relationship that honours both their individual authenticity and their shared commitment to building something beautiful together.

Relationships Are Hard Work

A marriage or long-term committed relationship is inevitably very different and harder than expected. In the words of poet and author David Whyte (2009):

> If we feel we're being tested during the engagement, then marriage itself is a fearsome examination during which we are almost always found wanting. It's interesting to discover in a search through all periods of literature and culture that happy marriages are seldom depicted. If they are depicted at all it is usually as a prelude to a story of happiness soon to be disturbed or destroyed
>
> This may be not because there are no happy marriages but because what defines happiness in marriage might look so different from the inside that we cannot recognise it or describe it from the outside. Most marriages are dynamic moving frontiers, hardly recognisable to the participants themselves; moving frontiers that occupy edges of happiness and unhappiness all at the same time.
>
> (p. 265)

It usually takes months, even years, for the couple to discuss the problem and agree on the next step. The cycle of change with pre-contemplation and contemplation can be very prolonged (Prochaska & Norcross, 2001).

Every couple is unique and fascinating in their differences. We are working with a system of infinite complexity where one small change can create a dramatic improvement. The skill is in knowing where to look and what buttons to press.

When working with a couple, there are many layers, many dimensions that need to be revealed and understood to get the full picture of how a couple and two individuals have got to where they are right now. We are dealing not just in the now but with many years of emotional echoes. With an understanding of their journey and their charts, we can help them move to their desired destination. This is one of many wise observations of the author, commentator, and filmmaker Nora Bateson (2023b).

You do a thing and then something happens so more things happen mostly in ways that are impossible to track or correlate. The variables excite the other variables into inter calculable storms of consequences and consequences of consequences. It is tricky because these consequences of consequences can unfurl and tear apart relation and interdependence as well as generate possibilities.

(p. 9)

These are words that very much resonate with me and my personal philosophy, which inform my own practice and writings.

My insights from Duo Coaching, my life experiences, and my research are that a couple bring with them shadows from the past and unrealised ghosts that are anchoring them to the rocks and preventing them from moving forward in the right direction. Diving below the surface and freeing the snagged anchors requires several different approaches as they need to understand what is below both of their surfaces. Reflecting on this has led me to research into transcontextuality and warm data. I explore these in the remainder of this chapter.

"The larger the number of perspectives we can bring to bear on a problem, the more likely it is that we will achieve a solution that work" (Bateson, 1972). These are the words of Nora Bateson's father, Gregory, the noted anthropologist and cyberneticist, with which I concur. "Conventional" relationship counselling will often deal with what is presented in the room, which is largely the spoken conscious feelings. We need to go much deeper and understand the patterns of behaviour that have been created in their lives. These will include the following:

Warm Data

The identification of warm data is one of those insights I have had during my engagement with this critique. Warm data (Bateson, 2023b) is defined as transcontextual information produced through communication forms, both direct and indirect, that combine contexts. We exude warm data in our eyes, our smiles, our verbal and non-verbal conversations, and the importance we call to relationships with others at the personal, family, and community levels and in local national and global contexts.

A couple is a complex system, and warm data is key to understanding the interrelationships that connect elements of them with each other and the wider world. Warm data captures the qualitative dynamics and offers another dimension of understanding to what is learned through quantitative (cold) data. It is a specific kind of information about the way a couple comes together to give vitality to that system. By contrast, other data will describe only the parts, while warm data describes their interplay in context.

Qualitative data from the test scores, calibration, and responses are surrounded by a cloud of more data and energy. Warm data is certainly alive in our therapy room and is used to create a holistic understanding of the individuals, the couples, and their place in the world.

Hero's Journey

I have been reflecting on my journey through life, sea, and my professional practice. I have also read many of the inspiring stories of journeys of exploration and discovery by sea, including books on and by Columbus (1942), Vespucci (2007), De Gama (1997), Magellan (1969, 2003), Drake (1998), Cook (1994), Darwin (2019), Slocum (1978), Amunsden (1999), Shackleton (2015), Scott (1913), Heyerdahl (1950), Chichester (1967, 1975), Rose (1968), and Moitessier (2019).They all have at their core a passion for finding more, uncertainty on how to get there and the knowledge that the journey will be challenging and perilous. These follow the pattern set out by Joseph Campbell (1949) in the Hero's Journey.

The Hero's Journey is a fundamental paradigm in storytelling that involves a heroic character who goes on an adventure, facing a series of trials and meeting archetypal figures. The journey typically follows a cyclical pattern: the call to adventure, supernatural aid, the road of trials, the approach to the inmost cave, the ordeal, the reward, the return, and the reintegration with society. This monomyth represents the Hero's internal and external struggle, their transformation, and the attainment of wisdom or elixir that they can bring back to their community. Campbell's (1949) work explores the ubiquity of this narrative pattern across diverse cultures and its significance in human experience.

An insight has been that I have been on a Hero's journey many times, albeit on a much smaller scale. I want to use my insights to help clients on their Hero's journey to find the wisdom to change their lives for the better. They also need to understand that they have to rebuild their lives, often resetting their whole relationship. They may still be carrying the dissonance of when they first committed to each other expecting their individual lives to be only enhanced. The "me" may have got swamped by the "us."

In the words of David Whyte (2009):

> …We often enter marriage with images of how it will enhance our sense of self, increase the happiness we already possess and end a sense of aloneness. After the initial euphoria we just as often find that in the marriage itself our sense of self is obliterated, previous sources of happiness disappear and our sense of isolation is made more acute through the constant proximity of the other. Their never-ending presence suddenly seeming to give us no time to think or gain a larger view. What is difficult about the imagined happiness of marriage is that the hard reality that both sides of the partnership have to rebuild their lives from the razed foundations of their former individual existences, and faced with this discovery we cannot really believe this radical rebuilding from scratch is necessary. We want to remain intact and untouched and we soon intuit it is impossible. The temptation at this point is to hold ourselves back from a full participation. Ironically if we want to preserve ourselves, we have to make a new home for that self and not retreat into the old house. Marriages often begin to fail when

one side or the other refuses to begin building from this new joint foundation but wants all the development on their previously planned side of the street.

(p. 266)

What is fascinating and almost existentially mischievous about marriage is that whatever one side of the partnership wants will not occur; whatever the other side of the partnership desires will not occur and that whatever does occur is the combined life that emerges from first the collision and then the conversation between the two, the conversation that may seem foreign to both to begin with; something they might not recognise or even think they want.

(p. 267)

On my journey through life, the sea is transcontextual, as a reservoir of all possibilities and infinite variations of colour, waves, currents, and depths. The journeys that I embark on into the unknown are liminal journeys like the Hero's journey. I am using this mythology of journeying to more deeply explore this public work at the micro (individuals and couples) and macro (practice and sector) levels.

There are multiple journeys that our clients need to go on as "Me," "You," and "Us." We are their guides on their own Hero's journey. We need to ensure that they own their change and become self-sufficient. Having achieved their desired outcomes, they also have the relationship tools to cope with the vagaries of future life.

A realisation for me has been that, all along, our clients are the Heroes of their own story going on an important and perilous journey and that we are the guides. This feels to be a very different relationship than exists in most forms of relationship therapy where the therapist can often be seen as the wailing wall, to help the clients to offload and create their own learning, or the mountain top guru, dispensing wisdom. In Duo Coaching, we are in the room and beyond the room, using our skills, experience, and intuition to create significant energetic shifts. This journey is about transitions, helping them to open up the closed doors in themselves where they have put pain and disappointment.

The Male

In the room we normally have one male and one female client. We are very happy to work with all sexual preferences and non-binary states, but the clients that we have, so far, have all been heterosexual couples from all walks of life. They, like all individuals, will have different perceptions of the situation and the solutions. The fact that there are two of us in the room, Maria and myself, a male and female, allows the male to relax into the safe space of feeling that *he will understand me and we can talk man to man.*

Social stereotyping will often have made the male feel that expressing feeling is a sign of weakness and *big boys don't cry*. Guiding the male to express their feelings, listen to their partner's feelings, and show emotions is often hugely transformational to their sense of self.

I find that there is often a young boy hiding inside, desperate to please their father or teacher and to receive unrequited praise and affirmation. For the grown man to understand that and to be able to, in a dissociated way, talk to their younger self, express their supressed feelings, and achieve internal validation is often life changing.

Another pattern that needs to be understood and resolved is the ego roles that are being played out in the relationship (Berne, 1961). Is it an adult-to-adult one or does the female partner slip into a nurturing parent role and allow the male to be a free child. Has the woman married the hero or the child? In conflict does it deteriorate to a critical parent to adapted child, with the male normally filling the child role. It is fascinating to see these patterns being played out, so frequently, in front of us, often with the two individuals being blissfully unaware of this and the dissonance it creates.

I am in the very fortunate position, through my life experiences, of being able to see, understand, and empathise with the male (as well as female) perspectives. Through my responses and guidance to the male, they can feel that they are not alone on their pathway.

An insight for me has been the burden I have carried for over 60 years of the internal conflict between the big, strong, silent stereotypical male, the person that would have been praised by my father, and the sensitive, empathic me. This has frequently helped me to liberate deep feelings from male clients and give them permission to be vulnerable.

The Female

Maria provides a safe space for the female to relate to, and in my interactions with Maria, I can model positive male/female communication and understanding. My resonance with the male perspective of her partner also helps her to see what is happening for her in the relationship. The fact that Maria and I are male and female and are actively demonstrating the adult-to-adult roles in our interventions and relationships can give the female a different reference point. We can help her to realise if she has slipped into the parent role without realisation of the impact it is having on the relationship, where she has unknowingly encouraged her adult partner to become a child.

Ghosts

In the room there is not just me, Maria, and the couple. The couple bring in a sense of many ghosts, and the session is often an attempt to give a body to the ghost so we can all see them and have a conversation with them. In my own early experience of couple counselling, it was as if we brought in many ghosts that were haunting us and then left them there on that not very seaworthy craft with an inattentive captain—a ghost ship which we abandoned.

Here is a description of the metaphorical ghost ship that we encounter in our first session with some clients:

> *We observed the couple's interaction as if witnessing a spectral vessel adrift on a misty sea of unresolved conflicts. The ship, once a proud and sturdy craft, now creaked with the weight of unspoken resentments and unfulfilled expectations. Its sails, tattered by years of emotional storms, hung limply in the absence of shared purpose.*
>
> *At the helm, the partners stood locked in silent struggle, each grasping for control of a phantom wheel that no longer steered their course. Their eyes, hollow and distant, gazed past one another into the fog of their own perceptions, failing to recognise the shared isolation of their journey.*
>
> *Maria and I, acting as a lighthouse on a distant shore, sought to penetrate the haze with beams of insight and reflection. Each illumination revealed spectral crew members—past traumas, family-of-origin issues, and maladaptive patterns—that haunted the decks, influencing the couple's every move yet remaining largely unseen.*
>
> *As the session progressed, our interventions served to calm the turbulent waters of their communication, allowing the couple to gradually perceive the true state of their vessel. Moments of clarity broke through like shafts of sunlight, revealing glimpses of the vibrant ship that once was and could be again.*
>
> *The challenge lay in guiding this ethereal craft back to corporeal waters, where the couple could jointly repair and recommit to their shared voyage. Our role was to help them exorcise the ghosts of their past, rekindle the spark of connection, and chart a course through the fog towards shores of mutual understanding and renewed intimacy.*

Here are some of the ghost phenomena which we work together to describe and get to know better.

Conversational Styles

The most frequent presenting problem is the inability to have important conversations with each other. One will often feel unheard, or conversations will turn into arguments, blame, and defensiveness, and resolution will be avoided.

Using the Gottman model of Bids for Connection (Gottman, 2008) can help unlock where the conversational problems have started and show the importance of giving a turning towards response when their partner makes a bid.

Other important dimensions are expressing clearly what is wanted, rather than expecting their partner to mind-read them. *If they love me, they will know what I want*. We coach our couples in being able to express their feelings to each other and to be truly listened to. They also need to clarify whether they just want to vent, have empathy, or help in finding a solution. A common pattern for males is that they will not listen having defaulted to problem-solving mode.

Sex

I find it fascinating that a topic that is so important to many couples is rarely talked about because *it is too embarrassing*. The frustration, resentments, and misunderstanding fester; the elephant in the room grows, and resolution drifts further away. We create a safe space where clients can, metaphorically, take all their clothes off and express their long-hidden desires and needs.

I am also fascinated that, with our guidance and gentle questions, how easy it becomes for a couple to talk about something that is so elemental and important in their lives.

Shadows of the Past

Individuals may be consciously aware of the patterns created by their pasts, or they may be buried in their unconscious. Here are the main areas.

Parental Relationships

Increasing numbers of our couples are coming from broken families where their parents are separated or divorced. When this has happened during their childhood, it can leave them feeling rejected or damaged. This can also resonate in a fear of the same happening to their children, so a reluctance to address their relationship issues in case this triggers an ending of their current relationship. This becomes a strong presence in the room.

Death of a parent or important relative at a young age can also resonate many years later with a continuing sense of loss or abandonment. This can become conflated with their current state, and the inner child emerges, often feeling that the loss of their parent is their fault. This can be transferred into a fear of loss of their current relationship.

Intergenerational Trauma

Another presence in the room can be intergenerational trauma. My experience is that trauma of loss and rejection can continue down the family line for several generations. This is confirmed by the many pieces of research and writings on the issue that I have investigated (Bowers et al., 2016; Brothers, 2014; Danieli et al., 2016; Isobel et al., 2019; Lev-Wiesel, 2007; Yehuda & Lehrner., 2018). We learn not just from what our parents teach us but also from their unspoken unconscious. A vital part of our work is to guide parents to have a great relationship and inoculate future generations from the traumas of the past. Nora Bateson's wise observations again (2023b).

> Family is where we live. The next decades of human life on this planet will reveal how much each of us is nourished the relationships we live within today, tomorrow and next week. Did we perceive the complexity in ourselves, each other, and the world. Did we tend to the relationships that build more relationships. Attention to words spoken in the child that set the tone for the

> grandchildren's stories—the gift of a weekend conversation with the elders that holds a meta message of care for the past and future—willingness to be wrong, willingness to be angry willingness to be on the swirling time boat together.
>
> (pp. 316–317)

To quote Bruno Bettelheim (1960) on the power of the individual to sink or rise in difficult circumstances.

> In the concentration camp, all circumstances conspired to make the prisoner feel that his life was determined from without, and that he had no influence at all on his fate, which was entirely in the hands of his oppressors. The prisoner felt that his very self was invaded, and that he was turned into a powerless object, and his oppressors into omnipotent subjects.
>
> (p. 147)

Marx's (1959) concept of alienation—the disconnection from one's authentic self and capacity for genuine human connection—applies powerfully to relationship dynamics. When early family experiences create alienation from emotional authenticity, individuals struggle to form intimate bonds, perpetuating cycles of disconnection across generations. His thoughts are relevant to intergenerational trauma as poor familial relationships can create alienation from other human beings and feed difficulty in forming genuine social connections.

Upbringing

Early years development is vital to the creation of the neural pathways that facilitate empathy and understanding of others (Levy et al., 2019). We often find that the problems in a current relationship are rooted in each individual's experiences when they were very young—how their parents talked to each other and how they argued and showed love, or not, to each other. These are important foundations.

Siblings are also important; did they feel equal or less than equal? Were they first, middle, or last? Were their siblings from both birth parents, or were they step siblings? All these can have a disproportionate importance in the feelings of a young child that can plant an unconscious seed that grows, unseen.

It can be helpful to look at each individual through the lens of the Bowlby—Ainsworth Attachment theory (Bowlby, 1979) as well as Erikson's stages of development (Erickson, 1991). These can give great insights into what shadows have followed them into their current, adult state. A person can often, in terms of their behaviours, thinking patterns and engagement with the world, be stuck at the developmental age they were when they experienced traumatic events preventing healthy maturing.

Schooling

Many men that I have worked with have been unconsciously affected by their school days. If they had been sent to boarding school, a sense of rejection may linger. The power of a few words from a teacher such as *"you will never succeed, you are lazy"* is often still resonating many decades later in the unconscious and constraining their lives. Exorcising these ghosts is really important.

Previous Relationships

Increasing numbers of our clients have been in previous relationships that have not ended well. The adversarial legal approach in this country often comes at a high financial cost and at a huge emotional cost. It is also vital to learn what went wrong in the old relationship to enable lessons to be learned and blame to no longer inhabit the current couple relationship.

If there is the legacy of children brought from the previous relationship, there may still be unresolved conflict with the ex that causes collateral damage to the children and creates significant problems with the new partner who has become a step-parent.

In the words of Nora Bateson (2023b):

> A system responds as it has been honed to respond…A broken heart makes one more cautious. The past traumas are the filters through which new learning takes place. you cannot return to how you were before the heartbreak or trauma. You have changed, your relationships have changed and you see the world differently and the world sees you differently. Learning and healing from now on include those experiences. The submerged events are in the soil and while they cannot be removed the alchemy, the tone, and the contextual resonance can be shifted.
>
> (p. 133)

Children

Having children creates a paradigm shift in the relationship. Fortunate couples will have lovely children, be aligned on parenting styles, and share the load and the joy equitably. When this is not the case, children can cause resentment and division. A couple need to work as a team to get through the sleeplessness and new life.

Many couples put the "us" on hold in their focus on the children. If one gives up work to be the main carer, then when the children leave home, the purpose of the main carer will have largely left with them. The "me" will be depleted, and the "us" will have dissipated leaving an empty shell.

Sex, intimacy, and couple fun are often casualties of the onset of children. It takes focus and determination to keep these alive.

Couples in difficulty will often put off doing anything about their relationship until the children leave home with the belief that "they need to stay together for the sake of the children." My strong view is that relationship problems need to be dealt with quickly to prevent them from becoming embedded and creating years of misery. An amicable parting may be much better than subjecting the children to the misery of years of unhappy parents (Hetherington, 1999). Another study from over 20 years ago shows the impact on young children of their parent's divorce, but this was from a time when divorce was much rarer and the support for the children significantly less (Wallerstein & Lewis, 2004). Children can adapt to change as long as their parents actively co-parent and demonstrate love.

Childlessness

Desire to have children and an inability to have them can put a huge strain on the relationship. It often leaves one feeling *"it is my fault"* and the disappointment may resonate more strongly as they get older. The problem is increasing as couples are leaving it later in life, often for career and financial reasons. One in seven women have problems in conceiving, and about 20% of women have children after the age of 35 (Delbaere et al., 2020; NHS, 2023).

In Vitro Fertilisation (IVF) may provide a solution but comes at a significant financial and emotional cost and stress at the uncertainty of a positive outcome.

Adoption is another alternative but is a long and invasive process. There are currently 2410 children in the UK waiting to be adopted (UK Government, 2023), 80% of whom are from a difficult or abusive background. It takes an average of two years and five months for a child to be adopted. I know from my personal experience that it is a process that is failing to meet the urgent needs of the children as well as parents (Wilkie, 1994). The children are often traumatised by their previous experiences, and the impact of their rejection by their birth parents can emerge many years later.

Values

It is rare for a couple to explore their own values and share these with each other.

Without this shared foundation, how can they truly understand themselves and each other? How can they trust if the behaviour is aligned or not? We facilitate this exploration and guide clients through the impact this will have on each other.

Lack

We are all lacking many things in life; some of what we feel we lack may be illusory or fundamentally unnecessary. A Ferrari might seem a nice dream, but would it provide lasting happiness and fulfilment? We help clients express what they feel they are lacking in their lives and explore what will provide them with true fulfilment as an individual and as a couple.

An interpretation of Lacan's (Lacan, 1992) arguments is that:

> There is no particular philosophy of existence that is capable of providing us the answers we are looking for. The purpose of obliterating the subject's illusory convictions about his ontological security is to create an opening for the "truth" of his desire—for unconscious communications that break through the deceptive edifices of the ego.

The more we are able to liberate ourselves from the spell of fantasies—including the fantasy of the omnipotent analyst (Other) who is able to fill our lack—the better our chances for singularity. The act of accepting our lack—and of developing a measure of self-reflexivity with regard to the meanings of the Other— empowers us to move from unconscious repetition of inert existential patterns to a more active and life-enriching (poetic) connection with the world.

Future Goals

Who were we, who are we, and who do we want to be? There are an infinite number of possibilities for the future. We help our clients to explore this and ensure their future goals exist, are underpinned by their values, and are understood and aligned with their partner.

Without a chart and a destination, they will just drift.

The Art of Rhythm

Unlike traditional therapy models that impose a rigid weekly cadence, Duo Coaching recognises that meaningful transformation requires a more nuanced approach to timing and rhythm. We understand that a week may not provide sufficient space for couples to fully digest profound insights, complete meaningful exercises, or integrate new ways of being into their relationship dynamic. Instead, we collaborate with each couple to establish a bespoke rhythm that honours both their commitment to growth and the realities of their lived experience. This might mean spacing sessions two or three weeks apart, allowing time for deep self-exploration, examining relationship patterns, and genuinely applying the learning that emerges from our work together.

We navigate carefully around the natural ebb and flow of life—demanding work periods, school holidays, family commitments—ensuring that the coaching process enhances rather than burdens their journey. The art lies in finding that optimal frequency where momentum is maintained without overwhelm, where there's sufficient time for reflection and practice, yet not so much distance that continuity is lost. By attuning to each couple's unique capacity for processing and change, we create a rhythm that becomes a supportive framework for transformation rather than an additional pressure in already complex lives.

A Transformative Space

We consciously create transformative spaces that transcend the ordinary boundaries of conversation and reflection (Wilkie, 2025). This begins with establishing a liminal threshold—a deliberate crossing from the everyday world into a container held with intention, safety, and possibility. The physical environment, the quality of our presence as co-coaches, and the agreements we create together all contribute to forming this sacred space where clients can shed familiar personas and explore new ways of being. Within this transformative container, the usual rules of social interaction are suspended, allowing for deeper vulnerability, authentic expression, and the emergence of previously hidden aspects of self.

The power of such spaces lies in their capacity to accelerate insight and change—when people feel truly seen and held by two coaches working in harmony, they access parts of themselves that remain dormant in conventional settings. Here, limiting beliefs can be examined without judgement, new possibilities can be imagined without constraint, and profound shifts in perspective can occur naturally. The transformative space becomes a crucible for renewal, where clients don't merely discuss change but actively experience it, creating lasting transformation that extends far beyond the coaching room itself.

Face to Face and Online

The majority of our work is face to face, and couples may travel a long distance to come and see us. The fact that there are six intense sessions makes this more manageable. Clients have come from as far as Greece. The travel time can also be a rare opportunity for a couple to talk before and after a session, free from distractions. Where there is a crisis, we may have an intensive weekend of three sessions to get the couple back from the precipice. We do also work using Zoom if urgent support is needed. Many therapists moved to online during COVID-19. This may still be convenient for the therapist, but they should assess what is most effective for their clients.

I have a strong preference for face to face as this gives a much clearer understanding of their energy flows, opens up the warm data, and allows us to work somatically and utilise space to change state.

> *I started to read the stories of voyagers in the world of relationships and psychotherapy. They all had very different approaches to mine, and the voyages their passengers had been on seemed to be much longer and less fulfilling than mine. Was I wrong and were they right or did we just have different approaches. I felt that my approach had a clearer outcome and a clearer passage plan. Apart from their stories of voyages, I wanted to construct charts of how to get from now to the desired destination. There will inevitably be storms, adverse currents, and hidden rocks on the way as well as more clearly visible islands. I have tried to address these differing approaches below and question whether these are better, worse, or just different. After all, for the passenger it is not just about the destination, it is what they will experience and learn on the journey.*

Psychotherapeutic Approaches

There are many different approaches used in psychotherapy, with well over 50 different types, and the number is growing as people continue to develop new approaches. Most therapists are strong adherents to the one modality that they were trained in and use this in all their client interactions.

As explored extensively in Chapter 3, each approach offers valuable insights while also having inherent limitations when applied to relationship work. The efficacy of an approach is subjective to each client, each context, and each temporality, making direct comparison difficult. In summary, our Duo Coaching approach differs from accepted norms by:

- Using an integrative mix of approaches rather than single-modality adherence
- Having much longer sessions than the standard 50 minutes
- Working as co-therapists rather than solo practitioners
- Positioning ourselves as guides who utilise appropriate power dynamics
- Focusing on clear outcomes rather than open-ended exploration

Morals and Ethics

I believe that it is the responsibility of a therapist to use their skills and judgement to help their clients achieve significant progress towards better lives. I only want to work with clients where I am facilitating meaningful change.

While British Association of Counselling and Psychotherapy (BACP's) ethical principles of Autonomy, Beneficence, Non-maleficence, and Justice provide important foundations, they don't address areas of potential dissonance in relationship work, including whether:

- We are the right therapists for each specific client
- Clients are genuinely committed to improvement or locked in victim mode
- We're creating dependency rather than independence
- There are clear outcomes and ability to calibrate progress

I have worked with many clients who have had therapy in the past and, in their words, "spent a lot of time and money getting nowhere." The desire for a counsellor to earn a living may sometimes override what I believe to be ethical behaviour towards achieving client outcomes.

My Internal Navigation: The Confluence of Conscious and Unconscious Awareness

The Symphony of Internal Cues

During a session with clients, I'm simultaneously conducting and participating in a complex symphony of internal awareness. My head, heart, and gut are each providing different but equally valuable streams of information—cognitive analysis, emotional resonance, and somatic wisdom—all of which inform how I respond to what's unfolding in the room.

In my head, there's the cognitive processing: tracking patterns, making connections to previous sessions, noting inconsistencies between what's being said and what was shared before. I'm mentally cataloguing the techniques that might be useful, assessing the timing of interventions, and maintaining awareness of the session's arc and objectives. This is the "cold data"—the factual, analytical information that my training and experience help me organise and interpret.

But my heart is simultaneously gathering different intelligence. I'm feeling into the emotional undercurrents—the sadness beneath the anger, the fear hiding behind the defensiveness, the love that's struggling to express itself through layers of hurt. Sometimes I'll notice my own heart rate changing, a tightness in my chest, or a sudden warmth that seems to mirror what one of the clients is experiencing. These empathic responses aren't just emotional reactions; they're diagnostic tools that help me understand what's really happening beneath the surface conversation.

My gut provides perhaps the most mysterious but often most accurate guidance. There's a quality of knowing that emerges from my solar plexus—a sense of when to speak and when to stay silent, when to push gently and when to back off entirely. Sometimes I'll feel a sudden urge to shift direction in the session, or I'll sense that something important is about to emerge if I just create the right space for it. Other times, my gut will signal danger—that we're approaching territory that isn't safe to explore yet, or that one partner is reaching their capacity for the day.

The Dance Between Conscious and Unconscious Competence

What fascinates me about this work is how these different streams of awareness weave together. Sometimes I'm very conscious of what I'm picking up—I can feel my body responding to tension in the room, I can name the emotion I'm sensing, I can articulate why I want to try a particular intervention. In these moments, I might check with clients: "I'm noticing some tension between you right now—is that landing for you?" or "Something shifted in your face when she said that—what's happening for you?"

But increasingly, as my competence has deepened over the years, I find myself operating from unconscious competence. In these moments, things simply flow. I'll find myself saying exactly what needs to be said without having consciously planned it, or moving into a technique that perfectly matches the moment without having deliberately chosen it. My body will lean forward or back in just the right way, my voice will modulate to exactly the tone that's needed, my timing will be precisely calibrated to what the couple can receive.

This unconscious competence isn't about abandoning awareness—it's about trusting a deeper level of integration where my training, experience, intuition, and empathic attunement have become so seamlessly woven together that responses emerge organically from this unified field of knowledge and sensitivity.

The Multidimensional Field of Awareness

Adding another layer of complexity is my simultaneous awareness of Maria's experience alongside my own. I'm not just tracking what I'm picking up from the clients; I'm also sensing what she's receiving, how she's responding, and what the interplay between our different perspectives might reveal.

Sometimes I'll notice her body language changing before I've consciously registered what's happening with the clients. Other times, I'll sense that she's picking up something I've missed, and I'll create space for her to share her observations. There's a kind of peripheral vision that develops—I can feel when she wants to interject, when she's having a different response than I am, or when she's about to offer an insight that will shift the entire dynamic.

This creates what I think of as a multidimensional field of awareness. I'm simultaneously holding:

- What I'm consciously observing about each client
- What I'm unconsciously sensing from each client
- What I'm experiencing in my own body and emotions
- What I'm picking up about Maria's responses and insights
- What I'm noticing about the dynamic between all four of us
- The interplay between all these different streams of information

What's remarkable is how Maria and I have developed an unconscious choreography in these moments. Like musicians who've played together for years, we intuitively sense when one should lead and when one should follow, when to step forward into an active intervention role and when to step back into pure sensing and noticing. Sometimes I'll feel her about to speak and naturally create the space for her voice. Other times, she'll sense I'm building towards something and hold back, letting me complete the musical phrase. We switch roles fluidly—one moment I'm leading an exploration while she observes and tracks, the next moment she's guiding the couple while I notice what's shifting in the background.

This coordination happens largely below the level of conscious decision-making; it emerges from the same unconscious competence that guides our individual responses but applied to our partnership as co-facilitators.

Observing Language Patterns

In our sessions, one of the most revealing indicators of a client's mindset emerges through their habitual responses to simple questions like "How are you?" Defensive patterns like "not too bad," "can't complain," or "surviving" reveal underlying neural wiring that keeps clients in survival mode rather than thriving mode. These seemingly innocuous phrases actually require complex neurological processing—the brain must first activate representations of "bad," then suppress them through negation, finally extracting implied meaning. This cognitive overhead strengthens threat-detection circuits while weakening reward-processing pathways, creating a neurological bias towards caution and limitation that extends far beyond the conversation.

The transformation work involves helping clients recognise these automatic patterns and consciously choose life-affirming alternatives. When we guide clients from "not too bad" to "life's good" or "I'm thriving," we're literally rewiring their brains through neuroplasticity. The most effective approach combines awareness building—recording their language patterns for a week—with systematic replacement through implementation intentions: "When someone asks how I'm doing, I will respond with genuine enthusiasm about something positive in my life." Within, allegedly, 66 days of consistent practice, these new responses become automatic, creating measurable changes in brain structure and social outcomes. The ripple effects extend beyond the individual, as positive language patterns spread through social networks, improving relationships, workplace dynamics, and family systems.

The Integration Challenge

The art lies in integrating all of this information without becoming overwhelmed by it. It's like being a conductor who's not just following the sheet music, but listening to each instrument, feeling the acoustics of the hall, reading the audience's energy, and sensing the emotional journey that wants to emerge through the performance.

Sometimes the conscious and unconscious streams align perfectly—my gut instinct matches my cognitive assessment, my emotional response dovetails with what I'm observing, and Maria and I are in complete sync. These are the moments when everything clicks, when the intervention lands exactly as intended, when the couple experiences a breakthrough that feels almost effortless.

Other times, there's dissonance between these different streams, and that dissonance itself becomes important information. When my head says one thing but my gut says another, when I'm feeling something that doesn't match what I'm observing, when Maria and I are picking up different signals—these moments of internal conflict often point towards something crucial that's happening beneath the surface.

And then there are those rarer moments of conscious incompetence—when I simply don't know what to do next. In these instances, rather than rushing to fill the void with activity, I've learned to lean into the uncertainty. Sometimes I'll consciously create space for Maria to step in, trusting that what I'm missing, she might be seeing clearly. Other times, I'll choose silence, allowing the space itself to work its magic. There's tremendous power in those moments of not-knowing, when we resist the urge to solve or fix and instead let the couple's own wisdom emerge. These pauses often become the most profound moments of a session, when something authentic and unexpected can finally surface in the stillness we've created.

Learning to navigate this confluence of conscious and unconscious awareness, warm and cold data, and individual and collective sensing, has been one of the most challenging and rewarding aspects of developing as a practitioner. It requires cultivating a kind of internal spaciousness—the ability to hold multiple streams of awareness simultaneously without needing to immediately resolve them into action, trusting that the right response will emerge from this rich field of integrated knowing.

The Invisible Work: Before They Arrive: Getting into the Right Headspace

Our work begins long before the couple walks through the door. As a practitioner, I've learned that the quality of a session often depends as much on my internal preparation as it does on any technique or framework I might employ.

There's a particular kind of mental calibration required—a state that's both rested and prepared, open yet focused. I need to be emotionally available enough to receive whatever the couple brings into the room, while simultaneously maintaining the professional boundaries and clarity of thought that effective intervention requires.

With new clients, there's an additional layer of uncertainty that requires careful navigation. Yes, I have their consultation forms, their written accounts of their struggles and hopes. But these are static snapshots—they tell me nothing about the subtle dance of their interaction, the micro-expressions that speak volumes, or the energy that flows between them when they're in the same space. Unless they've had a joint Zoom consultation, I'm essentially meeting not just two individuals, but a third entity: their relationship dynamic.

This uncertainty isn't something to be eliminated—it's something to be embraced with curiosity and readiness. I prepare by centring myself in a state of what I call "informed openness"—grounded in my knowledge and experience, yet receptive to whatever unfolds.

I think of this like a tree: deeply rooted with a strong foundation, yet flexible enough to bend with whatever winds of change blow through the session. Many therapists, I've observed, have firm foundations but remain rigid when the unexpected arises. They hold fast to their predetermined approaches regardless of what's actually happening in the room. Our practice requires something different—that foundational strength combined with fluid responsiveness.

Being in this state means I'm energetically available, with all of my senses and energy focused on what's happening in front of me. I'm fluidly responsive because I'm able to go wherever I need to go in response to whatever's unfolding. But there's another layer to this dynamic that makes our approach unique: Maria is beside me, equally attuned and responsive.

What emerges is what I can only describe as an infinitely flexible dyad. I'm not just processing what I'm noticing and responding to—I'm also aware of what she is noticing and responding to, and I'm conscious of what I'm noticing that she's noticing. The dynamic between the two of us creates a rich, multidimensional response system that has a profound impact on the quality of our interventions. Where one of us might miss a subtle shift, the other catches it. Where I might lean towards one approach, she might sense the need for something entirely different.

With returning clients, the preparation takes on a different character. Here, I'm not just preparing for who they are but for who they might have become since our last session. What has shifted? What homework have they attempted? What crises or breakthroughs have occurred in the intervening days or weeks? The consultation form provides a baseline, but the real assessment begins the moment they enter the room.

I've learned to tune into what I call the "warm data"—the immediate, felt sense of their connection. How do they move through the space? Do they sit closer together or further apart than last time? Is there a lightness between them, or does tension fill the room before they even speak? These subtle indicators often tell me more about their progress than any verbal update could.

After They Leave: The Emotional Overhang

The end of a session doesn't mark the end of my involvement—it marks a transition into a different kind of work. Unlike traditional therapy models where practitioners can close the door at the end of an hour and move on to the next client, our approach creates what I can only describe as "emotional overhang."

When you work intensively with couples, when you allow yourself to become genuinely invested in their healing, you can't simply switch off at 5 PM. Part of me goes home with each couple, carrying fragments of their story, wondering about their next conversation, hoping they'll remember to use the tools we practiced.

This is particularly pronounced after sessions that haven't gone as well as I'd hoped. In those moments, I find myself in a reflective spiral: What could I have done differently? What intervention might have landed better? What did I miss? This isn't self-flagellation—it's professional growth. But it's also emotionally taxing in a way that's unique to this deeply connective work.

The challenge is compounded by the nature of our 24/7 support model. Most counsellors and coaches have the luxury of clear boundaries—they see their clients for 50 minutes, offer some closing words, and schedule the next appointment. The responsibility for growth and change rests squarely with the client until they meet again.

Our approach is fundamentally different. We become part of the couple's support system in real time. When they text at 10 PM because they're in the middle of a difficult conversation, when they need guidance before a challenging family event, when they're experiencing a breakthrough and want to share it—we're available. This level of involvement creates profound results, but it also means we're never completely "off."

The emotional connection that develops across the four of us—the couple, Maria, and myself—is both the source of our effectiveness and the reason why decompression becomes so crucial. We don't just work with couples; we enter into a kind of temporary extended family system with them.

Learning to carry this responsibility without becoming overwhelmed by it is an ongoing practice. It requires developing professional resilience—the ability to care deeply while maintaining perspective, to invest emotionally while preserving energy for the next couple who needs our support.

This is the invisible work of transformational couples therapy: the preparation that happens in quiet moments before clients arrive and the processing that continues long after they've left. It's work that doesn't appear on any schedule or invoice, but it's perhaps the most crucial component of creating lasting change in relationships.

Post-Session Decompression

After each couple leaves our office, there's an immediate emotional residue—either the satisfaction of knowing a session went well or the frustration of sensing missed opportunities for deeper connection. Maria and I have developed a ritual of immediate debriefing, discussing what we both noticed during the session: the moments of breakthrough, the patterns that emerged, and areas where we could have intervened more effectively.

However, the real work of decompression requires more than just intellectual processing. To avoid carrying the emotional overhang from one couple into the next session, I've learned that I need at least an hour to physiologically and psychologically reset. This involves attending to basic needs—eating, drinking water—but equally important is movement: walking to a different space, doing light exercise, anything that helps my body release the tension held from the previous encounter. This deliberate transition allows me to tune out of the emotional frequency of the couple who just left and tune into a state of internal tranquillity, preparing myself to meet the unique needs and expectations of whoever walks through our door next.

Equally important is preparing the physical space itself—effectively cleansing it so that the new couple enters what feels like a blank canvas, ready to be filled with their own feelings and experiences. This might involve opening windows for fresh air, lighting candles, or simply rearranging cushions to create a sense of renewal. Before the next couple arrives, Maria and I reconvene to discuss what we want to focus our attention on in the upcoming session, drawing on what we've both noticed after our reflection on their previous visits.

While I may enter each session with a plan forming in my head, I've learned to hold it lightly—more often than not, that plan dissolves in the face of what emerges from the couple's lived experience between our sessions. It's in this emergence, this unplanned revelation of their real-time struggles and discoveries, where the most meaningful work often happens.

The most skilled navigators know that successful passage through challenging waters requires attending to multiple information streams simultaneously—wind direction, current flow, barometric pressure, celestial positioning, and the subtle signals that indicate changing conditions ahead. In the transformative space of therapy, practitioners must develop similar multidimensional awareness, tracking not just what couples say but the warm data they emanate, the historical patterns they embody, and the invisible forces that either support or sabotage their journey towards deeper connection. The art lies not in managing each element separately, but in reading the complex interplay of forces that create the unique conditions each couple navigates together.

Chapter 8

Duo Coaching—A New Framework for Relationship Therapy

The Essential Elements of Effective Practice

A revolutionary boat design isn't built by discarding everything learned from previous vessels but by understanding why existing boats struggle in certain conditions and engineering solutions that address those specific limitations. The Duo Coaching framework emerged from careful analysis of where traditional therapy moves slowly or runs aground.

Through years of working with couples in the Duo Coaching framework, I have distilled what I believe are the essential conditions for relationship therapy to be truly effective. These conditions are not theoretical abstractions but practical observations derived from hundreds of cases—some where profound transformation occurred and others where progress remained elusive.

What makes the difference between these outcomes? Why do some couples experience significant breakthroughs while others remain trapped in their patterns despite investing considerable time, energy, and resources in therapy? The answer lies not in any single technique or approach, but in the presence or absence of certain fundamental conditions that must exist both within the couple and within the therapeutic relationship.

The Essential Conditions for Effective Relationship Therapy

Here is a summary of what I believe to be essential for relationship therapy to be effective: what is needed from the clients and from the therapist. This is drawn from my years of intuitive enquiry (Table 8.1 and Figure 8.1).

Client Responsibility

Presence and Commitment

The first two conditions—both partners being physically present and both being genuinely committed to the process—might seem obvious, yet they are frequently lacking. Physical presence without emotional commitment creates the illusion of participation while virtually guaranteeing failure.

Table 8.1 The Essential Conditions for Effective Relationship Therapy

From Clients	From Therapist	Comments
Both to be present	Holding this as a necessity	Working with only one client gives only their perspective. The one that is not include will be marginalised. The dyad is needed to understand the positions and create sustainable change
Both to be committed to the process	Setting boundaries and expectations	If one wants to make it work and the other is going through the motions, change will not be sustained
Both prepared to invest time and energy	Clarity on how long, what is needed from them, and the cost	Dedication and desire are needed
Clarity on desired outcomes	Asking about the desired outcomes and ensuring they are coherent and compatible and progress is tracked	Without this, it could just drift
Openness and honesty	Creating a safe, liminal space and asking deepening questions	We need to uncover the known unknowns as well as the unknown unknowns
Understanding each other's perspectives	Creating space and questioning to highlight this	As established earlier, couples must learn that different perceptions of the same reality can be equally valid
Acceptance that they have co-created the situation	Focusing on how they have both got to where they are and moving from blame to understanding	Blame—"if only they hadn't, didn't" is an echoing excuse that blocks progress
Strong desire for a resolution to the relationship problems	Challenging their desires for this	This must be a top priority for them both
Prepared to work on the "me" "you" and "us"	Resolving couple and individual issues in parallel	Both the couple and individuals need to change and improve through the progress
Moving from blame to resolution	Holding that boundary	Blame is a trap that prevents change and progress
Outcome focused and prepared to fly free	Avoiding dependency	It is easy for the therapist to become a crutch rather than the solution facilitator. This can also be a comfortable business model
Willingness to explore themselves and each other	Holding that space	Without this deep work, there is unlikely to be sustainable or significant change

(Continued)

114 Reinventing Relationship Therapy

Table 8.1 (Continued)

From Clients	From Therapist	Comments
Going beyond "just talking" about the past	Creating a space to explore the unconscious and unhelpful patterns of behaviour	Using tools such as Constellations, Time Line Therapy, Hypnotic language patterns, parts negotiation, Clean Language, Clean Space, Symbolic modelling may deliver this
Feeling safe in the care of the therapists	Able to use a wide range of tools and techniques to uncover the patterns of behaviour and create change	Different approaches are needed for different people, at different times and contexts. There is no one universal tool
To be treated equally and without preference	Two therapists, in a working relationship, of different sexes and training	This creates multiple dyads and ensures that each of the couple feel listened to and supported
Short time between first contact and commencement	Maintaining availability within 1–2 weeks	The trigger point to wanting counselling often comes after a long period of unhappiness and a period of discussion within the couple. To have to wait a long time for the first appointment often means the opportunity has passed

True commitment manifests as prioritising the therapeutic process, completing agreed-upon practices between sessions, and maintaining openness to change even when it becomes uncomfortable. When both partners bring this level of commitment, even the most entrenched patterns can shift remarkably quickly.

Investment and Clarity

The willingness to invest both time and energy in the process correlates directly with outcomes. Couples who view therapy as something to fit in around other priorities rarely achieve the depth of change possible for those who make their relationship a central focus during the therapeutic process.

Equally important is clarity about desired outcomes. Vague aspirations like "better communication" or "more happiness" provide insufficient direction. Specific, well-articulated outcomes create a compass for the work.

Openness and Perspective-Taking

No therapeutic approach, regardless of its sophistication, can overcome a fundamental lack of honesty. Partners who withhold important information create informational gaps that make effective intervention impossible.

Duo Coaching 115

Duo Coaching Framework
Reinventing Relationship Therapy

Core Principles

Two Therapists
Balanced perspective with male/female co-therapists creating natural equilibrium and preventing triangulation

Extended Sessions
3.5-hour initial session, 2.5-hour follow-ups allowing depth without time pressure

Outcome Focused
Clear goals established upfront with progress tracking throughout 6-session journey

Integrative Approach
Drawing from 15+ modalities based on what each unique couple needs in the moment

24/7 Support
Unlimited contact between sessions to address issues as they emerge, not aftermath

Brief & Intensive
Finite 6-session framework creating urgency and preventing dependency

The "Me, You, Us" Triad

Working simultaneously on individual growth and relationship dynamics - addressing unconscious patterns alongside conscious communication

Session Structure

Session 1 (3.5 hours)	Sessions 2-5 (2.5 hours each)	Session 6 (2.5 hours)
Comprehensive assessment, outcome clarification, pattern identification, constellation work	Deep work on identified patterns, skills development, experiential exercises, progress tracking	Integration, future planning, relapse prevention, celebrating progress, graduation

Figure 8.1a The Duo Coaching Framework: an overview of core principles, the "Me, You, Us" triad, and the session structure that together create the conditions for relationship transformation.

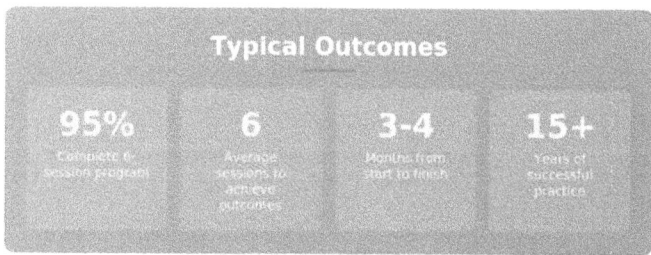

Figure 8.1b The Duo Coaching Framework: therapeutic toolkit, typical outcomes, and key differentiators that distinguish this integrative, outcome-focused approach from traditional relationship therapy.

Alongside honesty must come willingness to understand each other's perspectives. As I often tell couples, "In a relationship there is no reality, there is only perception. These perceptions can be very different but equally correct."

Therapist Responsibility

Creating Container and Expectations

The therapist's role begins with establishing clear boundaries and expectations. This includes explicit discussion of commitment requirements, timeframes, costs, and the nature of the therapeutic relationship.

An essential element of this container is the liminal space—a threshold environment where normal rules are suspended and new possibilities can emerge. The physical setting, session pacing, emotional atmosphere, and therapist presence all contribute to creating this space.

Outcome Focus and Tracking

While many therapeutic approaches emphasise process over outcomes, effective relationship therapy maintains clear focus on desired results. This begins with helping couples articulate specific, observable outcomes rather than vague aspirations.

This tracking provides both direction and motivation. When couples can see tangible progress towards their stated goals, their engagement with the therapeutic process deepens.

Facilitating Depth and Pattern Recognition

Perhaps the most distinctive aspect of the therapist's role in the Duo Coaching framework is creating space for exploration of unconscious patterns. Rather than remaining at the level of conscious communication and behavioural changes, effective relationship therapy facilitates awareness of the deeper patterns driving surface conflicts.

This requires a diverse therapeutic toolkit. Different couples respond to different approaches. The therapist's ability to select and apply the right tool at the right moment significantly impacts therapeutic effectiveness.

The Synergy of Conditions

While each condition described above is important, their real power emerges through their interaction. When all conditions are present, they create a synergistic effect that accelerates and deepens the therapeutic process.

Consider the relationship between openness and safety: clients cannot be fully open without feeling safe, yet the therapist cannot create complete safety without client openness. As each element strengthens, it enables the others to develop further, creating positive feedback loops that transform the therapeutic environment.

Case Example: When Conditions Align

> To illustrate how these conditions work together in practice, consider the case of Emma and James, who sought help after James's emotional affair with a colleague. Their initial sessions revealed high commitment from both, clear desired outcomes, and willingness to explore deeper patterns.
>
> Emma and James moved beyond the immediate issue of the affair to discover longstanding patterns in their relationship. Through constellation work, parts negotiation, and targeted communication practices, they not only healed from the immediate breach of trust but also transformed the underlying relationship patterns. Six months after our work concluded, they reported not just recovery but renewal—a relationship stronger and more vibrant than before the crisis.

Case Example: When Conditions Are Missing

> Contrast this with Michael and Rebecca, who appeared committed to therapy but whose work progressed much more slowly. Over time, it became clear that while Rebecca was fully committed to the process, Michael was primarily motivated by avoiding the financial implications of divorce rather than genuinely rebuilding the relationship.
>
> His partial honesty created a foundation of sand—interventions that appeared effective would collapse when hidden information eventually emerged. After four sessions, we had a direct conversation about what we were observing and mutually agreed to end the therapeutic relationship, as continuing would likely create more frustration than progress.

The Duo Coaching Advantages

The framework addresses several limitations inherent in traditional approaches:

Balance through co-therapy: Two therapists, typically male and female, create natural balance and prevent the triangulation that often occurs in single-therapist models.

Extended sessions: The first session of 3.5 hours and subsequent sessions of 2.5 hours allow couples to work through complete emotional cycles rather than being cut off mid-breakthrough.

Finite timeline: Typically six sessions over 3–4 months creates momentum rather than open-ended drift while maintaining sufficient space for integration between sessions.

Integrative approach: Drawing from 15+ therapeutic modalities allows selection of whatever tools best serve each unique couple.

Table 8.2 Summary of Therapeutic Approaches: Benefits and Limitations for Relationship Work

Therapeutic Approach	Key Benefits	Key Limitations
Person-Centred Counselling	• Creates profound safety through empathy and unconditional positive regard • Excellent foundation for vulnerable expression • Helps couples feel genuinely heard and validated • Develops trust through non-judgemental presence • Builds self-awareness and emotional intelligence	• Non-directive stance can leave couples "drowning without a lifeboat" • Understanding problems doesn't create solutions • May inadvertently enable destructive cycles to continue • Limited ability to interrupt harmful patterns • Insufficient guidance for couples needing active intervention
Psychodynamic Therapy	• Reveals unconscious patterns driving relationship dynamics • Understands how childhood experiences shape adult partnerships • Provides "X-ray vision" for seeing beneath surface conflicts • Recognises repetition compulsion and defence mechanisms • Offers profound insight into emotional logic of behaviours	• Designed for individual work, not couple systems • Creates "individual submarines that can't dock together" • Partner exclusion leads to imbalanced perspective • Risk of creating echo chambers that reinforce victim narratives • Progress can be frustratingly slow for couples in crisis
Systemic Counselling	• Sees interaction patterns rather than individual problems • Focuses on "the dance, not just the dancers" • Practical, present-moment focus on changing patterns • No need for extensive historical exploration • Understanding that problems are maintained by current interactions	• May miss deeper emotional currents that drive patterns • Can address surface symptoms while deeper dynamics remain • Limited attention to individual psychological needs • May lack tools for processing emotional trauma • Generic pattern interruption may not address unique dynamics

(Continued)

Table 8.2 (Continued)

Therapeutic Approach	Key Benefits	Key Limitations
Transactional Analysis	• Provides "instant relationship X-ray vision" • Clear, accessible language for understanding roles • Immediate recognition of ego state interactions • Practical tools for shifting communication patterns • Helps identify "games" couples unconsciously play	• Individual focus within relationship context • May miss deeper attachment needs and fears • Limited attention to somatic and unconscious processes • Can become overly cognitive without emotional depth • May not address systemic family-of-origin influences
Cognitive Behavioural Therapy	• Provides practical, concrete tools for change • Clear structure and measurable progress • Evidence-based approach with research support • Excellent skill-building for communication and conflict resolution • Helps identify and change destructive thought patterns	• "Engine room vs. navigation bridge"—fixes mechanics but may miss direction • Focus on symptoms rather than underlying emotional sources • May miss attachment needs and deeper relationship dynamics • Limited attention to unconscious processes • Can neglect the "heart beneath the head"
Integrative Therapy	• Adaptive flexibility to meet unique couple needs • Can address multiple dimensions simultaneously • Avoids limitations of single-approach thinking • Seamless blending of complementary methods • Responds to what emerges rather than following rigid protocols	• Risk of being "jack of all trades, master of none" • Requires competence across multiple modalities • May lack coherent theoretical framework • Training challenges—how to master integration? • Potential for scattered, unfocused interventions
Eclectic Therapy	• Pure responsiveness to immediate needs • Freedom from theoretical constraints • Outcome-focused rather than approach-focused • Intuitive flexibility and surprise factor • "Whatever works, works" philosophy	• Competence limitations across diverse approaches • Difficulty providing rationale for intervention choices • Training challenges for developing eclectic skills • Risk of incoherent, random technique selection • May lack depth in any particular modality

(Continued)

Table 8.2 (Continued)

Therapeutic Approach	Key Benefits	Key Limitations
Duo Coaching	• Two therapists create natural balance and prevent triangulation • Extended sessions (3.5–2.5 hours) allow genuine depth work • Finite framework (typically 6 sessions) creates momentum and accountability • Integrative approach draws from 15+ modalities as needed • Works simultaneously on "Me, You, Us" dimensions • 24/7 support between sessions for real-time guidance • Outcome-focused with clear success criteria • Addresses both conscious and unconscious patterns • Creates liminal space for profound transformation • Fixed cost provides certainty and reduces dependency risk	• Requires two skilled therapists working in partnership • Higher cost due to two practitioners involved • Significant time commitment may not suit all clients • Intensive approach may overwhelm some couples • Limited availability of trained Duo Coaching practitioners • Requires strong therapeutic alliance between co-therapists • May be "too much, too fast" for couples preferring gradual change • Success depends heavily on both partners' genuine commitment • Approach still developing research evidence base

"Me, You, Us" focus: Addressing individual growth alongside relationship dynamics recognises that couple health requires individual foundation.

24/7 Support: Availability between sessions helps couples navigate challenges as they emerge rather than dealing with aftermath weeks later.

I summarise the main therapeutic modalities and contrast them with Duo Coaching below (Table 8.2):

Key Insights from This Expanded Comparison

What Makes Duo Coaching Distinctive

- **Systematic integration**: Unlike eclectic approaches, combines multiple modalities within a coherent framework
- **Structural innovation**: Addresses format limitations (time, single-therapist, open-ended process) that constrain other approaches

- **Balanced depth and practicality**: Provides both profound insight and practical skills within the same framework
- **Outcome accountability**: Creates clear success criteria while maintaining process sensitivity

Duo Coaching's Response to Common Limitations

- **Individual vs. systems**: Explicitly works with "Me, You, Us" simultaneously
- **Time constraints**: Extended sessions allow complete emotional cycles to unfold
- **Single-therapist issues**: Two therapists prevent alliance problems and provide multiple perspectives
- **Depth vs. skills**: Integrates insight-oriented and practical approaches seamlessly
- **Open-ended drift**: Finite framework with clear outcomes creates direction and momentum

For practitioners considering different approaches: This comparison reveals that Duo Coaching represents an evolution that:

- Preserves the strengths of multiple traditions while addressing their limitations
- Requires significant practitioner development but offers enhanced effectiveness
- May not be suitable for all practice contexts but demonstrates possibilities for innovation
- Suggests that effectiveness improvements may require structural as well as theoretical changes

The innovation challenge: Duo Coaching's benefits come at the cost of complexity and resource requirements, raising important questions for the field:

- How can effective innovations be made more accessible?
- What elements could be adapted for single-therapist practice?
- How might traditional approaches evolve to address their own limitations?
- What training and support would help practitioners integrate multiple modalities effectively?

The Evolution of Practice

The framework presented here is not static but continually evolving through clinical experience and integration of new insights. The current formulation represents understanding based on work with hundreds of couples across diverse circumstances, ages, cultural backgrounds, and relationship structures.

I invite practitioners to engage with this framework, not as a rigid prescription, but as a foundation for reflection. The ultimate measure of any therapeutic approach is not its theoretical elegance but its practical effectiveness in creating lasting positive change.

The journey of developing more effective approaches to relationship therapy is itself a relationship—between practitioner and methodology, between established wisdom and innovative exploration, between theoretical understanding and practical application. Like all meaningful relationships, it requires both respect for what exists and openness to what might become.

In the second book in the trilogy, *Reframe*, I will provide detailed, step-by-step guidance for implementing these approaches across various practice contexts.

Applying This Framework in Your Practice

Whether you are a coach expanding into relationship work, a counsellor seeking to enhance your effectiveness with couples, or a psychoanalyst integrating systemic perspectives, the conditions outlined in this chapter provide a practical framework for assessment and intervention.

You might begin by evaluating your current approach: Does it explicitly address each of these conditions? Are there elements you emphasise more than others? Are there conditions you haven't previously considered essential that might merit greater attention?

For those working within institutional contexts with established protocols, consider how you might adapt this framework to work within your constraints. Even small shifts can significantly enhance effectiveness.

For independent practitioners with greater flexibility, experiment with more substantial adaptations: co-therapy arrangements with colleagues, extended session formats, or integration of experiential methods from outside your primary modality.

Understanding the necessary conditions for effective relationship therapy provides the foundation, but couples also need practical navigation tools—a compass that can guide them through the inevitable storms and doldrums of long-term partnership. The Relationship Paradigm emerged from observing what thriving couples actually do differently.

Chapter 9

The Relationship Paradigm

Figure 9.1 The Relationship Paradigm: a compass for couple navigation, mapping the six essential elements—Communication, Connection, Commitment, Fun, Growth, and Trust—that distinguish thriving relationships from those merely surviving.

A Compass for Couple Navigation

Every navigator needs a compass—a reliable instrument that points towards magnetic north regardless of weather, current, or tides. The Relationship Paradigm serves as such a compass, helping couples orient themselves amid the confusion of conflicting emotions and identify their authentic direction forward.

Throughout my years of working with couples, I've observed recurring patterns in relationships that thrive vs. those that struggle. This observation led me to develop the Relationship Paradigm, a framework that identifies six essential elements present in successful relationships. I first introduced this model in my book "Reset: Finding a New Course After Drifting Apart," and since then, it has helped countless couples understand, assess, and strengthen their partnerships (Figure 9.1).

The Relationship Paradigm isn't merely theoretical—it's a practical tool born from real-world experience with hundreds of couples at different stages of their relationships. Whether working with pairs in crisis or those wanting to move from good to great, this framework provides a clear map of what matters most in creating and sustaining a healthy relationship.

Understanding the Six Elements

At its core, the Relationship Paradigm consists of six fundamental elements that connect "You" and "Me" to create "Us." These elements are Communication, Connection, Commitment, Fun, Growth, and Trust—with Trust serving as the foundation upon which all other elements rest.

Let's explore each element and how it contributes to relationship health.

Communication: The Bridge Between Worlds

Communication extends far beyond merely exchanging information. It encompasses our ability to express thoughts, feelings, and needs clearly and to be truly heard and understood by our partner. In thriving relationships, couples have learned to navigate differences without allowing them to contaminate the rest of their relationship.

The quality of communication often determines the quality of the relationship itself. When communication breaks down, misunderstandings multiply, emotional distance grows, and resentment builds. Conversely, when couples communicate effectively, they create a bridge between their separate perceptual worlds, fostering intimacy and understanding even when they disagree.

Effective communicators in relationships have moved beyond the golden rule of "treat others as you would like to be treated" to the platinum rule: "treat others as they would like to be treated." They've learned to adjust their communication style to match their partner's needs rather than expecting their partner to adapt to theirs.

Remember that "the meaning of any communication is the response it gets." If your partner consistently misunderstands you, the issue may not be with their listening but with how you're communicating. Small adjustments in phrasing, timing, or tone can transform a conversation from frustrating to connecting.

Connection: The Invisible Threads That Bind

Connection encompasses all the ways partners make contact—from small daily moments to deep physical and emotional intimacy. It includes physical touch and affection, emotional vulnerability, being fully present when together, shared experiences, sexual intimacy, and the rituals of greeting and parting.

Dr. John Gottman's (2008) research on "bids for connection" highlights how crucial these small moments are. In successful relationships, partners respond positively to each other's bids for connection at least 86% of the time, while failing relationships show a "turning towards" rate of just 33%. These responses—a smile, a touch, a question about their day—may seem insignificant, but cumulatively they build a foundation of connection.

In our digitally distracted age, genuine connection requires mindfulness—being truly present rather than physically together but mentally elsewhere. Many couples exist in the same space while their attention remains on screens, creating what I call "together loneliness"—physically present but emotionally absent.

Connection doesn't require grand gestures. Often it's found in small moments: morning coffee together, a knowing glance across a crowded room, or a reassuring touch during a difficult day. These moments create the invisible threads that weave two lives together in meaningful ways.

Commitment: The Foundation of Security

Commitment extends far beyond wedding vows or relationship agreements. It encompasses clarity about what both partners want from the relationship, willingness to invest time and energy, alignment on life direction, support for each other's individual goals, and prioritising the relationship amid competing demands.

When commitment is strong, both partners make decisions with "us" in mind, not just "me." They're willing to work through difficulties rather than abandon ship when waters get rough. This creates the security needed for vulnerability and growth—partners feel safe being authentic when they trust in each other's commitment.

Many relationship problems stem from misaligned commitment. One partner may be fully invested while the other maintains escape routes—emotional, financial, or social. This imbalance creates uncertainty that undermines all other elements of the relationship.

Commitment doesn't mean losing individuality or autonomy. Rather, it means choosing to intertwine your life with another's while supporting each other's individual growth and goals. It's about creating a partnership that enhances both lives rather than diminishing either.

Fun: The Antidote to Life's Pressures

Fun is often the first casualty of busy, stressful lives, yet it's essential for relationship vitality. It includes playfulness and humour, shared activities that both enjoy, new experiences, laughter, breaking routines, and rediscovering your inner child together.

Fun creates positive shared experiences that strengthen bonds and build resilience against stress. It generates the neurochemicals—dopamine, oxytocin, and endorphins—that fuel attraction and attachment. Without fun, relationships become all work and no play, creating a joyless environment where connection withers.

When I ask couples in distress, "When did you last have fun together?," many struggle to answer. They've gradually allowed the serious business of life—careers, parenting, finances—to crowd out playfulness. Yet fun isn't frivolous; it's fundamental to relationship health.

Reintroducing fun doesn't require elaborate plans or expensive holidays. It might be a spontaneous pillow fight, trying a new restaurant, dancing in the kitchen, or revisiting activities you enjoyed when you were first together. The key is breaking routine and creating moments of shared joy that become treasured memories.

Growth: The Path to Fulfilment

Like all living things, relationships must grow to thrive. Growth encompasses personal development for both individuals, evolution of the relationship itself, adapting to life's changes together, supporting each other's aspirations, challenging each other to be your best selves, and creating shared goals.

Many relationships stagnate because partners assume that once formed, relationships naturally sustain themselves. In reality, relationships require continuing attention and development. As individuals change—and we all do throughout life—the relationship must evolve to accommodate new interests, priorities, and understandings.

A great relationship requires two fulfilled individuals and an "us" that is also fulfilled. When both partners are growing individually and the relationship is evolving, the partnership remains dynamic and engaging rather than becoming a constraint on either person's development.

Growth prevents the stagnation that often leads to affairs or separation. When partners feel alive, challenged, and supported in their relationship, they're less likely to seek fulfilment elsewhere. They see their relationship as enhancing rather than limiting their life possibilities.

Trust: The Essential Foundation

Trust forms the foundation upon which all other elements rest. It encompasses reliability (doing what you say you'll do), transparency (openness about thoughts, feelings, and actions), consistency (being the same person in different contexts), accountability (taking responsibility for mistakes), fidelity (honouring agreements about exclusivity), and respect for boundaries.

Trust is built slowly through consistent actions but can be damaged quickly through betrayal. When trust is strong, it's like a clear blue sky—barely noticed but creating the perfect conditions for relationship health. When trust is damaged, storm clouds gather, affecting every other element of the relationship.

Rebuilding broken trust requires time, transparency, and consistent behaviour. The betraying partner must demonstrate trustworthiness through actions, not just words, while the betrayed partner works through hurt and gradually opens themselves to trusting again. This delicate dance requires patience from both partners.

Trust isn't just about fidelity. It also encompasses financial transparency, emotional reliability, and keeping small promises. Each time you do what you say you'll do—whether it's arriving when promised or following through on household responsibilities—you make a deposit in your "trust account" with your partner.

How the Elements Interact

The six elements don't operate independently—they form an interconnected system where changes in one area create ripple effects throughout the relationship:

Communication and Trust create a reinforcing cycle. Poor communication erodes trust over time, as misunderstandings accumulate and partners feel unheard or misrepresented. Conversely, broken trust makes honest communication feel dangerous—why risk vulnerability with someone who might use it against you? When both elements are strong, they reinforce each other: skilled communication builds trust through understanding, while strong trust enables more vulnerable, authentic sharing.

Connection and Fun feed each other. Playful interactions create emotional connection by generating positive shared experiences and neurochemical bonding. Simultaneously, feeling emotionally connected makes couples more willing to be spontaneous, silly, and playful together. Couples who've lost their sense of fun often find their emotional connection suffering, while those who prioritise playfulness maintain stronger bonds.

Commitment and Growth support mutual development. Strong commitment provides the safety needed for individual growth—partners can explore new aspects of themselves knowing their relationship is secure. Personal development, in turn, keeps partners interesting and attractive to each other, reinforcing commitment. Stagnant individuals often create stagnant relationships, while growing people energise their partnerships.

The Foundation Effect of Trust. Trust acts as the foundation that either supports or undermines all other elements. When trust is strong, partners interpret ambiguous situations generously, give each other benefit of the doubt, and feel safe being vulnerable. When trust is damaged, even positive interactions in other areas feel tentative and fragile—fun feels forced, communication becomes guarded, and commitment feels uncertain.

Positive and Negative Spirals. These interactions can create upward spirals where improvement in one area catalyses growth in others, or downward spirals where deterioration in one element undermines the rest. Understanding these dynamics helps couples see why working on one element often creates unexpected improvements in others and why some persistent problems require addressing multiple elements simultaneously rather than focusing on symptoms in isolation.

The Relationship Paradigm in Practice

Understanding these six elements provides a framework for assessing and strengthening relationships. Rather than feeling overwhelmed by relationship problems, couples can identify specific areas needing attention and focus their efforts where they'll have the greatest impact.

To use this framework effectively, I've developed an online questionnaire available at www.relationshipparadigm.com. I encourage both partners to complete this assessment independently, then compare results. The process often reveals illuminating differences in perception—one partner might rate communication as strong while the other experiences it as weak, highlighting an important area for exploration.

The discrepancies between ratings often reveal the most valuable insights. If you rate connection as eight while your partner rates it as four, this suggests significantly different perceptions about intimacy in your relationship. These differences aren't about right or wrong—they're opportunities to understand each other's experience more deeply.

Low scores indicate areas needing immediate attention, while high scores represent relationship strengths you can leverage. If trust receives high marks from both partners but communication scores low, you can build on your foundation of trust to improve how you talk with each other.

Using the Assessment Effectively

Interpreting Your Scores.

8–10: Relationship strength to celebrate and leverage—understand what you're doing well here and consider how to apply those same principles to weaker areas

5–7: Functional but with significant room for enhancement—these areas aren't in crisis but could benefit from focused attention.

1–4: Priority areas needing immediate focused attention—these gaps are probably creating ongoing frustration and disconnection.

Creating Your Action Plan.

Choose 1–2 elements for initial focus rather than trying to address everything simultaneously.

Start with areas where small changes could create disproportionately large improvements. Consider which elements, if strengthened, would most naturally support improvement in others.

Set specific, observable goals: "We will have one 20-minute conversation each week without phones" rather than "We will communicate better."

Schedule regular check-ins to reassess progress and adjust your focus as needed.

Common Assessment Patterns Include

The efficiency trap. These have high scores on Commitment and Trust (8–10), but low scores on Fun and Connection (3–5). These couples have created secure, stable relationships but have lost vitality and intimacy in the process. They function like well-oiled business partnerships but feel more like roommates than lovers. The priority is rediscovering playfulness and emotional intimacy without sacrificing the reliability they've built.

Passion paradox. They have high Connection and Fun scores (7–9) but lower Commitment and Trust (4–6). These relationships feel exciting and emotionally intense but lack security and depth for long-term sustainability. Partners enjoy each other but struggle with reliability and future planning. The priority is building consistent trustworthiness and aligned vision for the future.

Communication crisis. Low Communication scores (1–4) drag down performance in all other areas. When partners can't express needs, navigate differences, or feel heard, every other element suffers. Trust erodes through misunderstanding, connection weakens through unexpressed needs, and fun disappears under accumulated resentment. Their priority is learning specific communication skills before addressing other areas.

Trust recovery. One or more trust-damaging events (affairs, financial betrayals, broken promises) affecting the entire relationship system. Even when partners are working hard on other elements, progress feels tentative and fragile when the foundation is cracked. Their systematic trust rebuilding often requires professional support.

Stagnation. Moderate scores (5–7) across all elements; not in crisis but not thriving either. These relationships feel "fine" but lack the vitality and growth that create long-term satisfaction. Partners often feel like they're living parallel lives rather than building something together. Priority is revitalisation through intentional growth experiences and new shared challenges.

Individual imbalance. Significant score differences across multiple elements, suggesting partners are living in different relationship realities. This often indicates that individual needs, communication styles, or relationship expectations haven't been adequately explored or accommodated. The priority is understanding and bridging the perceptual gaps before focusing on specific elements.

The "You," "Me," and "Us" Dynamic

Notice how the paradigm connects "You" and "Me" to create "Us." This visual representation emphasises an important truth: a healthy relationship requires both individual wellbeing and partnership.

The most sustainable relationships balance individual fulfilment and identity ("Me"), understanding and supporting your partner ("You"), and creating a shared life together ("Us"). Problems often arise when one aspect dominates at the expense of others.

When "Us" consumes everything, individuals lose their identity, leading to resentment or dependency. When "Me" dominates, connection suffers as partners live parallel rather than intertwined lives. The paradigm helps maintain this crucial balance between autonomy and togetherness.

Balancing Individual and Relationship Growth

Each element requires attention at both individual and couple levels. The strongest relationships actively nurture both dimensions, recognising that personal growth enhances partnership while healthy partnership supports individual flourishing.

Communication

Individual work: developing emotional intelligence, learning to identify and express feelings, understanding your communication style and triggers, building self-regulation skills for difficult conversations

Couple work: creating safe dialogue practices, establishing ground rules for conflict, learning each other's communication needs, developing shared vocabulary for emotions and needs

Connection

Individual work: addressing personal barriers to intimacy, healing past relationship wounds, developing capacity for presence and mindfulness, understanding your attachment style and needs

Couple work: creating daily connection rituals, scheduling quality time, learning each other's "love languages," building physical and emotional intimacy practices

Commitment

Individual work: clarifying personal values and life vision, understanding what you want from partnership, developing personal integrity and follow-through, examining commitment fears or patterns

Couple work: aligning life visions and goals, creating shared meaning and purpose, making explicit commitments and agreements, building "we" identity while maintaining individual selves

Fun

Individual work: reconnecting with personal joy and playfulness, exploring individual interests and hobbies, addressing barriers to spontaneity, healing "inner critic" voices that inhibit play

Couple work: discovering mutually enjoyable activities, breaking routine patterns together, creating adventure and novelty, learning to be silly and spontaneous with each other

Growth

Individual work: pursuing personal development goals, expanding skills and interests, addressing individual therapy needs, maintaining friendships and individual identity

Couple work: supporting each other's individual growth, growing together through shared challenges, learning new skills as a team, evolving the relationship as both people change

Trust

Individual work: building personal integrity and reliability, understanding your trust patterns from family of origin, developing emotional regulation for trust-building conversations, addressing individual factors that impact trustworthiness

Couple work: establishing transparency practices, creating accountability systems, rebuilding trust after breaches, developing rituals that reinforce security and reliability

The Integration Challenge

The art lies in pursuing both individual and couple growth simultaneously without creating competition between them. When individual development threatens the relationship or relationship needs stifle individual growth, couples need help finding the balance that honours both "me" and "us" dimensions of each element.

Focusing Efforts

If the assessment reveals challenges across multiple elements, don't try to address everything at once. Start with one or two areas where improvement will create the greatest positive impact. Often, strengthening one element creates a ripple effect that enhances others.

For many couples, communication provides the best starting point, as improved communication facilitates progress in other areas. For others, rebuilding trust must come first, as trust forms the foundation for everything else.

With clear principles and practical tools established, the question becomes: how can different types of practitioners integrate these insights into their existing work? Coaches often sail in familiar waters of goal-setting and performance enhancement, but relationship work demands ventures into deeper emotional territories.

Reflection on Part 2: Discovering New Frameworks

From the reconnaissance of existing approaches, we have voyaged into uncharted waters where innovation meets necessity. You've witnessed the organic creation of Duo Coaching—born not from academic theory but from lived frustration with inadequate therapeutic vessels, evolved through intuition and refined through work with hundreds of couples seeking genuine transformation.

You've explored the systematic framework that consistently creates change: two therapists providing balance, extended sessions allowing depth, finite timelines creating momentum, and integrative approaches selecting whatever tools best serve each unique couple. The Relationship Paradigm has provided you with a practical compass—six essential elements that distinguish thriving relationships from those merely surviving.

These frameworks represent more than alternative techniques; they demonstrate what becomes possible when we prioritise effectiveness over convention, when we design therapeutic containers that match the complexity of relationship challenges rather than forcing couples into pre-existing structures.

Now comes the crucial question: how can practitioners from diverse traditions adapt these insights to enhance their own work? The frameworks exist, and the principles are clear—but implementation requires thoughtful guidance for the specific challenges facing coaches, counsellors, and psychoanalysts as they expand beyond familiar shores.

Part 3

Guidance for Coaches, Counsellors, and Psychoanalysts on Extending Your Practice

The frameworks exist, the principles are clear, the innovations have proven their effectiveness—but how do practitioners from diverse traditions thoughtfully integrate these insights without abandoning the foundations that serve them well? This section provides specific guidance for the respectful evolution of professional practice across therapeutic boundaries.

Rather than asking you to discard your training, these chapters show how to build upon existing strengths while adding dimensions that enhance effectiveness with relationship challenges. Coaches discover how to venture beyond performance-focused work into deeper emotional territories. Counsellors explore pathways beyond single-modality constraints while honouring their therapeutic expertise. Psychoanalysts learn how their sophisticated understanding of unconscious processes can be extended into the intersubjective waters where relationships actually exist.

There are four chapters in this section. Each one addresses practitioners where they are, acknowledging both the valuable contributions of different traditions and their inherent limitations when working with couple systems. You'll find practical tools, ethical considerations, and step-by-step guidance for thoughtful expansion that strengthens rather than dilutes your professional identity.

The section culminates with Maria's authentic perspective—the irreplaceable voice of someone who has actually navigated the transition from traditional counselling to innovative practice. Her insights reveal what theoretical descriptions cannot: the lived experience of implementing change, the challenges encountered, the discoveries made, and the profound satisfaction that comes from serving couples more effectively.

This isn't about abandoning your therapeutic identity but about expanding the possibilities of what that identity can encompass in service of healthier relationships.

Chapter 10
Guidance for Coaches

Figure 10.1 Scanning the horizon: a figure with a telescope looks beyond the immediate, representing coaches who are ready to extend their vision past performance-focused work into the deeper emotional waters of relationship practice.

Expanding Beyond Familiar Coastal Waters

Coaches often sail in familiar coastal waters—goal-focused, performance-oriented territories where they've developed expertise. But when clients need guidance in the deeper emotional seas of relationship dynamics, even experienced coaches may find themselves in waters that require new navigation skills.

Beyond the Boundaries of Traditional Coaching

As a coach, you've probably heard it a thousand times—that invisible wall between coaching and therapy. It's treated almost like a sacred boundary, something to be feared rather than thoughtfully explored (Figure 10.1). But what if that boundary isn't a wall at all but more of a permeable membrane? What if respecting

DOI: 10.4324/9781003715467-13

boundaries doesn't mean avoiding them entirely but engaging with them intelligently, with both care and courage?

I know firsthand how coaching tends to plant its flag firmly in the here-and-now. We focus on goals, actions, performance, and outcomes—all valuable territory, especially when working with executives who need to deliver results yesterday. But when it comes to relationships? That's when things get wonderfully messy. The relationship challenges clients bring rarely exist in isolation from the deeper patterns that have been forming throughout their lives.

So the question isn't whether to respect professional boundaries—of course we should. It's how to navigate them skilfully while honouring both your limitations and your potential to facilitate deeper change. This requires a new frame of reference—a reframing of what coaching can be when applied to the complex domain of human relationships.

The Artificial Divide

Let's be honest about something: the division between coaching and therapy might be administratively convenient, but it doesn't reflect how humans actually experience life. As we explored in Chapter 5 on Transdisciplinarity, human relationships operate across multiple interconnected contexts. When we artificially separate "performance issues" from "psychological issues," we fragment the very experience we're trying to help our clients integrate.

Picture a client who struggles with assertiveness in their relationship. The traditional coaching approach might focus on communication strategies and goal-setting around specific conversations. Useful? Yes. Sufficient? Rarely. Without acknowledging the deeper currents—perhaps established in childhood—that maintain the client's difficulty with assertiveness, coaching interventions often create only temporary shifts rather than lasting transformation.

The reality is that many coaching clients are seeking help with issues that have psychological dimensions. They don't come because they've neatly segmented their concerns into "coaching-appropriate" packages. They come because they trust you to help them navigate real-life challenges in all their messy complexity.

The Coach's Edge: Your Unique Advantages

Before you start wondering if you need to go back to school for a psychology degree, let me assure you: as a coach, you bring distinct advantages to relationship work that differ from those of traditional therapists.

Your orientation towards the future helps clients envision and create relationship possibilities rather than merely resolving problems. Your emphasis on concrete actions and accountability supports the practical implementation of relationship changes. Your strengths perspective provides a powerful foundation for growth-oriented relationship work that builds on capability rather than fixating on pathology.

You're also free from the constraints of the traditional therapeutic "hour" and setting, allowing you to create more adaptable engagement models. And many coaches, particularly those with organisational backgrounds, already understand systems dynamics—providing a valuable foundation for understanding relationship systems.

These aren't minor advantages—they're substantive differences in approach that position you to make unique contributions to relationship work. Not as a pseudo-therapist, but as a skilled facilitator of change who approaches relationships from a distinct and valuable perspective.

Expanding Your Range: Depth Without Overreaching

Expanding your practice to include deeper relationship work doesn't mean becoming a therapist without proper training. Instead, it means thoughtfully extending your existing skills while remaining acutely aware of your limitations. Here are five principles for navigating this expansion.

Develop Pattern Recognition

Learn to recognise recurring patterns in your clients' relationships. These often appear as consistent stories with changing characters—the same fundamental dynamics playing out across different contexts. The client who consistently chooses unavailable partners. The repeated cycle of initial connection followed by withdrawal. The persistent pattern of prioritising others' needs over one's own.

When you notice these patterns, gentle observation can be powerful: "I notice that this situation with your partner feels similar to what you described with your previous relationship. I'm curious about that pattern."

This observation alone often catalyses awareness, which is the essential first step towards change. You need not analyse or interpret the pattern's origins (which would venture into therapeutic territory); simply bringing it into conscious awareness creates space for new choices.

Work with the Whole Person, Not Just Their Goals

Traditional coaching often focuses narrowly on articulated goals. Relationship coaching requires a broader engagement with the whole person—their values, beliefs, emotions, and ways of being. This doesn't mean conducting therapy; it means acknowledging that relationship goals are deeply intertwined with identity and meaning.

Explore values underlying relationship desires. Acknowledge emotions as information rather than obstacles. Investigate how relationship patterns align with or contradict the client's sense of self. Use outcome-focused questions that address being, not just doing: "How would you like to be in this relationship?" rather than just "What do you want to achieve?"

Incorporate Relationship Systems Thinking

Coaching often focuses on the individual client, but relationship coaching requires a systems perspective. A relationship is more than the sum of two individuals—it is a dynamic system with its own patterns, rules, and emergent properties.

Even without formal training in systems therapy, you can bring systems awareness by considering how changes in one partner will affect the system, exploring the "dance" between partners rather than isolated behaviours, and acknowledging that relationship patterns often serve functions, even dysfunctional ones. Use visual representations to help clients see relationship dynamics—simple diagrams can be remarkably effective.

Remember that relationship therapists often make the mistake of focusing exclusively on the "us" while neglecting the "me" and "you." As a coach, your individual focus can be an advantage if you learn to toggle between individual and systemic perspectives.

Create Experiments, Not Just Action Plans

Traditional coaching often emphasises straightforward action plans. Relationship coaching benefits from a more experimental approach that acknowledges the complex, responsive nature of relationship systems.

Instead of saying, "Your action step is to have a conversation about finances this week," try, "What if you experimented with a different approach to the financial conversation this week? We could design a small experiment, see what happens, and learn from the results."

This framing reduces pressure and perfectionism, acknowledges the unpredictable nature of relationship dynamics, creates a learning orientation rather than a success/failure binary, and builds the client's capacity for ongoing adaptation.

Know Your Boundaries and Build Your Network

Expanding your practice doesn't mean eliminating boundaries. In fact, clearer boundaries—thoughtfully established—are essential for ethical relationship coaching.

Develop explicit criteria for when to refer clients to therapeutic resources. Build relationships with qualified therapists, including those specialising in relationship therapy. A strong referral network allows you to maintain appropriate boundaries while ensuring clients receive the support they need.

Consider developing collaborative relationships with therapists where appropriate, creating complementary support for clients who might benefit from both modalities.

Working with Couples as a Coach

While many coaches work primarily with individuals, the principles and tools above can be adapted for direct work with couples. If you choose to work with couples, here are some additional considerations.

Create Clear Contracts

Establish explicit agreements about confidentiality (including what happens if you speak with partners separately), goals and outcomes for the coaching relationship, process and structure of sessions, boundaries of your role as a coach vs. a therapist, and criteria for when referral to relationship therapy might be appropriate.

Balance Attention and Alliance

Working with two people simultaneously requires careful attention to balance. Monitor your own potential biases or stronger connection with one partner. Ensure both partners have equal voice and influence. Pay attention to power dynamics within the relationship. Consider whether having a co-coach of a different gender might provide better balance (as in the Duo Coaching model described in Chapter 6).

Focus on Interaction Patterns

With couples, focus on the patterns between them rather than individual issues. Observe and reflect on communication patterns in real time. Help partners identify recurring cycles of interaction. Create experiments that interrupt problematic patterns. Build capacity for constructive conversations about difficult topics.

Utilise the Session as a Laboratory

The coaching session provides a unique opportunity to observe and shift relationship dynamics in real time. Notice how partners interact during the session. Create opportunities for new interaction patterns within the session. Use what happens between partners as data for exploration. Provide real-time feedback about communication patterns.

The Ethical Dimension

Expanding your coaching practice to include deeper relationship work carries ethical responsibilities that deserve thoughtful consideration.

Be transparent about your qualifications. Clearly communicate your training and credentials, the boundaries of your expertise, the difference between coaching and therapy, and when and why you might refer to a therapist.

Commit to ongoing learning about relationship dynamics and patterns, basic understanding of attachment theory, ethical considerations specific to relationship work, and signs that might indicate the need for therapeutic intervention.

Regular supervision is essential when doing relationship-focused coaching. Work with a supervisor experienced in relationship dynamics. Use supervision to explore your own reactions and potential blind spots. Discuss challenging cases and boundary questions. Consider periodic consultation with qualified relationship therapists.

In relationship coaching, clients often ask directly or indirectly about your own relationship experiences. Develop thoughtful guidelines for when self-disclosure might serve the client, how to disclose without making the session about you, maintaining appropriate boundaries while being authentic, and using your experiences as context rather than prescription.

A Coach's Expanded Horizon: Mark and Joanna's Story

> George had been coaching executives for 15 years before he began working with couples. His approach had always been firmly future-focused and action-oriented—identifying goals, creating plans, and holding clients accountable for progress. When Mark and Joanna came to him, he initially approached their relationship challenges in the same way.
>
> "We keep having the same argument about our finances," Mark explained in their first session. "We never reach a resolution."
>
> "And what would you like to have happen instead?" George asked, falling into his familiar pattern.
>
> "We'd like to be able to discuss money without it turning into a fight," Joanna replied.
>
> George nodded and began to outline a communication strategy, complete with structured conversation templates and feedback loops. It was the kind of practical solution he'd offered countless executives facing team conflicts. But as the couple attempted to implement his suggestions over the following weeks, something felt incomplete. The tools weren't taking root.
>
> During their fourth session, George decided to try something different—an approach he'd learned from studying the Duo Coaching framework. Rather than focusing exclusively on creating new patterns for the future, he invited the couple to explore the historical roots of their financial conflicts.
>
> "I know this is a shift from our previous work," he acknowledged, "but I'm curious if we might look more deeply at what each of you brings to these financial discussions. Not just your current positions, but how your relationship with money was shaped earlier in your lives."
>
> Mark looked sceptical. "Isn't that more therapy than coaching? I thought we were here to find solutions."
>
> "It's a fair question," George replied.
>
>> What I've discovered is that sometimes understanding the origins of patterns can help us create more effective solutions. We won't get lost in the past—we'll use what we learn to inform our path forward. Would you be willing to experiment with this approach today?
>
> The couple cautiously agreed. George began by asking them each to share their earliest memories of money in their families. Joanna described growing

up with parents who fought constantly about finances after her father lost his job during a recession.

"I remember hiding in my room during their arguments," she said quietly. "I swore I'd never be financially vulnerable when I grew up."

Mark, in turn, revealed that his family rarely discussed money. "It was considered impolite to talk about finances. Problems were handled privately by my father. I just knew that sometimes we couldn't afford things, but no one ever explained why."

As they continued exploring, George used Clean Language questioning to deepen their awareness without imposing his interpretations:

"And when you hear discussions about spending, Joanna, what kind of feeling is that feeling from your childhood?"

"It's a tightness, like I can't breathe," she replied. "Like something bad is about to happen."

"And for you, Mark, when financial topics need to be discussed, what happens just before you go quiet?"

Mark considered this. "I feel... unprepared. Like I'm supposed to know what to do but don't have all the information."

Through this exploration, a new understanding emerged. What had appeared to be a disagreement about current spending habits was actually triggered by deeper patterns. Joanna's hypervigilance about finances and Mark's tendency to withdraw from financial discussions both made perfect sense in light of their early experiences.

George then helped them design experiments that acknowledged these patterns while creating new possibilities:

"Given what we've discovered, what would be a small, manageable step toward discussing finances differently?"

The couple decided to begin with a weekly "financial check-in" with clear time boundaries and a structured format that helped Joanna feel secure and gave Mark time to prepare. They also created a signal they could use when past patterns were being triggered, allowing them to pause and reset.

Three months later, the couple reported a significant shift. "Understanding where our reactions were coming from changed everything," Mark explained. "I used to think Joanna didn't trust me when she questioned every purchase. Now I understand she's responding to old fears."

"And I see that when Mark goes quiet, it's not because he's hiding something," Joanna added. "It's because he never learned how to have these conversations."

For George, this experience transformed his approach to relationship coaching. While he maintained his strengths in goal-setting and accountability, he now integrated thoughtful exploration of formative patterns. He didn't position himself as a therapist—he stayed firmly in his coaching role—but he expanded his perspective to include the historical dimension that shapes current challenges.

"I used to believe that looking backward wasn't part of coaching," he reflected.

> Now I understand that knowing where patterns originated doesn't keep us stuck in the past—it actually liberates us to create more effective paths forward. The Duo Coaching framework helped me see that integration of past, present, and future creates more sustainable change than focusing on any single timeframe.

George continued to define clear boundaries for his practice, referring couples to therapists when deeper trauma work was needed. But within his coaching role, he found that this expanded perspective allowed him to help couples make more meaningful, lasting changes in their relationships.

The Courage to Explore

The ancient mariners who first ventured beyond sight of land didn't do so recklessly. They prepared meticulously, developed new navigation tools, studied the patterns of stars and currents, and built vessels capable of withstanding unknown challenges. Most importantly, they proceeded with both courage and humility, knowing that the journey would reveal both wonders and dangers they couldn't anticipate.

As you expand your coaching practice to include deeper relationship work, you're embarking on a similar journey. The frameworks and approaches I've shared provide navigation tools, but they can't eliminate the inherent risks of venturing into deeper waters. What will carry you forward is the same combination of courage and humility that has guided explorers throughout history.

You'll need the courage to move beyond comfortable boundaries. The humility to recognise what you don't know. The commitment to ongoing learning and development. And above all, the unwavering dedication to serving your clients with integrity and care.

In my forthcoming book, *Reframe*, I'll provide a more detailed, step-by-step guide to implementing these approaches. For now, I invite you to begin exploring the expanded possibilities of relationship coaching—not by abandoning your coaching identity, but by enriching it with new dimensions of awareness and skill.

The couples you work with need guides who can help them navigate their relationship challenges with wisdom and practical support. By thoughtfully expanding your practice to include deeper relationship dynamics, you become precisely the guide they need—someone who can help them not only achieve their stated goals but also transform the patterns that have limited their relationship potential.

Welcome to the journey beyond the traditional boundaries of coaching. The waters may sometimes be challenging, but the destinations they reveal will be worth every moment of the voyage.

In my forthcoming book, *Reframe*, I will provide a more detailed, step-by-step guide to implementing these approaches. For now, I invite you to begin exploring the expanded possibilities of relationship coaching—not by abandoning your coaching identity, but by enriching it with new dimensions of awareness and skill.

The couples you want to work with need guides who can help them navigate their relationship challenges with wisdom and practical support. By thoughtfully expanding your practice to include deeper relationship dynamics, you become precisely the guide they need—someone who can help them not only achieve their stated goals but also transform the patterns that have limited their relationship potential.

Welcome to the journey beyond the traditional boundaries of coaching. The waters may sometimes be challenging, but the destinations they reveal will be worth every moment of the voyage.

While coaches may need to expand beyond their comfort zones into deeper waters, counsellors face a different challenge: they're already skilled in emotional depths but may be constrained by single.

Chapter 11

Guidance for Counsellors

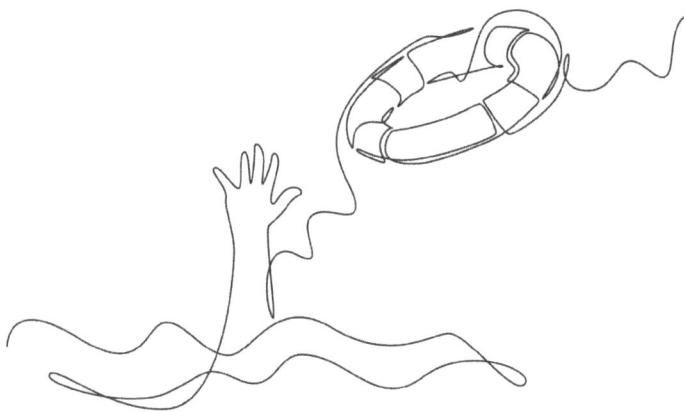

Figure 11.1 A hand reaches from the waves towards a life ring: the essential act of rescue that counsellors perform, and the invitation to expand their therapeutic repertoire so they can reach couples who are struggling to stay afloat.

From Single-Handed Sailing to Coordinated Navigation

Many counsellors master one particular type of sailing—perhaps the steady, methodical approach of traditional therapy. But relationship work often demands the ability to switch between different sailing techniques as conditions change, sometimes within the same session.

Expanding Your Horizons Beyond Familiar Waters

As a counsellor, you've invested years in developing expertise within your chosen modality. Whether your foundation is person-centred, psychodynamic, CBT, or another established approach, this training has given you valuable tools and a coherent framework for understanding human experience. Yet when working with relationship issues, you might sometimes feel like a sailor with an excellent boat but only one type of sail—well-equipped for certain conditions but limited when the winds change (Figure 11.1).

I'm not suggesting you abandon ship. Far from it! This chapter is an invitation to expand your therapeutic repertoire while honouring the foundations that have brought you this far. Think of it as adding a few more sails to your collection, allowing you to navigate a broader range of relationship waters with greater confidence and effectiveness.

The Limitations of Single-Modality Approaches

In Chapter 3, we explored various psychotherapeutic approaches and their applications to relationship work. Let's be honest—each modality offers valuable insights while also having inherent blind spots when applied to the complex dynamics of couple relationships.

Person-centred approaches provide that wonderful foundation of empathy, congruence, and unconditional positive regard—qualities essential for creating safety in therapeutic work. But as I noted in Chapter 3, "this approach is of limited value in Relationship Therapy as the clients are often adrift at sea and need a lifeboat. If no guidance is given, the couple would be likely to sink." The non-directive stance can leave couples floundering when they need active intervention in destructive patterns.

Psychodynamic approaches excel at exploring unconscious patterns and early influences on current behaviour. Yet they are "inappropriate for use with couples' relationships as [they] can only accommodate one client at a time and [are] not suited to working with a couple system." The focus on individual intrapsychic dynamics often neglects the systemic nature of relationship challenges.

CBT approaches offer practical tools for changing thought patterns and behaviours, providing couples with concrete skills. However, the emphasis on conscious cognition may miss deeper emotional currents and attachment needs that drive relationship dynamics below awareness.

Systemic approaches address the relationship as a system, examining patterns and interactions rather than individual pathology. While powerful, this perspective sometimes neglects individual psychological needs and internal experiences that contribute to relationship difficulties.

The reality of relationship work is that no single modality provides all the tools needed to address the multilayered complexity of couple dynamics. As we saw in Chapter 5 on Transdisciplinarity, relationships exist across multiple interconnected contexts that require diverse lenses to fully comprehend and address.

The Case for Integrative Practice in Relationship Work

In Duo Coaching, as described in Chapter 6, we use "an eclectic approach." This gives us the flexibility to tailor our approach to what intuitively feels right for each client and each couple in the moment. This flexibility isn't haphazard but a thoughtful integration of approaches based on careful assessment of what each unique situation requires.

The benefits of an integrative approach to relationship work are rather like having a well-stocked galley on a long voyage. You don't know exactly what conditions you'll encounter, but you've prepared for a range of possibilities. This approach allows you to meet clients where they are, with their unique communication styles and readiness for various interventions. It enables you to address multiple dimensions simultaneously—cognitive, emotional, behavioural, systemic, and historical. You can avoid the limitations of any single perspective by complementing one approach with the strengths of another.

Relationships are among the most complex human systems. Their multidimensional nature demands a similarly multifaceted therapeutic approach. And perhaps most excitingly, the intersection of different theoretical frameworks often generates breakthrough insights that might never emerge from any single perspective.

Expanding Your Practice: Key Dimensions

If you primarily practice within a single modality, consider expanding your approach along these key dimensions that are particularly relevant to relationship work.

From Individual to Systemic Perspective

Many counselling traditions focus primarily on the individual client, even when working with relationships. Expanding to a systemic perspective means viewing the relationship as an entity with its own properties, greater than the sum of the two individuals.

It's rather like the difference between studying two individual musicians vs. studying the music they create together. Both approaches have value, but understanding the duet requires attention to the interaction, the harmonies and dissonances that emerge between them, not just their individual techniques.

When you attend to patterns of interaction rather than just individual behaviours or feelings, you begin to see the dance rather than just the dancers. You consider how changes in one person will inevitably affect the entire system. You explore the function that problematic patterns might serve within the relationship system. And you examine how external systems (families of origin, work, culture) influence the couple's dynamics.

For person-centred counsellors, while maintaining your stance of empathic understanding, try expanding your empathy to include the relationship itself as an entity deserving of attention. Consider what the relationship needs to flourish, not just what each individual needs.

For psychodynamic counsellors, connect individual intrapsychic material to the co-created patterns between partners. How do unconscious processes manifest in and get reinforced by interaction patterns?

For CBT counsellors, explore how individual cognitive patterns become interlinked in relationship dynamics. Consider the "relationship dance" that emerges from two sets of thoughts, feelings, and behaviours interacting.

From Past/Present to Multi-Temporal Perspective

Different therapeutic traditions emphasise different timeframes: psychodynamic approaches focus on the past, person-centred and CBT approaches often emphasise the present, and coaching approaches look towards the future. Relationship work benefits from integration across all three time dimensions.

Think of it as having a map that shows not just where you are, but where you've been and possible routes forward. Understanding how each partner's history shapes current expectations and reactions provides crucial context. Working with in-the-moment patterns and experiences as they emerge creates immediate awareness and opportunities for change. And helping couples envision and create their desired relationship provides direction and motivation.

Regardless of your current focus, try expanding to include exploration of how past experiences (particularly in family of origin and previous relationships) create templates for current relationship expectations. Pay attention to what is happening in the room between partners during sessions. Create a clear vision for the desired future of the relationship. And build bridges between historical understanding, present awareness, and future orientation.

This integration of timeframes creates a more complete picture of the relationship journey and increases the potential for meaningful change. It's like having access to all dimensions of time rather than being stuck in just one.

From Verbal to Multi-Channel Communication

Traditional counselling relies heavily on verbal exchange. Relationship dynamics, however, are communicated through multiple channels that deserve attention.

Have you ever noticed how much is conveyed between a couple without a single word being spoken? Body language and non-verbal cues often tell a more truthful story than words. Emotional energy and atmospheric feeling in the room can shift dramatically within seconds. Physical positioning and proximity between partners reveal volumes about their emotional connection. Voice tone, volume, and pacing carry emotional messages that words alone might contradict. And what remains unsaid or actively avoided often holds the key to understanding core issues.

Consider expanding your awareness and interventions to include noticing and commenting on non-verbal patterns between partners. Use the "warm data" (mentioned in Chapter 5) that emerges through indirect communication. Incorporate body-based awareness into your work. Work with the energy and emotional atmosphere between partners. And create experiential exercises that engage multiple channels of experience and expression.

As noted in Chapter 6, in Duo Coaching we pay attention to "what is happening in the unconscious (out of full awareness), what are the embedded patterns of behaviour which need to be changed." Many of these patterns are visible only when we attend to multiple channels of communication.

From Single-Tool to Multi-Method Approach

Each therapeutic tradition has preferred interventions and techniques. Relationship work benefits from a broader toolkit that can address different aspects of relationship dynamics.

Imagine being a carpenter with only a hammer. You'd be limited to hammer-appropriate tasks. But with a complete toolkit, you can select precisely the right tool for each unique situation.

Consider adding experiential exercises that allow couples to experience new patterns rather than just talking about them. Try visualisation techniques to help partners access emotional states and possibilities. Experiment with structural interventions that physically reorganise how couples interact during sessions. Develop homework assignments that extend therapeutic work beyond sessions. And explore creative methods such as drawing, metaphor, or narrative techniques that access different modes of understanding.

As described in Chapter 6, our work with couples draws from a diverse range of approaches, including psychodynamic counselling, client-centred therapy, coaching, Neuro Linguistic Programming (NLP), Gestalt, Clean Language, Clean Space, Symbolic Modelling, Time Line Therapy, Transactional Analysis, Drama Triangle, Clinical Hypnotherapy, Parts Negotiation, visual and aural exploration, Systemic Constellations, Human Constellations, and Personality Profiling.

While you needn't master all these approaches, expanding your toolkit beyond your primary modality will significantly enhance your effectiveness with relationship issues. It's about having more options, more ways to help couples break through stuck patterns and discover new possibilities.

From Neutral to Strategic Balance

Many counselling traditions emphasise therapist neutrality. While this has value, relationship work often requires a more active stance that maintains strategic balance.

Imagine a sailing boat with two people trying to steer in different directions. As the captain, remaining completely neutral might mean the boat goes nowhere or, worse, capsizes. Sometimes you need to provide more guidance to help the sailors coordinate their efforts towards a shared destination.

This means ensuring both partners feel equally heard and understood. It involves preventing dominant partners from controlling the therapeutic space. It requires actively interrupting destructive interaction patterns. It sometimes calls for providing more direct guidance when couples are stuck in harmful cycles. And it entails balancing attention to individual needs with focus on the relationship system.

This doesn't mean abandoning therapeutic boundaries or imposing your values. Rather, it means recognising that relationship dynamics can replicate themselves in the therapeutic setting if the counsellor maintains strict neutrality.

As we've seen in Chapter 6, the Duo Coaching framework addresses this issue by having two therapists—typically one male and one female—to create natural balance in the room. If you work alone with couples, you must be particularly attentive to maintaining this balance yourself, like a captain constantly adjusting to keep the boat on an even keel.

Working with Relationship Issues in Individual Therapy

Many counsellors encounter relationship issues in the context of individual therapy. While Chapter 4 noted the limitations of working with only one partner ("The therapist will only hear one perspective, the other part of the couple will not be represented and may feel threatened"), there are ways to make this work more effective when couple therapy is not possible.

Maintain a systemic perspective even when working with just one partner. Help the client see their role in co-created patterns. Avoid reinforcing a simplistic "victim/persecutor" narrative. Explore how changes in the client's behaviour might affect the relationship system.

Actively consider the absent partner. Bring the partner's perspective into the room. Help the client imagine how situations might look from their partner's viewpoint. Use empty-chair techniques to create dialogue with the absent partner.

Focus on the client's agency. Emphasise what the client can change rather than focusing on the partner's behaviour. Explore how shifts in the client's responses might interrupt problematic patterns. Build the client's capacity for emotional self-regulation.

Develop the individual foundation. Work on the client's self-awareness and personal growth. Address individual issues that impact relationship functioning. Strengthen the client's clarity about their needs and boundaries.

And when appropriate, consider inviting the partner. Suggest including the partner for some sessions. Create a safe space where both perspectives can be heard. Use these joint sessions strategically, returning to individual work as needed.

Remember that while individual therapy for relationship issues has limitations, it can still create meaningful change by shifting one part of the relationship system. It's like adjusting one sail—not as effective as coordinating both, but still capable of altering the course.

Shifting from 50-Minute Sessions to More Effective Timeframes

In Chapter 3, we explored how the traditional 50-minute session may not be optimal for relationship work. As noted, there is "limited research into whether 50 minutes is the most effective duration for therapy, or whether clients would do just as well or better with shorter or, conversely, longer sessions."

In Duo Coaching, we use significantly longer sessions: "Experience has shown that the first session needs to be about three and a half hours to explore how the couple have got to where they are right now… Subsequent sessions are typically about two and a half hours long."

While your practice context may not allow for such extensive sessions, consider experimenting with alternative timeframes. Try extended initial sessions to allow for comprehensive assessment. Explore variable session lengths based on the needs of the particular couple and stage of work. Offer occasional double sessions for more in-depth work on complex issues. Consider intensive periods of more frequent sessions when needed. And develop more flexible scheduling that responds to couple needs rather than rigid weekly appointments.

As Professor Timothy Carey's research (cited in Chapter 3) suggests, giving clients more autonomy over scheduling can significantly improve engagement and outcomes. It's about creating a container that fits the work, rather than forcing the work to fit an arbitrary container.

Developing a Clearer Outcome Focus

Traditional counselling approaches often emphasise process over specific outcomes. While this open-ended exploration has value, relationship work typically benefits from a clearer focus on desired results.

In Duo Coaching,

> we clarify the outcomes that they both want because we are driven very much by outcomes that are wanted. That way we can make sure they are coherent and compatible and can calibrate the progress that is being made. It feels like the traditional approach is just drifting along and seeing if anything happens.

Consider enhancing your practice by establishing clear outcome criteria at the beginning of the work. Regularly revisit and refine these outcomes as the work progresses. Track progress more explicitly. Create a defined timeline rather than an open-ended process. And celebrate achievements and mark progress along the way.

This outcome focus needn't mean abandoning depth or rushing the process. Rather, it provides direction and momentum while allowing for the organic unfolding of the therapeutic journey. It's like having a destination in mind—you might take detours or stop to explore interesting territory along the way, but you maintain a sense of where you're ultimately heading.

Ethical Considerations When Expanding Your Practice

As you expand your approach to relationship work, several ethical considerations deserve attention:

Competence Boundaries

Be clear about the distinction between expanding within your competence and practising beyond it. This requires honest self-assessment of your skills and knowledge. Pursue appropriate training before implementing new approaches. Seek supervision with someone experienced in relationship work. Refer couples to specialists when issues exceed your competence. And maintain transparency with clients about your experience and limitations.

Managing Multiple Relationships

Working with couples inherently involves multiple relationships and potential conflicts of interest. Consider how you will handle requests for individual sessions with one partner. Develop a clear policy on secrets between partners. Decide how you will manage situations where one partner wants to continue while the other wishes to end therapy. Determine whether and when you would see one partner individually after couple work ends. And establish how you will maintain therapeutic boundaries with both partners.

Avoiding Triangulation

The presence of two clients creates potential for triangulation, where one partner attempts to align you against the other, you find yourself more sympathetic to one partner's perspective, or the therapeutic relationship becomes a recreation of family-of-origin triangles. Develop strategies for recognising and addressing these dynamics when they emerge.

Cultural and Value Considerations

Relationship norms vary significantly across cultures and individual value systems. Be attentive to your own assumptions about "healthy" relationships. Respect cultural differences in relationship expectations. Acknowledge diverse relationship structures beyond traditional monogamy. Be sensitive to religious or spiritual frameworks that inform clients' relationship values. And guard against the risk of imposing your own values rather than helping clients clarify theirs.

Self-Care and Support

Relationship work can be emotionally demanding, particularly when expanding beyond familiar approaches. Ensure you have regular supervision with someone experienced in relationship therapy. Develop peer support or consultation groups. Pay attention to your own emotional responses and potential countertransference. Establish clear boundaries around availability between sessions. And commit to ongoing professional development in relationship-specific approaches.

Learning from the Duo Coaching Framework

While you may not implement the full Duo Coaching framework in your practice, several of its key elements can inform and enhance your work with relationships.

The Value of Co-Therapy

If your practice context allows, consider the benefits of working with a co-therapist for relationship cases. As noted in Chapter 3, co-therapy offers "a greater opportunity for learning through discussion and collaboration with a therapist," "widened perspectives for therapists," "widened transference possibilities for clients," "greater learning opportunities," and "opportunities for therapists to check and balance their complimentary behaviours."

Even occasional collaboration with colleagues can provide some of these benefits without requiring a full co-therapy model. It's like having a second set of eyes and ears—you'll notice things together that neither might catch alone.

The Power of the "Me," "You," and "Us" Framework

The Duo Coaching approach works:

> on the triad of the 'You', 'Me' and 'Us'. The normal relationship counselling approach is to look at the couple, their dynamics and the present state. My view is that a couple cannot have strong foundations unless the individuals do too.

Incorporate this perspective by assessing individual wellbeing alongside relationship dynamics. Address personal growth needs that impact the relationship. Help partners balance individual and relationship needs. And create space for individual expression within the couple context.

The Importance of Practical Support Between Sessions

In Duo Coaching, "unlimited telephone and email support between sessions 24/7" is offered because it would be better dealing with problems as they are emerging rather than dealing with the aftermath.

While this specific model may not be feasible in your practice, consider how you might provide more accessible support during difficult periods. This might include brief check-in calls at critical junctures, email availability for urgent situations, crisis management protocols, or referrals to appropriate resources for between-session support.

The Value of Deeper Pattern Recognition

The Duo Coaching approach emphasises working with "what is happening in the unconscious (out of full awareness) and what are the embedded patterns of behaviour which need to be changed."

Develop your capacity to identify recurring relationship patterns. Connect current dynamics to historical influences. Recognise attachment patterns in action. And address the unconscious dimensions of relationship challenges.

Creating a Comprehensive Assessment Process

In Duo Coaching, couples "complete a comprehensive consultation form before they start, giving their background, timeline of their life, perspective on the relationship problems and what they would like to have happen."

Consider enhancing your assessment process to gather more comprehensive information at the outset, creating a stronger foundation for the work to follow. It's like making sure you have a good map before setting sail.

Expanding the Therapeutic Space: Claire's Discovery

> Claire had been a person-centred counsellor for nearly two decades. Her small practice room with its comfortable chairs, soft lighting, and meticulously maintained 50-minute sessions had been the setting for countless therapeutic journeys. She prided herself on creating a safe, nurturing space where clients could explore their experiences without judgement or directive intervention.
>
> For three months, she had been working with Robert and Sarah, a couple in their mid-forties who had been together for twelve years. Their presenting issues included communication breakdowns, emotional distance, and disagreements about parenting their two children. Despite Claire's empathic listening and gentle reflections, the sessions had fallen into a predictable pattern: Robert would express frustration about Sarah's emotional withdrawal; Sarah would defend herself by pointing to Robert's critical tone; Claire would reflect their feelings and encourage deeper expression; and the session would end with little tangible progress.
>
> After one particularly circular session, Claire found herself feeling restless. She had recently attended a workshop on the Duo Coaching framework and had been intrigued by its emphasis on longer sessions and outcome-focused work. Though initially sceptical—"How could extending session time alone make such a difference?"—she decided to propose an experiment to Robert and Sarah.
>
> "I've been reflecting on our work together," she began at their next appointment, "and I'm wondering if our current format is serving you as effectively as it could. Would you be open to trying something different? Instead of our usual 50 minutes, we could meet for a two-hour session next time."
>
> The couple looked surprised but agreed to try the extended format. Claire also suggested a second modification: "I'd also like us to spend some time clarifying what specific outcomes you're both hoping for from our work together. Not just 'better communication,' but what that would actually look like and feel like for each of you."
>
> When Robert and Sarah arrived for their extended session the following week, Claire had rearranged her room slightly, adding a small table with water and tea facilities. "Make yourselves comfortable," she invited. "We have time today."
>
> The session began with Claire's invitation to clarify outcomes. "If our work together is completely successful," she asked, "what would be different in your relationship? Let's be specific."

Initially, their responses were vague—"We'd communicate better" and "There would be less conflict." But with gentle persistence and the luxury of time, Claire helped them articulate more precise desires:

Robert: "I want to be able to express concerns without Sarah shutting down. I want to feel heard, not like I'm always the bad guy."

Sarah: "I want to feel safe being vulnerable, not constantly on guard. And I want us to make decisions together about the children instead of undermining each other."

As they explored these outcomes, Claire noticed a shift in the room's energy. With the pressure of the clock removed, both partners began to speak more slowly, pause more often, and listen more attentively. The usual defensive patterns were still present but less pronounced.

"What's happening now feels different," Claire observed. "I notice you're both taking more time to consider your words and to really hear each other. What are you experiencing?"

"I don't feel as rushed," Sarah admitted. "Usually, I'm just thinking about what to say next because our time is so limited. Now I can actually process what Robert is saying."

With the extended timeframe, Claire felt confident to suggest an experiential exercise she would normally have considered too time-consuming. She invited the couple to sit facing each other and, for two minutes just look into each other's eyes without speaking. Initially awkward, the exercise gradually led to moments of genuine connection that had been absent in previous sessions.

In the second hour, Claire guided them to explore the patterns in their communication cycle, drawing it out visually to help them see their interactional dance. With time for both reflection and practical application, they were able to not only identify the cycle but also practice interrupting it with new responses. When difficult emotions arose, there was space to explore them fully rather than having to contain them as the session's end approached.

"I'm noticing that we've been able to move through several layers today," Claire reflected towards the end of the two hours. "We've named specific outcomes, identified patterns, experienced emotional connection, and practiced new responses. How has this extended format felt for you?"

"It's completely different," Robert said. "In our usual sessions, just as I start to feel like we're getting somewhere, it's time to go. Today I feel like we actually accomplished something."

Sarah nodded. "I was sceptical that just having more time would make a difference, but it's not just about the minutes. It's about having space to breathe, to feel, to process. I don't feel cut off mid-thought."

As Claire continued working with Robert and Sarah over the following months, she maintained the extended format for every third session, finding that this rhythm allowed for both depth work and integration time. She also began each session by reconnecting with their desired outcomes, gauging progress and adjusting their focus accordingly.

The clarity about outcomes proved particularly valuable. Rather than an open-ended exploration, their work now had direction and measurable markers of progress. When Robert reported that Sarah had stayed engaged during a difficult conversation about their son's academic struggles, they could recognise this as movement towards their articulated goal. When Sarah acknowledged feeling safe enough to express vulnerability about work pressures, this too was acknowledged as meaningful progress.

Six months into this adjusted approach, Claire reflected on the transformation in her practice:

> I realised I had been unconsciously constrained by the traditional therapeutic hour, not because it was the most effective timeframe but because it was what I had always done. The extended sessions haven't just given my clients more minutes; they've created a fundamentally different therapeutic space where deeper work can unfold.
>
> Similarly, I had been hesitant about focusing explicitly on outcomes, concerned it might feel too directive or create pressure. But I've found that clarity about desired change actually creates more freedom, not less. It provides a compass for our work together without prescribing the exact path.
>
> I haven't abandoned my person-centred foundations—empathy, unconditional positive regard, and authenticity remain central to my approach. But I've expanded beyond these foundations to incorporate elements that enhance effectiveness with couples specifically. The Duo Coaching framework helped me see possibilities I had been missing, not because they contradicted my therapeutic orientation, but simply because they lay outside my familiar territory.
>
> The most powerful realisation has been that small changes in structure can create significant shifts in process and outcome. By simply expanding the therapeutic container—both in terms of time and explicit direction—I've created space for deeper, more transformative work within my existing practice framework.

As Claire continued to integrate elements of the Duo Coaching approach, she found that her effectiveness with couples increased significantly. The success with Robert and Sarah led her to selectively implement extended sessions with other couples, always with attention to their specific needs and preferences. What had begun as a tentative experiment became an integral part of her therapeutic repertoire—not replacing but enhancing the person-centred foundation that remained at the heart of her practice.

Conclusion: The Courage to Integrate

Expanding beyond the familiar shores of your primary modality requires courage—the willingness to venture into less charted waters and to risk temporary discomfort as you develop new skills. Yet this journey offers rich rewards: greater effectiveness with the couples you serve, renewed engagement with your practice, and the satisfaction of meeting complex relationship challenges with a more complete therapeutic repertoire.

Integration does not mean abandoning what you already know and do well. Rather, it means building upon that foundation, adding dimensions that complement and enhance your existing strengths. The most effective relationship counsellors are not those who rigidly adhere to a single approach, but those who thoughtfully integrate diverse perspectives and methods based on a clear understanding of what each unique situation requires.

The frameworks and approaches outlined in this chapter provide a starting point for this integration. The specific ways you implement these ideas will depend on your current modality, practice context, and personal style. The invitation is not to adopt a prescribed formula but to engage in thoughtful experimentation guided by a commitment to serving your clients more effectively.

In my forthcoming book, *Reframe*, I will provide more detailed, step-by-step guidance for implementing these approaches in various counselling contexts. For now, I encourage you to begin exploring the expanded possibilities that emerge when you venture beyond the familiar boundaries of your primary modality.

The couples who seek your help are navigating some of life's most challenging waters. By expanding your therapeutic repertoire, you become better equipped to guide them through storms and calm seas alike, helping them chart a course towards the relationships they truly desire.

Chapter 12

Guidance for Psychoanalysts

Figure 12.1 Above the clouds with a telescope: a figure surveys the landscape from an elevated vantage point, representing the psychoanalyst's capacity for depth and perspective—and the expanded view that emerges when that understanding is brought into the relational waters below.

Bringing Deep-Sea Discoveries to Shared Waters

Psychoanalysts are the deep-sea explorers of therapy—trained to navigate the profound depths of the unconscious mind. Yet even the most sophisticated submersible may need surface support vessels when bringing findings up to where two people can breathe the same air and build a life together.

Navigating New Waters with Ancient Maps

As a psychoanalyst, you possess perhaps the oldest and most detailed maps of the human psyche in the therapeutic world. Your training has immersed you in understanding the depths of unconscious processes, the power of early experience, the complexity of intrapsychic conflict, and the subtle manifestations of transference and countertransference. These are invaluable tools for understanding the hidden currents that shape human relationships (Figure 12.1).

Yet when working with couples, you may find yourself in a curious position—equipped with profound insights into individual psychological processes while potentially less versed in the intersubjective dynamics that emerge between partners. It's as if you possess exquisite depth soundings of individual harbours but less detailed charts of the open waters where two people navigate together.

I'm not suggesting you abandon your psychoanalytic compass—far from it. This chapter invites you to bring your psychoanalytic understanding into dialogue with complementary approaches that can enhance your effectiveness in relationship work. The goal isn't to dilute your psychoanalytic perspective but to extend it into the intersubjective space where relationships live and breathe.

The Psychoanalytic Contribution to Relationship Understanding

Before we explore extensions to your practice, let's acknowledge the significant contributions that psychoanalytic thinking already makes to relationship work. Your tradition brings unique gifts that other modalities often lack.

The Unconscious Dimension

Your training allows you to recognise that much of what drives relationship dynamics exists below the threshold of awareness. While other modalities may focus primarily on conscious communication and explicit agreements, you understand the profound influence of the unconscious.

You see how unconscious expectations from early attachment relationships shape adult partnerships in ways that partners rarely recognise. You observe the defences against vulnerability that create recurring patterns of disconnection despite conscious intentions to connect. You recognise the mechanisms of projection and projective identification that create complex emotional entanglements between partners, each unconsciously evoking and responding to disowned aspects of the other.

You understand how repetition compulsion leads couples to recreate familiar but painful relationship patterns, seemingly drawn to reproduce what they most wish to avoid. And you appreciate that transference phenomena apply not only to the therapeutic relationship but to intimate partnerships, with each partner unconsciously relating to aspects of significant figures from their past.

This awareness of the unconscious dimension provides a depth of understanding that more surface-oriented approaches often miss entirely. It's like having night vision when others can only see by daylight.

Developmental Perspective

Your appreciation for how early experience shapes adult functioning offers crucial insights into relationship dynamics. You bring understanding of how developmental arrests affect capacity for intimacy, seeing how childhood interruptions in emotional development manifest in adult relationship limitations.

You recognise how early attachment patterns manifest in adult relationships, creating predictable patterns of connection and disconnection under stress. The ways childhood experiences of love, loss, and conflict create templates for adult relationships become visible through your developmental lens. You can track how unresolved developmental tasks emerge as relationship challenges, particularly during life transitions that reactivate earlier developmental stages. And you perceive the echoes of early object relations in current partnerships, hearing the resonance between past and present relational patterns.

This developmental perspective provides a richness of understanding about the historical roots of present difficulties that few other approaches can match. It's like having access to the geological record of the relationship landscape, seeing how present formations were shaped by ancient forces.

Symbolic Processes

Your training in understanding symbolic expression and communication allows you to work with dimensions of relationship experience that might otherwise remain invisible. You recognise the metaphorical dimensions of relationship complaints, hearing how seemingly concrete grievances often speak to deeper emotional longings. You understand how dreams and fantasies reveal unconscious relationship dynamics, providing windows into feelings too threatening to acknowledge directly.

Symbolic enactments between partners—repetitive scenarios that express unspoken emotional material—become meaningful rather than merely frustrating to you. You can discern the meaning beneath the content of conflicts, hearing the underlying attachment messages in seemingly trivial disputes. And you perceive the ways partners serve as objects for each other's internal processes, sometimes relating more to internal representations than to the actual person before them.

This symbolic understanding helps you recognise deeper meanings in what might otherwise appear as merely practical or behavioural issues. It's like being able to read a second language that expresses what cannot be said directly in the first.

Transference and Countertransference

Your sophisticated understanding of transference and countertransference provides extraordinary insight into relationship dynamics. You recognise how partners' early relationships are projected onto each other, creating reactions that seem disproportionate until their historical roots are understood. Your awareness of the therapist's emotional responses as data about the couple's dynamics transforms personal reactions into valuable clinical information.

You understand how triangular configurations from family of origin reappear in the therapeutic system, with couples unconsciously inviting you into familiar triangulated positions. You appreciate how the therapeutic relationship can parallel the couple relationship, creating a lived experience of their dynamics within the session. And you bring sensitivity to the multiple transferences operating in couple work, tracking the complex web of projections and expectations flowing between all participants.

This transferential awareness creates opportunities for insight that might otherwise remain hidden beneath the surface of more pragmatic interventions. It's like having a barometer that registers subtle shifts in emotional pressure that others might miss entirely.

Challenges in Applying Psychoanalysis to Couple Work

Despite these valuable contributions, traditional psychoanalytic training and practice contain elements that may present challenges when working with couples.

The Individual Focus

Classical psychoanalysis developed as a treatment for individuals, with theories primarily addressing intrapsychic rather than interpersonal processes. This singular focus creates significant challenges in couple work.

When both partners are present, you must attend to multiple intrapsychic worlds simultaneously—a complexity that traditional analytic training rarely addresses. The necessary focus on the co-created relationship system rather than individual dynamics requires a conceptual shift from how psychoanalysis typically frames human experience.

Furthermore, couple work often necessitates immediate intervention in destructive patterns rather than allowing them to unfold for analysis. Where individual analysis might observe a defence mechanism developing over sessions, relationship work may require interrupting harmful interactions before they escalate and cause further damage.

The development of practical relationship skills alongside insight becomes essential, as understanding alone rarely creates sufficient change in entrenched relationship patterns. And perhaps most challenging, the timeframe for intervention is typically more limited than traditional analysis allows, requiring a pace and focus that may feel uncomfortably directive to classically trained analysts.

The Neutral Stance

The traditional analytic stance emphasises neutrality, minimal self-disclosure, and allowing transference to develop without interference. This carefully cultivated position becomes problematic in couple work where different demands emerge.

Active intervention is frequently needed to interrupt destructive patterns before they undermine the therapeutic alliance or further damage the relationship. More transparent communication about the therapeutic process often proves helpful, as couples benefit from clearer understanding of the work's direction and purpose.

The modelling of healthy interaction becomes increasingly important, with couples learning not just from interpretations but from how you navigate difficult conversations with them. As partners attempt to triangulate you—a nearly universal occurrence in couple work—more active boundary management becomes necessary than the traditional analytic stance typically provides. And psychoeducation about relationship dynamics frequently benefits couples, requiring a more directive teaching role than classical analysis embraces.

These demands require a thoughtful reconsideration of neutrality without abandoning the valuable observational stance that psychoanalysis cultivates.

The Emphasis on Past Over Present

While psychoanalysis has evolved to include more present-focused approaches, there remains a strong emphasis on historical understanding that can limit effectiveness in couple work. Relationship therapy often requires focusing on immediate behavioural changes to stop deterioration before deeper exploration becomes possible.

The development of present-moment awareness of interaction patterns becomes crucial, helping couples recognise and interrupt cycles as they begin rather than analysing them afterwards. Future-oriented planning and goal-setting frequently benefit couples, providing direction and hope that purely historical exploration may not offer.

The development of relationship skills requires substantial focus on current behaviours, with practice and feedback in the present moment. And importantly, couples often need help visualising possibilities rather than only understanding origins—crafting a vision of what their relationship could become, not just insight into how it came to its current state.

This balance between historical understanding and present intervention represents one of the most significant adaptations required of psychoanalysts in couple work.

The Primarily Verbal Process

Traditional analysis relies heavily on verbal expression and interpretation—a focus that may prove insufficient in relationship work. Partners frequently struggle to verbalise emotional experiences, particularly the vulnerable primary emotions that drive relationship patterns.

Body-based interventions often provide more direct access to emotional states, bypassing intellectual defences that verbal approaches may reinforce. For many couples, experiential learning proves more effective than intellectual understanding, creating embodied knowledge that discussion alone cannot provide.

The non-verbal dimensions of communication—body language, tone, proximity, facial expressions—contain crucial information about relationship dynamics that purely verbal approaches may miss. And perhaps most importantly, direct practice of new behaviours frequently catalyses change more effectively than discussion about those behaviours.

While maintaining the value of verbal exploration, relationship work invites integration of more experiential, embodied interventions that extend beyond traditional analytic technique.

The Extended Timeframe

The traditionally open-ended, long-term nature of psychoanalytic work often conflicts with the realities of couple therapy. Many couples arrive in crisis, needing more rapid intervention than classical analysis typically provides. Financial constraints frequently limit treatment duration, with many couples having resources for months rather than years of therapy.

The structure of a more time-limited approach often benefits couples, providing clearer direction and momentum than open-ended exploration. Couples typically need clearer markers of progress than individual analysis might provide, with concrete evidence that their investment is yielding results.

And ultimately, most couples would be better served by developing self-sufficiency rather than therapeutic dependence, learning to navigate their relationship challenges with increasing autonomy rather than ongoing reliance on the analyst. This shift towards a more defined therapeutic journey represents another significant adaptation of traditional analytic work for the relationship context.

Integrating Psychoanalytic Insights with Other Approaches

Your psychoanalytic understanding can be powerfully complemented by selective integration of concepts and techniques from other modalities. Think of these as additional navigational tools that enhance rather than replace your existing charts.

Attachment Theory

While rooted in psychoanalytic thinking, attachment theory has developed into a distinct framework that offers a focused lens on how early attachment experiences create templates for adult relationships. It provides research-based understanding of attachment styles and their interaction patterns. It offers specific interventions to foster secure attachment between partners. It provides accessible language for helping couples understand their emotional needs and fears. And it brings a developmental perspective that normalises rather than pathologises attachment needs.

Integrating attachment concepts can provide a bridge between psychoanalytic understanding and more accessible interventions for couples.

Systems Theory

Systemic perspectives complement psychoanalytic thinking by addressing the circular causality of relationship patterns. They help you understand how symptoms function within the relationship system. They illuminate the role of homeostasis in maintaining problematic patterns. They clarify how change in one part of the system affects the whole. And they reveal the influence of larger family and social systems on the couple.

This systemic view expands the focus beyond individual psychology to the relationship ecosystem.

Emotionally Focused Therapy (EFT)

Developed by Sue Johnson, EFT integrates attachment theory with experiential approaches to offer a structured model for working with attachment-based relationship distress. It provides clear delineation of typical negative interaction cycles. It offers specific interventions to access and restructure emotional responses. It outlines a process for creating corrective emotional experiences. And it brings a strong evidence base for effectiveness with couples.

EFT's focus on emotion and attachment complements psychoanalytic insights while providing more structured intervention protocols.

Mindfulness-Based Approaches

Mindfulness practices can enhance couple work by developing partners' capacity for present-moment awareness. They help reduce reactivity through enhanced self-regulation. They create space between trigger and response. They foster non-judgemental observation of patterns. And they build tolerance for difficult emotions.

These approaches offer practical tools for the self-awareness that psychoanalysis values.

Cognitive-Behavioural Techniques

Selective integration of CBT elements can provide structured tools for changing destructive thought patterns. They offer specific communication skills training. They suggest behavioural experiments to test new ways of interacting. They provide homework assignments to extend therapeutic work. And they establish measurable markers of progress.

These techniques can create concrete change while the deeper psychoanalytic work progresses.

Working with the Unconscious in Couple Therapy

Your psychoanalytic training provides sophisticated tools for working with unconscious material. Adapting these to couple work involves several key dimensions.

Tracking Parallel Processes

Notice how the couple's dynamics manifest in relation to you through how they position you in relation to their conflicts. Observe patterns of engagement that recreate their typical dynamics. Pay attention to emotional responses they evoke in you as countertransference. Notice ways they attempt to split or triangulate. And track how your interventions are received differently by each partner.

Use these observations to understand the couple's unconscious patterns.

Working with Projective Processes

Help partners recognise and reclaim projections by identifying when qualities or feelings are attributed to the partner that may be disowned aspects of self. Explore the origins of these projections in earlier relationships. Create safe space for reclaiming projected material. Notice complementary projections that lock partners into rigid patterns. And address projective identification as a two-person process.

This work helps partners see each other more clearly rather than through the distorting lens of projection.

Identifying Shared Defensive Structures

Recognise how partners co-create defensive patterns through collusion to avoid certain topics or feelings. Notice mutual enactment of family-of-origin dynamics. Identify shared fantasies that maintain distance or merge boundaries. Observe complementary defences that interlock. And bring attention to unconscious agreements about what remains unspoken.

Addressing these shared defences can create openings where individual interpretations might be resisted.

Using Dreams and Fantasies

Incorporate dream work into couple therapy by inviting sharing of dreams that feature the partner or relationship themes. Explore how dreams might express unconscious aspects of the relationship. Note recurring themes or symbols across both partners' dreams. Use dreams to access feelings that are difficult to express directly, and consider dreams as potentially speaking for the relationship system.

This dream work expands beyond individual analysis to illuminate the shared unconscious dimension of the relationship.

Working with Transference in Multiple Dimensions

Navigate the complex transferential field by tracking each partner's transference to you. Notice each partner's transference to the other. Pay attention to your countertransference to each partner. Be aware of your countertransference to the couple as a unit and recognise the couple's joint transference to you.

This multidimensional awareness can reveal patterns that might otherwise remain hidden.

Adapting the Setting and Frame

Traditional psychoanalytic practice involves specific parameters around frequency, duration, and structure of sessions. Consider these adaptations for couple work.

Session Length and Frequency

As noted in Chapter 3, the traditional "50-minute hour" may not be optimal for couple work. Consider longer initial sessions (90–210 minutes) to allow comprehensive assessment. Explore flexibility in session length based on the work's requirements. Try variable frequency rather than rigid weekly scheduling. Consider intensive periods of more frequent sessions when needed and experiment with extended sessions for specific deeper work.

This flexibility serves the needs of the relationship rather than adhering to convention.

Physical Setting

Adapt your physical space to support couple work. Arrange seating to allow partners to see each other as well as you. Create space for experiential exercises when appropriate. Ensure privacy sufficient for emotional expression. Consider the potential for recording sessions (with consent) for review and provide comfort that supports longer sessions.

The setting should facilitate direct engagement between partners rather than primarily with you.

Active Structuring

Take a more active role in structuring the therapeutic process. Create clear contracting about goals and process. Provide more explicit session structure. Offer direct guidance about how partners engage with each other. Give strategic direction of focus and create explicit transitions between different modes of work.

This structure contains the work more actively than the traditional analytic frame.

Conscious Use of Self

Consider more flexible boundaries around self-disclosure and authenticity. Provide more transparent sharing of process observations. Consider judicious self-disclosure when it serves the therapeutic work. Maintain a more visible emotional presence. Express clearer boundaries and expectations. And offer direct feedback about observed patterns.

This more active presence can model healthy relationship qualities while maintaining appropriate therapeutic boundaries.

Integration of Between-Session Work

Extend the therapeutic work beyond sessions through structured assignments to practice new skills. Suggest journaling exercises to track patterns and responses. Recommend reading materials that support the therapeutic process. Provide recorded exercises or meditations for home practice and consider check-ins during particularly challenging periods.

This extension helps integrate insights into daily life more effectively.

Ethical Considerations Specific to Psychoanalytic Couple Work

Working with couples presents ethical challenges that may differ from individual psychoanalytic practice.

Confidentiality and Secrets

Develop clear policies about how information shared in individual contacts will be handled. Decide your response to secrets disclosed by one partner. Establish under what circumstances you would meet individually with one partner. Create record-keeping that respects both individual and joint confidentiality. Clarify your approach if one partner asks you not to share something with the other.

These policies should be transparent from the outset of treatment.

Managing Multiple Relationships

Consider the complexity of holding multiple therapeutic relationships. Determine how to balance attention and alliance with both partners. Clarify your responsibility if the couple separates. Decide whether you would see either partner individually after couple work ends. Establish how to handle requests for testimony in legal proceedings. Consider your approach if referred by another professional treating one partner.

These boundary questions require thoughtful consideration before they arise.

Countertransference Complexities

Develop awareness of countertransference issues specific to couple work. Notice potential for stronger identification with one partner. Be aware of activation of your own relationship history and patterns. Pay attention to reactions to being triangulated or split. Notice feelings about partners who behave in ways that challenge your values. Track responses to criticism from one partner about your alignment with the other.

Regular supervision or consultation is essential for navigating these complexities.

Balancing Depth with Safety

Find the appropriate balance between exploring unconscious material deeply enough to create meaningful change while maintaining sufficient safety for both partners. Challenge defences without overwhelming coping capacities. Address sensitive material without destabilising the relationship. Pace the work to match both partners' readiness.

This balance requires ongoing attention to both individuals' states as well as the relationship system.

Addressing Power Dynamics

Be attentive to power imbalances within the relationship itself. Notice power dynamics between you and each partner. Consider implications of gender, culture, race, class, or other social dimensions. Be aware of differences in emotional expressiveness or verbal ability. Recognise power created by financial arrangements for therapy.

These power dynamics require conscious management rather than neutral observation.

Case Example: Psychoanalytic Principles in Integrative Couple Work

To illustrate the integration of psychoanalytic understanding with a more flexible approach to couple work, consider this brief case example:

> **Michael and Sarah**, both in their mid-40s, sought therapy after 15 years of marriage. Their presenting complaints included emotional distance, sexual disconnection, and escalating conflicts about parenting their two adolescent children. Both described a gradual deterioration in their relationship satisfaction, though neither could identify a clear turning point.
>
> ### Initial Assessment and Formulation
>
> A psychoanalytically informed assessment revealed complementary attachment patterns: Michael's anxious attachment manifested as criticism and pursuit, while Sarah's avoidant style was expressed through emotional withdrawal. Their family-of-origin dynamics showed interesting parallels: Michael grew up with an emotionally volatile mother and distant father; Sarah with a chronically ill mother who needed constant attention and a father who coped through workaholism.
>
> There was also unconscious collusion: both partners feared genuine emotional intimacy while consciously desiring it, creating a safe but unsatisfying distance. Projective patterns were evident: Michael projected his neediness onto their children and expected Sarah to meet these projected needs; Sarah projected her anger onto Michael, experiencing him as more hostile than his behaviour warranted. And both showed evidence of unresolved adolescent individuation, now being triggered by their children reaching adolescence.

This psychoanalytic understanding provided depth to the formulation, while the integrative approach included systemic assessment of current interaction patterns, attachment-based understanding of their emotional needs and fears, practical evaluation of communication skills and conflict management, assessment of external stressors affecting the relationship, and clarification of desired outcomes from therapy.

Therapeutic Process

The integrative approach included psychoanalytic elements alongside complementary interventions.

The psychoanalytic elements included interpretation of the unconscious fit between their defensive structures, exploration of how current parenting conflicts triggered unresolved issues from their own development, analysis of transferential dynamics as they emerged in the therapeutic relationship, attention to dreams that revealed unconscious feelings about the relationship, and working through of early attachment injuries that shaped current expectations.

Complementary elements included structured communication exercises to interrupt destructive interaction patterns, attachment-focused interventions to help express primary emotions and needs, mindfulness practices to increase tolerance for emotional intimacy, behavioural assignments to create new experiences of connection, and psychoeducation about developmental stages for both them and their children.

Adaptations to the traditional analytic frame included 150-minute sessions to allow sufficient engagement with both partners, more active interruption of destructive patterns as they emerged, clearer direction and structure within sessions, more transparent sharing of observations about process, and regular review of progress towards specified goals.

Outcome and Analysis

Over 20 sessions spanning eight months, Michael and Sarah achieved significant improvements: greater awareness of how their family-of-origin experiences shaped their expectations, recognition of their unconscious collusion to maintain emotional distance, more direct expression of vulnerable feelings and attachment needs, improved capacity for conflict resolution without escalation, and renewal of physical and emotional intimacy.

The psychoanalytic understanding provided depth and meaning to their work, while the integrative approach offered more rapid interruption of destructive patterns, practical tools for managing triggers and conflicts, experiential learning alongside intellectual insight, clearer direction and focus throughout the process, and concrete evidence of progress that sustained motivation.

This case illustrates how psychoanalytic principles can be integrated with complementary approaches to create more effective and efficient couple therapy.

Learning from the Duo Coaching Framework

As described in Chapter 6, the Duo Coaching framework offers several elements that psychoanalysts might fruitfully incorporate.

Time Structure

The Duo Coaching approach uses "six sessions spread over a few months... The first is normally 3½ hours and subsequent ones 2½ hours." While this exact structure may not fit your practice, consider longer initial sessions for comprehensive assessment, sufficient time between sessions for integration of insights, a clearer overall timeframe rather than an open-ended process, flexibility to extend sessions when important work is unfolding, and a defined ending that promotes self-sufficiency.

Outcome Focus

In Duo Coaching, "we clarify the outcomes that they both want because we are driven very much by outcomes that are wanted." This focus provides clearer direction for the therapeutic work, criteria for assessing progress, motivation for engaging with challenging material, balance to the process-oriented nature of psychoanalytic work, and a foundation for termination decisions.

Integration of Multiple Approaches

The Duo Coaching framework draws from a wide range of modalities, selecting what will be most effective for each specific situation. This integrative approach allows matching interventions to the unique needs of each couple, addressing different dimensions of experience (cognitive, emotional, somatic, systemic), moving between depth and more direct intervention as needed, combining insight-oriented and skill-building approaches, and drawing from the full range of therapeutic possibilities rather than being limited by a single model.

Balance of Individual and Relationship Focus

The Duo Coaching approach works "on the triad of the 'You', 'Me' and 'Us'." This balanced focus recognises that individual wellbeing forms the foundation for relationship health, personal growth and relationship development are interconnected, partners bring individual histories that shape their relationship patterns, both individual insight and relationship skills are needed, and the relationship system emerges from but is more than the sum of two individuals.

Accessibility Between Sessions

In Duo Coaching, "unlimited telephone and email support between sessions 24/7" is offered because "it would be better dealing with problems as they were emerging rather than dealing with the aftermath."

While this specific arrangement may not fit your practice model, consider how you might provide more support during particularly challenging periods, create resources for partners to use between sessions, develop protocols for addressing crises that arise between appointments, use technology to extend the therapeutic connection when appropriate, and balance boundaries with accessibility to better serve the therapy process.

Conclusion: The Integration of Depth and Pragmatism

As a psychoanalyst working with couples, you have the opportunity to integrate the profound depth of psychoanalytic understanding with the pragmatic effectiveness of more active approaches. This integration does not require abandoning your psychoanalytic identity or compromising your values as an analyst. Rather, it invites you to extend your analytic understanding into new territories, applying your insights in ways that more directly address the unique challenges of relationship work.

The most effective relationship therapists are not those who rigidly adhere to a single approach but those who can move fluidly between different levels of intervention—sometimes exploring unconscious dynamics in depth, sometimes actively interrupting destructive patterns, sometimes teaching specific skills, sometimes creating experiences that bypass intellectual defences. This flexibility, guided by a sophisticated understanding of what is needed in each moment, creates the conditions for profound and lasting change.

The unconscious dimensions of relationships that your psychoanalytic training allows you to recognise remain crucial to effective couple work. The invitation is not to abandon this depth but to complement it with approaches that address other dimensions of relationship functioning—creating a more complete therapeutic response to the complex challenges couples present.

In my forthcoming book, *Reframe*, I will provide more detailed, step-by-step guidance for implementing these integrated approaches. For now, I encourage you to begin exploring the expanded possibilities that emerge when you bring your psychoanalytic understanding into dialogue with complementary perspectives and methods.

The couples who seek your help are navigating relationships shaped by forces both conscious and unconscious. By expanding your therapeutic repertoire while maintaining your psychoanalytic depth, you become uniquely equipped to help them understand and transform these patterns, creating the possibility for relationships that are both more conscious and more fulfilling.

Theoretical understanding of how different practitioners might adapt their approaches is valuable, but nothing replaces the lived experience of actually implementing these changes. Maria's journey from traditional counselling to the Duo Coaching framework offers the perspective that can only come from having navigated these waters personally.

Chapter 13

The View from the Co-Therapist's Chair
A Practitioner's Perspective

In sailing, there's a profound difference between reading about navigation and actually feeling the deck move beneath your feet as the boat responds to wind and waves. Maria's perspective offers something equally valuable: the lived experience of adapting from single-handed sailing to the complex choreography of a two-person crew.

A Practitioner's Perspective on Transformation

It was February 2017 that I received an email out of the blue from Neil, stating that we hadn't met but, as a counsellor in the area, could he bounce a thought off me. I was then introduced to Duo Coaching, a very different dynamic of having two therapists working with a couple and offering a very intensive program of coaching and counselling. I was intrigued. As a Relate Counsellor and Supervisor working within a 50-minute systemic model with back-to-back clients in Southampton, this approach seemed both exciting and daunting.

He asked if I had capacity and desire to do more relationship counselling and if could there be synergy in us working together. It would take some rearrangement of working hours and childcare, but I could have the capacity. Whether there was synergy was yet to be seen.

The First Meeting: Anticipation and Discovery

I agreed to meet with Neil on 13 March 2017. I was somewhat anxious driving to Brockenhurst after a Group Supervision meeting in Winchester—counselling has always been individual work for me, so the thought of working with someone else was rather daunting, and I didn't know what to expect.

Neil was engaging, enthusiastic, and highly experienced. His calm and considered manner made it a comfortable meeting, and I came away with a feeling of really being able to help and support couples in their counselling journey to a greater extent than I had been achieving. We agreed to meet again that week, and I was offered the opportunity to join Neil as the second member of Duo Coaching on 17 March 2017.

The First Session: Everything I Thought I Knew Was Challenged

Our first clients arrived the following week for a 3½ hour initial session. It felt such a long time, and I had many imposter syndrome moments sitting next to Neil while he expertly navigated the couple through their relationship history and offered exercises to help them understand what and who were important. I was able to watch and learn and soon realised how beneficial the allowance of extra time enabled clients to move forward more than the traditional 50-minute model.

We were able to learn so much about the couple and how they had come to the impasse in their relationship. They both had the chance to reveal their perspective of events and the impact of them. It was easy to see how the two perspectives misaligned and how many assumptions had been made. This would have taken at least four sessions from my past experience.

It was a highly effective session, and both clients were able to convey their thanks for the time we had taken and the understanding we offered. They were given considerable homework, and a further session was arranged for two weeks' time.

It was exhausting and exhilarating at the same time. I found it so comfortable working with Neil, and I would say that the synergy in us both working together was there from the outset and remains today.

What Two Therapists Can Achieve That One Cannot

There is an understanding and respect of each other, and the way we offer different perspectives, styles, and unique experience provides our clients with a personalised service that neither of us could achieve alone. The difference isn't just about having twice the expertise—it's about creating a completely different dynamic in the room.

With one therapist, couples often unconsciously compete for alliance or worry about appearing "the bad one." With two of us, there's natural balance. I notice that men often relax differently when Neil is present—they don't have to carry the weight of being the only masculine energy in the room. Similarly, women sometimes find it easier to express vulnerability with me while knowing that Neil is witnessing and validating their partner's experience.

But perhaps most importantly, Neil and I model healthy partnership in real time. Couples see us disagree respectfully, support each other's interventions, and collaborate without losing our individual perspectives. Many of our clients have never witnessed this kind of adult cooperation.

Eight Years of Transformation

Eight years later, we have supported many clients with a wide range of issues in finding a way forward. My relationship with Neil remains strong and supportive. We have navigated our way through our own personal journeys and the trials and tribulations of life, always finding time to work around both our own and clients' busy schedules. We found a way of supporting our clients through the difficult years of COVID-19, moving to Zoom and distancing where appropriate.

The feedback we receive from clients shows a high level of support and understanding of their situation without judgement. We demonstrate high levels of empathy, and our calm and down-to-earth approach enables clients to feel at ease very quickly. We have learned that it is impossible to help everyone, especially with split agendas, but we are always honest with clients and take their lead in what the next steps could be.

The Extended Sessions: A Complete Game-Changer

The Duo Coaching Framework offers the precious commodity of time. Clients do not feel rushed or unheard by the end of a session. Those three-and-a-half-hour initial sessions seemed like a luxury at first, but now I can't imagine working any other way. In traditional 50-minute sessions, just as couples start accessing vulnerable territory, they have to stop. It's like being asked to run a marathon in 100-metre sprints.

Extended sessions allow for what I think of as complete emotional cycles. Couples can move through defensiveness into hurt, then into understanding, and often into genuine connection—all within one session. They're not left hanging with difficult emotions to manage alone for a week.

Following sessions of 2½ hours further support clients with their understanding of each other through a range of modalities, exercises, and interventions, all individually chosen for the uniqueness of the couple. With six sessions maximum, couples can also manage their time, and we offer a flexible approach to timing between sessions depending on their individual circumstances.

Multiple Modalities: Tools for Every Situation

The systemic model of working with relationships offers a framework to counsel couples; however, we incorporate a wider range of modalities and exercises to meet the unique needs of each couple. Before working with Neil, I was strictly person-centred within my systemic training. Using techniques from other modalities felt like betraying my training. Now I understand that rigid adherence to one approach often serves therapist comfort more than client need.

When verbal processing hits a wall, we might use constellation work to reveal family patterns. When intellectual understanding isn't creating change, we might access unconscious material through timeline therapy. When couples need practical skills, we teach communication techniques. When they need to experience their relationship differently, we create embodied exercises.

The person-centred foundation remains—the empathy, the unconditional positive regard, the trust in clients' wisdom. But now it's part of a much richer therapeutic palette.

Six Sessions and 24/7 Support: Intensive but Liberating

The extensive homework and 24/7 support mean that couples are able to continue the counselling process at home to become more self-aware as well as gain more understanding about their partner. The idea of being available to clients outside sessions initially seemed generous rather than problematic. In practice, knowing they can reach us often means couples don't need to. The security of available support paradoxically enables greater self-reliance.

This availability communicates our genuine commitment to their success. We're not just appointment-keepers; we're partners in their transformation.

How This Changed My Own Practice

I still offer relationship counselling from my own practice but often miss the discussion and support of Neil alongside me. However, I understand that the Duo Coaching Framework does not meet everyone's needs or budget, so I have adapted my practice to allow for this. I have, though, extended my sessions to enable clients time to talk and reach swifter conclusions. Having two counsellors gives an opportunity for longer sessions that would be far more difficult and exhausting as an individual counsellor.

Duo has informed my own practice, not only by learning from the extensive experience and philosophy of Neil but also from the many couples we have supported to create relationships that last. As a result of working with Duo, I have increased my time offering to couples and incorporated much of the knowledge I have gained over the past eight years.

What Could Be Better

If I'm being completely honest, this approach demands more from therapists than traditional practice. The extended sessions require significant emotional and mental stamina. The integrative approach means constantly learning new skills rather than relying on familiar routines.

The Duo Coaching Framework generally appeals to clients with higher incomes. As a result, a larger proportion of couples with middle or lower incomes would be discouraged from the process and find themselves in more traditional counselling programs. This accessibility challenge remains something we continue to consider.

The Future of This Work

The divorce rate is increasing, and more children are navigating the difficult change towards single or blended families. The future needs to address the problems that occur when the cracks start to appear in a relationship rather than the cavern of problems and resentments that have reached their peak and couples no longer want to engage with each other, never mind resolving the hurt and pain they have endured due to lack of communication.

Therefore, the future is about education for relationships and an emphasis on relationship therapy as it sits today rather than marriage counselling of the past. I believe we're pioneering something that could transform relationship therapy entirely.

My Message to the Future

I believe that the future as a whole begins with strong, united families. When families stay together—emotionally, physically, and financially—they create a powerful foundation for stability, resilience, and growth. This strength is rooted in open communication, shared goals, and a willingness to work through challenges together.

At the heart of every strong family is a committed partnership. When couples prioritise honest, respectful communication and actively work to resolve difficulties, they model healthy relationships for future generations and lay the groundwork for a secure, loving environment. Conflict is inevitable, but how couples handle it—by listening, compromising, and staying united—can either strengthen or weaken the family bond.

Our success rate speaks for itself: clients with a joint focus on creating a great relationship are able to achieve the outcomes they set at the beginning of sessions. Families that work together, sharing responsibilities, supporting each other's goals, and planning for the future are better equipped to handle financial challenges, promote healthy living, and build lasting success.

My Message to Readers

If you're considering expanding your practice beyond traditional boundaries, my experience suggests it's worth the initial uncertainty. Yes, there's a learning curve. Yes, you'll question your competence more often than feels comfortable. But the results—for both your clients and your own professional fulfilment—justify the effort.

Don't abandon what's working in your current practice, but don't let familiarity prevent you from exploring what might be possible. The couples seeking our help deserve our most effective approaches, not just our most comfortable ones.

The view from the co-therapist's chair has shown me that relationship therapy can be more dynamic, more transformative, and more effective than I ever imagined. Eight years later, I can't conceive of returning to the limitations I once accepted as necessary. Our couples deserve nothing less than our most innovative, responsive approaches—and they consistently reward our willingness to think beyond traditional boundaries with remarkable transformations in their relationships and lives.

Maria's transformation illustrates what becomes possible when individual practitioners embrace new approaches, but the implications extend far beyond any single therapy room. The ripples from more effective relationship work touch not just couples but entire communities and future generations.

Neil's Perspective: The Power of Shared Navigation

My partnership with Maria has transformed not just our effectiveness with clients but my entire experience as a practitioner.

Before co-therapy, I carried the full weight of each couple's journey alone—responsible for tracking every dynamic, catching every subtle shift, holding space for both partners while maintaining therapeutic balance. It was like single-handed sailing in challenging waters: possible, but exhausting and limiting. You can only be in one place at a time, see from one perspective, and respond to one element while potentially missing others.

Working with Maria has revealed what becomes possible when two skilled practitioners navigate together. While I'm focused on one partner's breakthrough, she's tracking the other's response. When I'm following one line of exploration, she's noticing patterns I might miss. We can literally be in different places in the room simultaneously, creating multiple perspectives on the same dynamic. It's like having depth perception for relationship work—seeing dimensions that remain invisible to single-vision approaches.

But perhaps most remarkably, our collaboration creates a quality of liminal space that neither of us could achieve alone. There's something about the dynamic between two therapists working in harmony that generates a profound sense of safety and possibility. Couples consistently tell us they feel able to share things they've never spoken aloud—not just to us, but to each other. Secrets held for decades, vulnerabilities they thought were too dangerous to express, and truths they believed would end their relationship.

This liminal space we co-create seems to suspend ordinary rules of interaction, allowing couples to access parts of themselves and their relationship that remain hidden in everyday life. Perhaps it's the modelling of healthy partnership they witness between us, or the sense that they're held by something larger than any individual perspective. Whatever creates it, this threshold space consistently enables the kind of authentic expression and emotional risk-taking that transformation requires.

The shared load transforms the work itself. Instead of carrying the entire responsibility for therapeutic progress, we share the holding, the noticing, and the responding. When one of us needs to take a step back to process what's emerging, the other maintains the therapeutic connection. When sessions become emotionally intense—which they often do in 3½-hour containers—we can support each other as well as the couple.

Perhaps most powerfully, our different backgrounds and perspectives create a richness of response that neither of us could achieve alone. Maria's integrative counselling foundation complements my more eclectic, business-informed approach. Her attention to emotional process balances my focus on practical outcomes. Together, we create a more complete therapeutic response than either could offer independently.

The loneliness of solo practice—that sense of carrying everything yourself—has been replaced by genuine collaboration that enhances rather than diminishes our individual contributions. We've discovered that two experienced practitioners working in harmony can indeed create something greater than the sum of their parts, benefiting not just our clients but our own professional fulfilment and continued growth.

Reflecting on Part 3: Guidance for Coaches, Counsellors, and Psychoanalysts

You have navigated the practical territories of professional expansion, discovering how practitioners from diverse traditions can thoughtfully extend their capabilities without abandoning their foundations. Coaches have explored ventures beyond performance-focused coastal waters into deeper emotional territories. Counsellors have examined pathways beyond single-modality constraints while honouring their therapeutic expertise. Psychoanalysts have discovered how their profound unconscious understanding can be adapted for the shared waters where relationships actually exist.

Through Maria's authentic account, you've witnessed the lived experience of transformation—the challenges, discoveries, and rewards of implementing revolutionary change in therapeutic practice. These aren't theoretical possibilities but practical realities demonstrated by practitioners who have successfully made these journeys.

The frameworks exist, the guidance is clear, and individual practitioners can expand their effectiveness—but relationship challenges extend far beyond any therapy room. The couples we serve return to communities, families, and societies that shape relationship possibilities. Our individual work, however excellent, cannot address the systemic forces that make relationships increasingly difficult to navigate.

The final stage of our voyage expands the horizon beyond individual practice to explore the broader transformation needed for relationship health across entire communities and cultures.

Part 4

The Essential Needs We Are Supporting

Our individual work with couples, however skilful and transformative, occurs within larger systems that either support or undermine relationship health across entire communities. This final section expands our perspective beyond therapy rooms to examine the broader implications of relationship work and the systemic changes needed for comprehensive cultural transformation.

You'll explore the profound societal consequences of relationship health—how the couples we serve create ripple effects that extend through families, communities, and future generations. The statistics reveal both crisis and opportunity: while relationship challenges have reached unprecedented levels, the potential for positive change through improved support systems has never been greater.

We'll examine what's needed beyond individual intervention: relationship education that prevents problems before they develop, policy frameworks that support connection across the lifespan, and cultural shifts that value emotional intelligence as much as academic achievement. The vision extends from therapeutic repair to relationship resilience—creating conditions where healthy partnerships can flourish rather than merely survive.

This section challenges practitioners to see their work not as isolated intervention but as contribution to broader social transformation. Every couple helped, every relationship strengthened, every pattern interrupted becomes part of a larger movement toward a more connected, emotionally intelligent society.

The journey concludes where it began—with relationships as the foundation of human flourishing—but now viewed through expanded vision of what becomes possible when individual excellence combines with systemic change to support love itself.

Chapter 14

The Importance of Relationships

Figure 14.1 Hands raised together—adult and child—each bearing a heart: the intergenerational transmission of love and connection, reminding us that healthy relationships create ripples that extend through families, communities, and future generations.

The Lighthouse Effect: Illuminating Wider Territories

A lighthouse doesn't just serve the ships currently visible on the horizon—its beam reaches far into the darkness, offering guidance to vessels not yet seen but surely coming. Our work with individual couples creates ripples that extend far beyond any single relationship, illuminating safer passages for generations yet to sail these waters.

Relationships are the foundation of a healthy, prosperous, and innovative future for humanity. Without an understanding of relationships and different models of the world, conflict and warfare will continue to create tension, death, misery, and wasted resources around the world. At a wider level the dissociation of people from society will amplify mental health problems and create larger numbers of sad and lonely "outsiders" (Figure 14.1).

Without a foundation of good relationships, future generations will lack the skills and abilities to work together and have a sense of purpose and community. Unless this is addressed, the future of humanity looks bleak.

DOI: 10.4324/9781003715467-18

This is also much wider than couples' relationships; it needs to expand to include families, friends, communities, work, countries, creatures, planet, and the future.

The Societal Crisis

We are at a critical tipping point. Beyond the environmental sustainability challenges facing our planet, we face a pandemic of loneliness and disconnection. Children—our successors—are growing up in circumstances that fundamentally compromise their capacity for healthy relationships.

The statistics are sobering:

- The majority of children are growing up in families that have been fractured by divorce or breakup (ONS, 2023a)
- The number of children in care has increased by 30% between 2010 and 2023 (Dept for Education, 2023)
- One million children in the UK have no meaningful contact at all with their fathers (Centre for Social Justice, 2023)
- One in five Britons aged 18–24 have one or no close friends. Gen Z is possibly the loneliest generation in human history (ONS, 2022)
- Twenty-three per cent of adults worldwide felt lonely, and 54% of those who felt lonely said they experienced sadness (Gallup, 2023)
- Teenagers spend an average of 8 hours 39 minutes a day on their screens (Ofcom, 2023)
- A quarter of Gen Z have never answered their phones, with 70% preferring texts to calls (Uswitch, 2022)
- Less than 10% of teenagers meet the recommended guidelines for sleep, exercise, and screen time (Public Health England, 2023)
- There is an unprecedented crisis in mental health problems among young people. One in five people aged 8–25 had a probable mental health disorder in 2023 (NHS Digital, 2023)
- A series of UK longitudinal studies has shown "strong correlations" between broken homes and delinquency, with some 70% of young offenders coming from lone-parent families (Ministry of Justice, 2022)

Why the Wider World Needs Good Relationships

Good couple relationships create ripple effects that positively impact society:

- **Healthy child development**: Happy couples are more likely to create stable and nurturing environments for children, leading to better emotional wellbeing, educational attainment, and social skills in the next generation

- **Community engagement**: Supportive couples are more likely to be involved in their communities and contribute positively through volunteering and civic participation
- **Public health**: People in strong relationships tend to have better mental and physical health, reducing healthcare costs and creating a healthier overall population
- **Social modelling**: Strong, healthy couples provide positive examples of communication, conflict resolution, and teamwork for others, inspiring healthier relationships throughout society
- **Violence prevention**: Research suggests a link between happy couples and lower rates of domestic violence, contributing to a safer environment for everyone

Overall, good couple relationships contribute to a stronger social fabric, healthier individuals, and a more positive and productive society.

A Systemic Approach to Transformation

Creating sustainable change in relationships requires moving beyond piecemeal approaches. A systemic approach, traditionally used in organisational development, has relevance to the scale of societal change needed. This blends:

- **Top-down initiatives** from central government or senior leaders in education
- **Bottom-up initiatives** mobilising couples, parents, and children to understand the benefits and implement new ways of relating

Drawing from Peter Senge's *The Fifth Discipline* (Senge, 1990), we can adapt his five disciplines for relationship transformation:

Personal mastery: Individuals would commit to self-awareness, emotional intelligence, and taking responsibility for their own happiness and wellbeing.

Mental models: People would identify and challenge their preconceptions about relationships, become aware of cultural influences on relationship expectations, and learn to see situations from their partner's perspective.

Shared vision: Couples would discuss and align their long-term goals and values, create a shared vision for their future together, and regularly revisit this vision as they grow.

Team learning: This involves learning together as couples and from other relationships through attending workshops, sharing experiences with other couples, and learning from successful relationship models.

Systems thinking: Couples would recognise how their actions affect each other and the relationship as a whole, understand the impact of external factors, and see patterns rather than isolated events.

Implementation Strategy

To create significant improvements in relationships worldwide requires:

Education: Integrate relationship concepts into curricula from school-age to adult learning. The challenge is not to improve existing relationships but to radically reset younger generations' understanding of the importance of sustainable, loving relationships. This requires education from seven years onwards as a key part of school curriculum.

Media and culture: Promote these ideas through various media channels to shift societal perceptions of relationships, addressing unrealistic portrayals and providing realistic models.

Therapy and counselling: Train relationship therapists and counsellors in effective principles and frameworks like Duo Coaching.

Technology: Develop apps and online platforms that help couples practice relationship skills in their daily lives.

Policy: Encourage policymakers to consider relationship health in social policies, potentially offering incentives for relationship education.

Research: Conduct studies on effective approaches in different cultural contexts and relationship types.

Community building: Create support groups and community events centred around relationship health principles.

Workplace integration: Encourage organisations to consider relationship health as part of employee wellbeing programs.

The Practitioner's Role in Larger Change

As relationship practitioners, we are not merely treating individual couples—we are contributing to a larger social transformation. Each couple we help creates ripples that extend through families, communities, and future generations.

> One small step can start to change the world. Like the parable of one person changing a life: A young girl walking along a beach began throwing starfish back into the ocean after a storm. When told she couldn't save them all, she picked up another starfish and said, "Well, I made a difference for that one!" Soon others joined, and all the starfish were saved.

My Mission

My insight into these experiences, distilled in writing this book, has been the immensely positive change possible in relationships. Working with clients has allowed me to help create wonderful shifts in their lives. For individuals, couples, and the world, great, loving, and fulfilling relationships are essential.

Without an understanding of relationships and different models of connection, conflict and warfare will continue. The dissociation of people from society will amplify mental health problems and create larger numbers of sad and lonely "outsiders."

The Importance of Relationships 185

Without a foundation of good relationships, future generations will lack the skills to work together and have a sense of purpose and community. Unless this is addressed, the future of humanity looks bleak.

The solution cannot come by decree—it must be a bottom-up approach combined with systemic support, getting people to understand how to have good relationships and apply this in their lives.

My mission, using my doctorate and this book as a springboard, is to open up dialogue with educational thought leaders on this topic. The ripples from our individual work with couples must expand to transform how society approaches relationships at every level (Figure 14.2).

The couples who seek our help are navigating some of life's most challenging waters. By expanding our therapeutic repertoire and contributing to broader cultural change, we become better equipped to guide them through storms and calm seas alike, helping them chart courses towards the relationships they truly desire—and the society we all need.

Recognising the profound importance of relationships to human flourishing makes our work feel both more urgent and more hopeful. As we conclude this journey through uncharted waters of relationship therapy, what new territories have become visible from this vantage point, and what course should we chart for the voyage ahead?

Figure 14.2 A lighthouse standing firm against the horizon: a beacon of guidance and safety, symbolising the broader vision of relationship education and policy that can illuminate the way for couples long before they encounter the rocks.

Chapter 15

Conclusions
Charting New Waters

From Voyage's End to New Horizons

As any long voyage draws towards harbour, the wise navigator charts not just where they've been, but the new territories now visible from this vantage point. The journey through these waters of relationship transformation reveals horizons that were invisible from our starting point—and charts a course towards possibilities we're only beginning to imagine.

The Journey Travelled

As we reach the conclusion of this voyage through the world of relationship therapy, it is worthwhile to pause and reflect on the waters we have navigated together. Our journey began with an exploration of why relationships matter—not merely as personal sanctuaries of connection, but as the fundamental building blocks of a healthy society. We examined the contemporary landscape of relationships, acknowledging both the timeless challenges couples face and the unprecedented pressures of our digital age.

Through our exploration of traditional psychotherapeutic approaches, we confronted the limitations of single-modality frameworks when applied to the complex dynamics of couple relationships. We delved into the transdisciplinary nature of relationship work, recognising that no single lens can capture the multifaceted reality of human connection. We witnessed how the artificial boundaries between disciplines—between therapy and coaching, between past-focused and future-oriented approaches, between intrapsychic and systemic perspectives—often constrain rather than enhance our ability to serve couples effectively.

At the heart of this book stands the Duo Coaching framework—an approach born not from theoretical abstraction but from lived experience, intuitive innovation, and a willingness to challenge entrenched practices. This framework represents a departure from conventional relationship therapy in several key dimensions:

- The presence of two therapists creating balance and multiple perspectives
- Longer, more spacious sessions that allow deeper exploration
- A finite, outcome-focused journey rather than an open-ended process

- Integration of multiple therapeutic modalities tailored to each unique couple
- Attention to the triad of "Me," "You," and "Us"
- Accessibility between sessions to address issues as they emerge
- A commitment to both depth and practicality

The chapters offering guidance for coaches, counsellors, and psychoanalysts have demonstrated how practitioners from diverse traditions can enhance their effectiveness by thoughtfully expanding their approaches. Not by abandoning their foundations, but by building upon them—adding dimensions that complement existing strengths and address inherent limitations.

Throughout this journey, we have been guided by a simple yet profound insight: in relationships, there is no reality, only perception. And these perceptions can be very different yet equally valid. This understanding calls for humility in our work as relationship professionals—a recognition that our role is not to impose our vision of "healthy" relationships but to help couples create their own unique connection based on mutual understanding and respect for differing perspectives.

The Wider Horizon

As we look to the horizon, we must acknowledge that our work with individual couples, while deeply meaningful, represents only one dimension of what is needed. The challenges facing relationships today are not merely individual but societal in nature. The statistics presented in Chapter 13 paint a sobering picture:

- The majority of children growing up in fractured families
- Increasing numbers of children in care
- One million UK children without meaningful contact with their fathers
- Rising rates of loneliness, particularly among younger generations
- Unprecedented screen time replacing face-to-face connection
- A mental health crisis among young people that threatens their capacity for healthy relationships

These challenges cannot be addressed through therapy alone, regardless of how effective our approaches become. They call for a more comprehensive response—one that combines individual intervention with broader societal change.

The solution, as suggested in Chapter 13, must blend top-down and bottom-up initiatives. It requires education that begins in childhood, policy that supports relationship health, media that portrays realistic relationship dynamics, and communities that value and nurture connection. It demands a cultural shift that recognises the centrality of relationships to human flourishing.

This is not a call for a return to some idealised past of "traditional" relationships. Rather, it is an invitation to envision and create a future where relationships of all kinds—regardless of structure, orientation, or context—are characterised by mutual respect, emotional intelligence, and authentic connection.

The Challenge to Practitioners

To my fellow practitioners—coaches, counsellors, psychoanalysts, and therapists of all traditions—I offer both challenge and invitation. The challenge is to examine our practices honestly, to question whether our adherence to particular modalities and timeframes serves our clients or merely our professional comfort and convenience. It is to ask ourselves whether we are truly fostering independence or subtly encouraging dependence through open-ended processes without clear outcomes.

The invitation is to expand our perspectives and approaches, to become more flexible and responsive to the unique needs of each couple. This expansion does not require abandoning our training or diluting our expertise. Rather, it calls for integrating complementary dimensions that enhance rather than replace our foundations.

For coaches, this might mean developing greater sensitivity to the deeper patterns that shape relationship dynamics while maintaining your strengths in goal-setting and future orientation.

For counsellors, it might involve adopting more active, structured approaches while preserving your capacity for empathic understanding and non-judgemental presence.

For psychoanalysts, it might entail incorporating more pragmatic, present-focused interventions while continuing to illuminate the unconscious dimensions of relationship dynamics.

For all practitioners, it means recognising that no single approach can address the full spectrum of relationship challenges. It requires humility to acknowledge the limitations of our preferred modalities and openness to learning from diverse traditions.

Reimagining Relationship Education

Beyond our work with couples in distress lies an even more important frontier: relationship education that prevents problems before they develop. The most effective intervention is not brilliant therapy but preparation that makes therapy unnecessary.

Imagine a world where children learn about healthy relationships from an early age—not through abstract lectures but through experiential education that develops emotional intelligence, communication skills, conflict resolution, and respect for differences. Imagine adolescents receiving guidance not just about the physical aspects of sexuality but about the emotional dimensions of intimacy and the skills needed to build and maintain healthy connections.

Imagine young adults entering relationships with realistic expectations and practical tools rather than romantic idealisations that set them up for disappointment. Imagine a culture that values relationship skills as much as academic or professional achievements—that recognises emotional intelligence as essential rather than optional.

This reimagining of relationship education represents perhaps the most significant opportunity for lasting change. It shifts our focus from treating relationship distress to fostering relationship health—from intervention to prevention. While this book has focused primarily on therapeutic approaches, my forthcoming work, *Reframe*, will explore this educational dimension in greater depth, offering practical frameworks for relationship education across the lifespan.

Your Personal Journey

For practitioners reading this book, I invite you to consider that the most powerful tool you bring to your work is not your technique or theoretical framework, but your presence and authenticity. Your willingness to engage with couples not from a position of expertise but from one of genuine curiosity and compassion.

This requires ongoing attention to your own relationship with yourself and others. It calls for continuous self-reflection and growth. The qualities we seek to foster in our clients—openness, vulnerability, willingness to change—must be cultivated in ourselves as well.

My own journey in creating the Duo Coaching framework has been one of constant evolution. What began as an intuitive response to limitations I had experienced both as a client and practitioner has developed through years of refinement in work with hundreds of couples. It continues to evolve as I remain open to new insights and approaches.

This journey has taught me that the most profound changes often begin with simple shifts in perspective—with reframing how we see ourselves, our relationships, and our possibilities. The title of this book reflects this essential truth: that lasting transformation often requires not merely new techniques but new ways of seeing.

An Invitation to Co-Creation

This book is not intended as a definitive statement but as an invitation to dialogue and co-creation. The frameworks and approaches presented here are not finished products but works in progress, offered in the spirit of ongoing exploration and refinement.

I welcome your engagement with these ideas—your questions, challenges, adaptations, and innovations. The field of relationship work advances not through adherence to dogma but through creative exploration and thoughtful integration of diverse perspectives.

In my forthcoming book, *Reframe*, I will provide more detailed, step-by-step guidance for implementing these approaches, including specific protocols, exercises, and tools for relationship education and therapy. But the most valuable developments will come not from my writing but from your application—from the ways you adapt and enhance these frameworks in your unique contexts with your unique clients.

Closing Thoughts: The Ripple Effect

Each relationship we help to heal or strengthen creates ripples that extend far beyond the couple themselves. Children grow up with healthier models of connection.

Friends and family witness possibilities for relationship repair and renewal. Communities become more cohesive as their fundamental building blocks—couples and families—become more stable and nurturing.

In a world facing unprecedented challenges—from climate change to political polarisation, from technological disruption to social fragmentation—healthy relationships provide essential resilience. They are the containers in which we process change, face uncertainty, and find meaning. They are the contexts in which we learn to navigate difference without descending into division.

The work we do with couples, while often hidden from public view, is among the most significant contributions we can make to a healthier society. Every couple who learns to transform conflict into understanding, to replace blame with curiosity, and to balance autonomy with connection becomes a force for positive change that extends far beyond their relationship.

As you close this book and return to your practice, I invite you to carry this awareness with you—to recognise the profound significance of your work not just for the couples you serve but for the wider world they inhabit. And I invite you to approach this work with both humility about what you know and confidence in what is possible when two people are guided skilfully towards deeper understanding and connection.

The journey of reframing relationship therapy has just begun. New horizons await as we continue to explore, innovate, and collaborate in service of healthier relationships and a more connected world. I look forward to continuing this journey with you (Figure 15.1).

Figure 15.1 A yacht sails towards a radiant sun on the horizon: the journey concludes not at a fixed destination but at an expanded horizon of possibilities, where the warmth of new understanding illuminates the waters ahead.

Reflections on the Journey

Our voyage concludes where it began—with recognition that relationships form the fundamental building blocks of human flourishing. Yet now we see this truth through expanded vision, understanding both the profound challenges facing relationship capacity across generations and the systemic approaches needed for comprehensive cultural change.

We've discovered that our work with individual couples creates ripples extending far beyond any single partnership, touching children who will carry new models of connection into their own relationships, communities that become more resilient through stronger foundational partnerships, and societies that benefit from the reduced violence, improved mental health, and enhanced cooperation that healthy relationships provide.

The frameworks and insights shared throughout this book represent both ending and beginning—the culmination of one practitioner's journey while launching countless others towards more effective, responsive, and transformative relationship work. The horizon ahead reveals possibilities we're only beginning to imagine: relationship education that prevents problems before they develop, practitioner networks supporting innovative approaches, and cultural changes that value emotional intelligence as much as academic achievement.

As you close this book and return to your practice, you carry not just new tools and frameworks but expanded vision of what becomes possible when skilled practitioners dare to venture beyond familiar shores in service of healthier, more fulfilling relationships. The waters ahead hold both challenges and rewards for those willing to continue exploring, innovating, and collaborating in service of love itself.

Welcome to the voyage. The most important discoveries lie ahead.

Case Studies

Each of these three case studies has been drawn from clients that we have worked with. They are composites and carefully anonymised to maintain confidentiality.

John and Sarah

Readers witness the complete transformation of a couple who had perfected domestic efficiency while losing their capacity for genuine connection. This detailed case study demonstrates how surface-level functioning can mask profound emotional disconnection and how the right therapeutic approach can help couples rediscover not just compatibility but passion. The case illustrates the "me, you, us" framework in action, showing how individual growth and relationship system change occur simultaneously.

From Co-Managers to Lovers: Rediscovering Each Other after 12 Years

John and Sarah arrived at our first session looking like business partners forced to attend the same board meeting. After twelve years together and eight years of marriage, they had perfected the art of domestic efficiency while losing the ability to connect as human beings.

"We're excellent co-managers," Sarah explained with the same tone she might use to describe a successful project. "Our children are thriving, our household runs smoothly, our finances are stable. We just don't... *feel* like partners anymore."

John nodded his agreement, but the distance between them on the sofa told a different story—two people who had somehow become strangers while sharing the same life.

The Invisible Erosion

Their disconnection had been so gradual it felt inevitable. John had learned to withdraw whenever conversations felt critical or emotionally charged. Sarah had compensated by becoming hyper-efficient, managing more and more of their shared life solo. Each response made perfect sense individually but had created a devastating cycle: the more she managed, the more he retreated; the more he retreated, the more she felt compelled to control.

"I started walking on eggshells," John explained. "Everything I did seemed wrong. Eventually, it felt safer to just... step back."

Sarah's experience was equally painful: "I needed a partner, not another child to manage. When John withdrew, I had to become hyper-organised just to keep everything functioning. But that made me feel more alone, not less."

They had become what they most feared: efficient roommates sharing childrearing duties, with no emotional or physical intimacy to sustain them through the inevitable challenges of life.

The Transformation That Surprised Everyone

A few months later, the same couple returned for a follow-up session that neither of us will forget.

The change was immediately visible—they sat closer together, made eye contact when discussing their relationship, and demonstrated an ease with each other that had been completely absent before. But the real transformation went much deeper.

"I learned that withdrawal wasn't protection—it was a slow form of disappearing," John reflected. "Every time I chose silence over speaking up, I wasn't avoiding conflict; I was erasing myself from our relationship. Now I can express my needs without feeling like I'm causing problems."

Sarah's insight was equally profound: "I realised that efficiency isn't the same as connection. I was so focused on optimising our family life that I forgot relationships aren't meant to be optimised—they're meant to be experienced, with all the messiness that involves."

The Moment Everything Changed

The breakthrough came when they finally understood that their conflicts weren't about the topics they argued over—parenting decisions, household responsibilities, scheduling—but about two fundamental human needs that weren't being met.

John needed to feel valued and included in family decisions. Sarah needed to feel emotionally supported rather than having to manage everything alone. Once they could see past the surface arguments to these deeper longings, everything shifted.

"It was like finally speaking the same language," Sarah said. "We'd been having the same argument for years about different topics, but we were really just saying 'I need to matter to you' in ways the other person couldn't hear."

Rediscovering Intimacy

Perhaps most remarkably, John and Sarah had rebuilt not just their emotional connection but their physical relationship as well. Years of emotional distance had created sexual disconnection that both had assumed was permanent.

"We learned to talk about our physical relationship for the first time in our marriage," Sarah shared with surprising openness. "Things we'd never discussed in twelve years together. We rediscovered not just physical intimacy, but the vulnerability that makes intimacy meaningful."

John added, "I realised that emotional withdrawal in daily life made physical intimacy impossible. You can't disconnect emotionally all week and then try to connect physically on the weekend. They're part of the same system."

The Skills That Transformed Everything

The change hadn't happened through years of weekly sessions. Their transformation emerged through six intensive sessions over four months that addressed both their interaction patterns and the individual histories that had created those patterns.

They learned to recognise when they were slipping into their old "manager-withdrawer" dance and developed new responses that created connection rather than distance. More importantly, they discovered that their different processing styles—his need for thinking time, her need to talk through decisions—could complement rather than frustrate each other.

"We stopped trying to make each other wrong for being different," John explained. "Sarah's systematic approach actually helps me make better decisions. My reflective style helps her avoid rushing into solutions before understanding the real issue."

The Lasting Changes

A year later, their transformation had not only sustained but continued deepening:

- They had successfully navigated several major stresses—job changes, family illness, financial decisions—using their new skills rather than falling back into old patterns
- Their children commented on the change: "Mum and Dad actually seem to like each other again"
- They had developed weekly connection rituals that maintained their emotional intimacy despite busy schedules
- Friends began asking them for relationship advice, recognising something different about their partnership

"We're better partners now than we were even in the beginning," Sarah reflected. "Back then we were just compatible. Now we're genuinely connected."

The Individual Growth

Each partner had also grown individually in ways that strengthened their relationship:

John had learned to engage with conflict constructively rather than withdrawing, discovering that expressing his needs actually improved rather than threatened their connection.

Sarah had learned to distinguish between helpful organisation and anxious control, finding that trusting John with more responsibility actually made their life easier, not harder.

"I spent years thinking the problem was that we were too different," John said. "I was wrong. The problem was that we weren't letting our differences enhance each other."

The Surprise Discovery

Perhaps the most unexpected outcome was how much they enjoyed each other's company. What had started as crisis management had evolved into genuine friendship and renewed romance.

"We actually have fun together now," Sarah laughed. "We'd forgotten that was possible. Last weekend we spent three hours just talking about ideas and dreams—not logistics or problems, but actual conversation. I'd forgotten how interesting John is when he's not trying to avoid saying the wrong thing."

What Made the Difference

Their transformation involved understanding that their surface conflicts were expressions of deeper attachment needs, learning to see their different processing styles as complementary rather than incompatible, and developing the skills to maintain emotional connection even during stressful periods.

But perhaps most importantly, they learned that creating a great relationship requires both individual growth and system change—becoming better partners to each other while also becoming more fulfilled individuals.

"We realise now that we were asking each other to meet needs we didn't even know we had," John reflected. "Once we could name what we actually needed, we could figure out how to give it to each other."

The Ripple Effects

The changes extended far beyond their marriage. Their improved partnership created a more stable, joyful home environment for their children. Extended family members noticed the difference in family gatherings. Their example began inspiring friends who were struggling in their own relationships.

"People ask us what happened," Sarah said. "They can see that something fundamental shifted, not just surface improvements."

The Deeper Message

John and Sarah's story challenges the common belief that relationship problems are inevitably about incompatibility or irreconcilable differences. Their transformation reveals that many "personality conflicts" are actually unmet attachment needs expressing themselves through surface-level disputes.

More importantly, their journey demonstrates that couples don't have to choose between individual fulfilment and relationship happiness. The most satisfied couples are often those who have learned to grow both individually and together, becoming better people *because* of their partnership rather than in spite of it.

"We thought we had to choose between being ourselves and being good partners," Sarah concluded. "We discovered that being truly ourselves made us better partners, and being better partners helped us become more ourselves."

What This Proves

John and Sarah's transformation from co-managers to genuine partners illustrates what becomes possible when couples receive support that addresses both their interaction patterns and the individual needs underlying those patterns.

Their story raises important questions: How many couples settle for functional but emotionally empty relationships because they don't realise that profound positive change remains possible? What would happen if more couples had access to approaches that could help them rediscover not just compatibility but genuine connection?

Most significantly, if a couple who had become "efficient roommates" could rediscover passion and partnership, what untapped potential might exist in your own relationship?

Carrie and Keith

This remarkable case follows a couple who had eliminated all conflict along with all genuine feeling, living as polite strangers for nearly three decades. Their transformation challenges assumptions about passion having expiration dates, proving that even long-term relationships can rediscover depths of connection previously unimagined. The case demonstrates how efficiency and intimacy differ fundamentally and how couples can learn to prioritise authentic connection over mere functionality.

When 27 Years of "Efficiency" Nearly Killed Love

Carrie and Keith arrived at our door like polite strangers forced to share a taxi. After 27 years of marriage, they had perfected the art of civilised coexistence—their home ran with Swiss precision, their children had launched successfully into the world, their finances were immaculate.

They were also dying inside.

The Portrait of a "Successful" Marriage

"We function beautifully," Carrie explained with characteristic precision, her words carrying the weight of decades spent optimising rather than connecting. "Our conversations are efficient. Our schedules coordinate seamlessly. We haven't had a real argument in years."

Keith nodded his agreement, but something in his eyes suggested that the absence of conflict had come at a devastating cost.

What they couldn't say—couldn't even whisper to each other—was that their physical relationship had vanished entirely three years earlier. Not gradually declined or become routine, but disappeared completely, like a vital organ that had simply stopped functioning.

The discovery of Keith using pornography had become the final confirmation of what both feared: they were no longer lovers, barely friends, just two competent people managing a household with ruthless efficiency.

"We're like flatmates who happen to share a bed," Keith admitted quietly, his usual composure cracking just enough to reveal the loneliness beneath.

The Transformation No One Expected

Six months later, the same couple sat in the same chairs, but everything had changed.

They leaned towards each other instead of away. When Keith spoke about rediscovering Carrie's "brilliant mind," she blushed like a teenager. When Carrie described feeling "desired again after thinking that part of my life was forever over," Keith reached for her hand with unconscious tenderness.

"We talk about everything now," Carrie marvelled, her professional composure replaced by something softer, more alive. "Things we never discussed in twenty-seven years of marriage. Our needs, our fears, even our sexual desires. I had no idea how lonely I'd been for genuine conversation."

Keith's transformation was equally striking: "I thought passion was something that belonged to young people. I was completely wrong. We're more intimate now than we were as newlyweds because now we actually *know* each other."

The Breakthrough That Changed Everything

The pivotal moment came in session three, when a simple observation about hand placement unlocked decades of unspoken grief and disconnection. What emerged wasn't just understanding, but a complete rewriting of their relationship story.

Instead of two people who had "grown apart," they discovered they were two people who had never learned to grow *together*—each becoming more competent and self-sufficient as a defence against the vulnerability that real intimacy requires.

"I've been hiding behind competence," Carrie realised. "It's safer than risking being needed for who I am rather than what I can do."

"And I've been hiding behind agreeableness," Keith responded. "It's easier than risking rejection for having different opinions."

The Return of Desire

Perhaps most remarkably, Carrie and Keith had successfully rebuilt their physical relationship—not just resuming sexual intimacy, but discovering a passion neither had experienced even in their youth.

"It's not just that we're being intimate again," Carrie shared with surprising boldness. "It's that we desire each other again. I feel attractive, wanted. Keith looks at me the way he used to when we were courting, but with a depth that comes from truly knowing someone."

Keith added, "We learned to communicate about what we wanted physically—things we'd never discussed in nearly three decades together. It's like discovering an entirely new dimension of our relationship."

The Skills That Lasted

Eighteen months after our final session, their transformation had not only sustained but also deepened:

- They had planned and enjoyed their first pleasure-focused vacation in years—no family obligations, no practical purposes, just time to enjoy each other
- Keith had begun involving Carrie in his architectural work, valuing her systematic thinking as a complement to his creative vision
- Carrie had started gardening with Keith, learning to appreciate the slower rhythms and seasonal patience that farming requires
- They were actively planning Keith's upcoming retirement together rather than as separate individuals

"We've learned to tend our relationship like a garden," Carrie reflected. "It needs regular attention, seasonal adjustments, and patience for things to bloom."

What Made the Difference

Their transformation didn't happen through years of weekly sessions or expensive weekend retreats. The change emerged through six intensive sessions over four months—sessions that addressed not just their communication patterns but the deeper currents that had created those patterns.

The work involved understanding how their different processing styles could complement rather than frustrate each other, helping them distinguish between efficiency and intimacy, and creating experiences that allowed them to fall in love not just with who they used to be, but with who they were becoming.

"The most powerful realisation," Keith reflected, "was that efficiency isn't always a virtue in relationships. We'd spent decades streamlining our life together, removing what we saw as unnecessary complications. But some of what we removed was essential—the messiness of genuine feeling, the unpredictability of authentic connection."

The Ripple Effects

Their adult children noticed the change immediately. "Mum and Dad are different," their daughter observed. "They actually seem to enjoy each other's company again."

Friends began asking what had happened. "You two seem like newlyweds," became a common observation—not because they were acting young, but because they were radiating the contentment of people who genuinely liked the person they'd chosen to share their life with.

The Bigger Message

Carrie and Keith's story challenges one of our culture's most damaging myths: that passion has an expiration date, that long-term relationships inevitably settle into comfortable but emotionally flat coexistence.

Their transformation proves that even after nearly three decades together, even after years of emotional disconnection, even after the complete cessation of physical intimacy, renewal is possible.

Not just getting back to where they were, but discovering depths of connection they'd never imagined possible.

"We thought that chapter of our lives was closed," Carrie said. "We were wrong. The most passionate chapter was just beginning."

What This Reveals

Carrie and Keith's transformation wasn't unique—it was representative of what becomes possible when couples receive therapeutic support that matches the complexity of their actual relationship challenges rather than forcing them into simplified frameworks designed for easier problems.

Their story raises profound questions: How many couples resign themselves to "good enough" relationships because they don't know that dramatic positive change remains possible? What would happen if more couples had access to approaches specifically designed to address the full complexity of long-term relationship renewal?

Most importantly: What could your relationship become if you had the right guidance, the right container, and the right tools for transformation?

Michael and Olivia

This challenging case study examines recovery from compound betrayal—not just infidelity but continued deception during therapy itself. This case reveals how some relationships can not only survive but also ultimately thrive after devastating breaches of trust while honestly addressing the extraordinary commitment required from both partners. The transformation illustrates how complete honesty, though initially more painful, creates foundations for intimacy stronger than what existed before the crisis.

Rebuilding after Betrayal: When Love Survives the Unthinkable

Michael and Olivia arrived at our door carrying the kind of pain that changes people forever. After twelve years of marriage and two children, suspicious text messages on Olivia's phone had shattered everything Michael thought he knew about their life together.

What began as marriage counselling for "communication issues" quickly became something much more complex when the full truth emerged—not just about the affair, but about the lies that followed, even within the therapy process itself.

The Double Betrayal

The initial discovery was devastating enough: eight months of emotional and physical infidelity that had nearly led to Olivia leaving the marriage entirely. But what made their situation even more complex was Olivia's continued deception during our early sessions.

For weeks, Michael attempted to heal from what he believed was an "emotional affair that went too far." Meanwhile, the reality was far more extensive—a full relationship that had continued even after the initial discovery, with detailed lies covering the true timeline, frequency, and depth of the betrayal.

"I was trying to rebuild trust with someone who was still lying to me," Michael explained months later. "Every day I worked to forgive something that wasn't even the real thing. It was impossible, and I was blaming myself for not being able to get past it."

When the complete truth finally emerged in our third session, both Michael and Olivia found themselves facing an even deeper crisis than the one that had brought them to therapy.

The Moment of Truth

The full disclosure was devastating. Michael's quiet response said everything: "So for weeks, we've been in therapy based on a lie. While I've been trying to heal from an emotional affair, the reality was much worse, and you've allowed me to base my forgiveness on false information."

Olivia's terror was palpable:

> I convinced myself that the physical part didn't matter if it was over. I thought if I could just get us to a better place, I could carry the secret forever. I was terrified that telling the whole truth would destroy any chance of saving our marriage.

What followed was a complete breakdown and rebuilding—not just of their relationship, but of their individual understanding of what commitment, honesty, and love actually meant.

The Decision Point

After learning the full extent of both the affair and the deception, Michael faced an impossible choice: leave a marriage that had been built on lies, or attempt to rebuild with complete knowledge of what had actually occurred.

"I realised I had been trying to heal from the wrong wound," he said. "The affair was one betrayal. The lies during therapy were another. I had to decide whether I could work with this new reality or if this was simply too much to overcome."

His decision to stay and rebuild wasn't immediate—it required weeks of individual reflection, consultation with trusted friends, and brutal honesty about what forgiveness would actually require.

The Reconstruction

Three months later, Michael and Olivia presented as a fundamentally different couple.

The transformation was evident not just in how they related to each other but in their individual presence. Michael carried himself with a quiet strength that spoke of someone who had faced his worst fear and survived. Olivia radiated a kind of grounded authenticity that comes only from taking complete responsibility for devastating choices.

"I learned that trying to protect Michael from the truth was actually cruelty disguised as kindness," Olivia reflected. "Every day I didn't tell him the whole truth, I was making decisions for him that weren't mine to make. I was robbing him of his agency."

Michael's insights were equally profound:

> I learned that I could survive betrayal—even compound betrayal. I also learned that my emotional withdrawal over the years had created a vacuum that made our marriage vulnerable. I can't control Olivia's choices, but I can control my own engagement with our relationship.

The Deeper Discovery

What emerged through their intensive work together was recognition that their marriage had been struggling long before the affair began. Years of emotional disconnection, a complete cessation of physical intimacy following their youngest child's birth, and an inability to communicate about vulnerable topics had created the conditions where outside connection became appealing.

"We realised we had drifted so far apart that we were essentially strangers living in the same house," Michael explained. "The affair was a symptom of something that had been dying slowly for years."

This recognition didn't excuse the betrayal, but it provided context that made rebuilding possible. Instead of just healing from infidelity, they were learning to create a genuinely intimate marriage for the first time.

The New Marriage

What they built together was stronger than what they'd lost—not because betrayal improved their relationship, but because complete honesty about everything finally became possible.

"We had to learn to talk about sex and physical needs openly—something we'd never done in twelve years of marriage," Michael shared. "The affair taught me that avoiding difficult conversations doesn't make problems go away; it just makes them worse."

Their new relationship included transparency protocols that might seem extreme to other couples but felt necessary for rebuilding trust: shared technology access, location sharing, and immediate discussion of any disconnection or unmet needs.

"We know we're not 'cured,'" Michael explained. "This will always be part of our story. But we've learned that a relationship can survive almost anything if both people are willing to do the work with complete honesty."

The Individual Growth

Both partners had grown individually in ways that strengthened their rebuilt marriage:

Olivia had confronted her tendency to avoid consequences through deception, developing the courage to face difficult truths immediately rather than hoping they would disappear.

Michael had learned to engage with conflict and express his needs directly rather than withdrawing, discovering that speaking up actually improved rather than threatened their connection.

"I'll never forgive myself for the additional pain I caused by lying during therapy," Olivia said. "But I'm grateful Michael gave me the chance to prove I could change. I'm a different person now, and we're a different couple."

The Unexpected Outcome

Perhaps most remarkably, 18 months after their crisis, Michael and Olivia described their relationship as "stronger than it was even in the beginning" because they now had conscious tools for maintaining connection and resolving differences.

They had successfully navigated two significant challenges—a job change and family illness—using their new skills rather than falling back into disconnection. More importantly, they had developed a level of emotional intimacy that hadn't existed in their original marriage.

"We thought that level of honesty would be too dangerous," Olivia reflected. "We were wrong. Complete honesty is what made real intimacy possible for the first time."

The Ripple Effects

Their transformation extended beyond their marriage to their entire family system. Their children, who had sensed the crisis without understanding it, began commenting on the positive change in their parents' relationship.

"The kids say we seem happier," Michael noted. "They were right to notice the difference—we're more genuinely connected now than we've ever been."

The Courage Required

Their story illustrates the extraordinary courage required for both betrayal recovery and authentic relationship building:

- Olivia's courage to face complete accountability without minimisation or excuse-making
- Michael's courage to risk trusting again after experiencing compound betrayal
- Their shared courage to build something entirely new rather than trying to return to what they'd had before

"We learned that some things can't be fixed—they have to be rebuilt from the ground up," Michael said. "What we have now isn't a repaired version of our old marriage. It's a completely different relationship built on a foundation of honesty we never had before."

The Message of Hope

Michael and Olivia's transformation challenges one of our culture's assumptions about infidelity: that betrayal inevitably destroys relationships beyond repair. While their journey was extraordinarily difficult and certainly not possible for every couple, it demonstrates that even the most devastating breaches of trust can sometimes become catalysts for creating relationships stronger than what existed before.

"We wouldn't wish this experience on anyone," Olivia concluded. "But we're grateful it led to complete honesty about everything. We have a kind of intimacy now that we never imagined was possible."

What This Reveals

Michael and Olivia's journey from betrayal to renewal illustrates that while infidelity creates profound trauma, it doesn't have to be the end of the story. Their transformation required not just affair recovery but learning to create genuine intimacy for the first time in their marriage.

Their story raises difficult but important questions: How many relationships end after infidelity not because love is truly dead, but because couples lack access to effective recovery support? What becomes possible when both partners commit to complete honesty and fundamental change rather than just damage control?

Most significantly, if a relationship could not only survive but thrive after compound betrayal and deception, what other relationship challenges might be more surmountable than we imagine?

Bibliography

Ali, A.I. and Wibowo, K. (2011) Online dating services-chronology and key features comparison with traditional dating. *Competition Forum*, 9(2), p. 481.

Allen, M. (2004) *Clinical hypnotherapy*. Crown House Publishing.

Amundsen, R. (1999) *The South Pole: An Account of the Norwegian Antarctic Expedition in the Fram, 1910–1912*. Edinburgh: Berlin.

Anderson, M., Kunkel, A. and Dennis, M.R. (2011) "Let's (not) talk about that": Bridging the past sexual experiences taboo to build healthy romantic relationships. *The Journal of Sex Research*, 48(4), pp. 381–391.

Andreas, S. and Faulkner, C. (1994) *NLP: The new technology of achievement*. William Morrow.

Aravind, K.K. (2002) *Hypnosis for beginners*. Llewellyn Publications.

Bandler, R. and Grinder, J. (1975) *The structure of magic I*. Science and Behavior Books.

Bandler, R. and Grinder, J. (1976) *The structure of magic II*. Science and Behavior Books.

Bandler, R. and Grinder, J. (1979) *Frogs into princes*. Real People Press.

Bandler, R. and Grinder, J. (1982) *Reframing*. Real People Press.

Bateson, G. (1972) *Steps to an ecology of mind*. University of Chicago Press.

Bateson, N. (2023a) *Combining*. Triarchy Press.

Bateson, N. (2023b) *Small arcs of larger circles*. Triarchy Press.

Beasley, C. and Holmes, M. (2021) *Internet dating: Intimacy and social change*. Routledge.

Bergreen, L. (2003) *Over the edge of the world: Magellan's terrifying circumnavigation of the globe*. New York: William Morrow.

Berne, E. (1961) *Transactional analysis in psychotherapy: A systematic individual and social psychiatry*. Souvenir Press.

Berne, E. (1964) *Games people play: The psychology of human relationships*. New York: Grove Press.

Bettelheim, B. (1960) *The informed heart: Autonomy in a Mass Age*. Glencoe, IL: Free Press.

Bierenbaum, H., Nichols, M.P. and Schwartz, A.J. (1976) Effects of varying session length and frequency in brief emotive psychotherapy. *Journal of Consulting and Clinical Psychology*, 44(5), pp. 790–798.

Bourdieu, P. (1977) *Outline of a theory of practice*. Cambridge University Press.

Bowers, M.E. and Yehuda, R. (2016) Intergenerational transmission of stress in humans. *Neuropsychopharmacology*, 41(1), pp. 232–244. doi: 10.1038/npp.2015.247.

Bowlby, J. (1979) The Bowlby-Ainsworth attachment theory. *Behavioral and Brain Sciences*, 2(4), pp. 637–638.

Bray, J.H. and Jouriles, E.N. (1995) Treatment of marital conflict and prevention of divorce. *Journal of Marital and Family Therapy*, 21(4), pp. 461–473.

Brothers, D. (2014) Traumatic attachments: Intergenerational trauma, dissociation, and the analytic relationship. *International Journal of Psychoanalytic Self Psychology*, 9(1), pp. 3–15.

Campbell, J. (1949) *The Hero with a thousand faces*. New York: Pantheon Books.

Carey, T.A. (2011) As you like it: Adopting a patient-led approach to psychological treatments. *Journal of Public Mental Health*, 10(1), pp. 6–16.

Carey, T.A. (2016) Boundaries: A pluralistic perspective and illustrative case study of the patient-led approach to appointment scheduling. In Cooper, M. and Dryden, W. (eds.) *The handbook of pluralistic counselling and psychotherapy*. London: Sage, pp. 288–299.

Centre for Social Justice. (2023) *Fractured families: Why 1 million children have lost meaningful contact with their fathers*. Centre for Social Justice.

Chichester, F. (1967) *Gipsy moth circles the world*. London: Hodder & Stoughton.

Chichester, F. (1975) *The romantic challenge*. London: Cassell.

Cohen, D.B. (2006) Family constellations: An innovative systemic phenomenological group process from Germany. *The Family Journal*, 14(3), pp. 226–233.

Coleridge, S.T. (1798) The rime of the Ancyent Marinere. In Brett, R.L. and Jones, A.R. (eds.) *Lyrical Ballads*. London: Methuen, pp. 9–34.

Cookerly, J.R. (1980) Does marital therapy do any lasting good? *Journal of Marital and Family Therapy*, 6(4), pp. 393–397.

Cooper, J.M. and Hutchinson, D.S. (eds.) (1997) *Plato: Complete works*. Hackett Publishing.

Crowhurst (2016).Tomalin, N. and Hall, R. (2016) *The Strange Last Voyage of Donald Crowhurst*. London: Hodder & Stoughton.

D'Antonio, W.V. (1980) The family and religion: Exploring a changing relationship. *Journal for the Scientific Study of Religion*, 19(2), pp. 89–104.

Danieli, Y., Norris, F.H. and Engdahl, B. (2016) Multigenerational legacies of trauma: Modeling the what and how of transmission. *American Journal of Orthopsychiatry*, 86(6), pp. 639–651.

Darwin, C. (2019) *The voyage of the Beagle: The Illustrated Edition of Charles Darwin's Travel Memoir and Field Journal*. Minneapolis: Voyageur Press.

David, P. and Stafford, L. (2015) A relational approach to religion and spirituality in marriage: The role of couples' religious communication in marital satisfaction. *Journal of Family Issues*, 36(2), pp. 232–249.

Day, A. (2012) *Coaching psychology*. Routledge.

Delbaere, I., Verbiest, S. and Tydén, T. (2020) Knowledge about the impact of age on fertility: A brief review. *Upsala Journal of Medical Sciences*, 125(2), pp. 167–174.

Department for Education. (2023) *Children looked after in England including adoptions: 2023*. Available at: https://explore-education-statistics.service.gov.uk/find-statistics/children-looked-after-in-england-including-adoptions/2023

Dilts, R. (1980) *Neuro-linguistic programming*. Meta Publications.

Dilts, R. (1990) *Changing belief systems with NLP*. Meta Publications.

Doss, B.D., Cicila, L.N., Georgia, E.J., Roddy, M.K., Nowlan, K.M., Benson, L.A. and Christensen, A. (2016) A randomized controlled trial of the web-based OurRelationship program: Effects on relationship and individual functioning. *Journal of Consulting and Clinical Psychology*, 84(4), pp. 285–296.

Dunbar, M. (2016) *Executive coaching*. McGraw-Hill.

Erickson, M.H. (1991) *The collected papers of Milton H. Erickson*. Irvington Publishers.

Farrugia, R.C. (2013) *Facebook and relationships: A study of how social media use is affecting long-term relationships*. Rochester Institute of Technology.
Fernández-Armesto, F. (2007) *Amerigo: The Man Who Gave His Name to America*. New York: Random House.
Fors, M. (2021) Power dynamics in the clinical situation: A confluence of perspectives. *Contemporary Psychoanalysis*, 57(2), pp. 242–269.
Francis, K.C. (1975) *Questions and answers: Two hours with Carl Rogers*. Department of Education Services Brooklyn College.
Mountford, C.P. (2005) One size does not fit all. *Counseling and Psychotherapy Journal*, 16(5), pp. 43–45.
Franke, U. (2003) *The river never looks back*. Carl-Auer-Systeme Verlag.
Freud, S. (2012) *The basic writings of Sigmund Freud*. Modern Library.
Funk, J.L. and Rogge, R.D. (2007) Testing the ruler with item response theory: Increasing precision of measurement for relationship satisfaction with the Couples Satisfaction Index. *Journal of Family Psychology*, 21(4), pp. 572–583.
Gafner, G. (2000) *Handbook of hypnotic inductions*. Norton.
Gallup. (2023) *State of the global workplace: 2023 report*. Gallup Press.
Gottman, J.M. (2008) Gottman method couple therapy. *Clinical Handbook of Couple Therapy*, 4(8), pp. 138–164.
Gottman, J. and Gottman, J. (2008) *Professional training programs*. The Gottman Institute.
Hall, L.M. (2005) *Meta-states*. Crown House Publishing.
Hall, M. (1997) *Time-lining*. Crown House Publishing.
Hammond, D.C. (1990) *Handbook of hypnotic suggestions and metaphors*. Norton.
Hand, M.M., Thomas, D., Buboltz, W.C., Deemer, E.D. and Buyanjargal, M. (2013) Facebook and romantic relationships: Intimacy and couple satisfaction associated with online social network use. *Cyberpsychology, Behavior, and Social Networking*, 16(1), pp. 8–13.
Hellinger, B. (1998) *Love's hidden symmetry*. Zeig, Tucker & Theisen.
Hellinger, B. (2001) *Love's own truths*. Zeig, Tucker & Theisen.
Hellinger, B. (2003) *Peace begins in the soul*. Carl-Auer-Systeme Verlag.
Hetherington, E.M. (1999) Should we stay together for the sake of the children? In E.M. Hetherington (Ed.), *Coping with Divorce, Single Parenting and Remarriage: A Risk and Resiliency Perspective* (pp. 93–116). Lawrence Erlbaum.
Heyerdahl, T. (1950) *The Kon-Tiki Expedition: By Raft Across the South Seas*. London: George Allen & Unwin.
Hodgson, P. (2010) *Symbolic modelling*. Crown House Publishing.
Hough, R. (1994) *Captain James Cook: A Biography*. London: Hodder & Stoughton.
House of Commons Library. (2024) *"Common law marriage" and cohabitation*. Research Briefing.
Hudson, P. (2000) *Clinical hypnosis*. Crown House Publishing.
Huntington, C., Stanley, S.M., Doss, B.D. and Rhoades, G.K. (2022) Happy, healthy, and wedded? How the transition to marriage affects mental and physical health. *Journal of Family Psychology*, 36(4), pp. 608–617.
Ingold, T. (2021) *Being alive: Essays on movement, knowledge and description*. Routledge.
Institute for Family Studies. (2023) *Marriage is disappearing from Britain*. Available at: https://ifstudies.org/blog/marriage-is-disappearing-from-britain
Isobel, S., Goodyear, M., Furness, T. and Foster, K. (2019) Preventing intergenerational trauma transmission: A critical interpretive synthesis. *Journal of Clinical Nursing*, 28(7–8), pp. 1100–1113.
Jacobs, M. (2017) *Psychodynamic counselling in action*. Sage.

Jacobs, S. (1993) John Stuart Mill on the tyranny of the majority. *Australian Journal of Political Science*, 28(2), pp. 306–321.
James, T. (1988) *Time line therapy*. Meta Publications.
James, T. (1989) *The secret of creating your future*. Advanced Neuro Dynamics.
James, T. (2009) *Hypnosis: A comprehensive guide*. Crown House Publishing.
James, T. (2017) *Timeline therapy and the basis of personality*. Crown House Publishing.
Joo, T.M. and Teng, C.E. (2017) Impacts of social media (Facebook) on human communication and relationships: A view on behavioral change and social unity. *International Journal of Knowledge Content Development & Technology*, 7(4), pp. 27–50.
Jung, C.G. (1921) *Psychological types. In: The collected works of C.G. Jung*, Vol. 6. Princeton, NJ: Princeton University Press.
Jung, C.G. (1953–1979) *The collected works of C.G. Jung*. Edited by Read, H., Fordham, M. and Adler, G. Routledge & Kegan Paul.
Kahler, T. (1975) Scripts: Process and content. *Transactional Analysis Journal*, 5(3), pp. 277–279.
Kansky, J. and Diener, E. (2017) Benefits of well-being: Health, social relationships, work, and resilience. *Journal of Positive Psychology and Wellbeing*, 1(2), pp. 129–169.
Kelsey, H. (1998) *Sir Francis Drake: The Queen's Pirate*. New Haven, CT: Yale University Press.
Klein, M. (1975) *The writings of Melanie Klein*. Hogarth Press.
Knapp, M.L. and Vangelisti, A.L. (2005) Stages of coming together and coming apart. In *Interpersonal communication and human relationships*, 5th edn. Boston: Allyn & Bacon, pp. 36–49.
Knox-Johnston, R. (2004) *A World of My Own: The First Ever Non-stop Solo Round the World Voyage*. London: Adlard Coles Nautical.
Kohut, T., Fisher, W.A. and Campbell, L. (2017) Perceived effects of pornography on the couple relationship: Initial findings of open-ended, participant-informed, "bottom-up" research. *Archives of Sexual Behavior*, 46, pp. 585–602.
Lacan, J. (1992) *The Seminar of Jacques Lacan, Book VII: The Ethics of Psychoanalysis 1959–1960*. Edited by J.-A. Miller. Translated by D. Porter. London: Routledge.
Lamidi, E., Manning, W.D. and Brown, S.L. (2019) Change in the stability of first premarital cohabitation among women in the United States, 1983-2013. *Demography*, 56(2), pp. 427–450.
Lawley, J. (2000) *Metaphors in mind*. The Developing Company Press.
Lawley, J. (2017) *Clean space*. The Developing Company Press.
Lev-Wiesel, R. (2007) Intergenerational transmission of trauma across three generations: A preliminary study. *Qualitative Social Work*, 6(1), pp. 75–94.
Levy, J., Goldstein, A. and Feldman, R. (2019) The neural development of empathy is sensitive to caregiving and early trauma. *Nature Communications*, 10(1), article 1905.
Lohan, A., Cao, Y., Petch, J., Murray, J. and Howe, E. (2021) Does relationship counselling for one work? An effectiveness study of routine relationship counselling services where only one individual attends. *Australian and New Zealand Journal of Family Therapy*, 42(3), pp. 320–335.
Machiavelli, N. (1993) *The prince (1513)*. Wordsworth Editions.
Mahoney, A. (2010) Religion in families, 1999-2009: A relational spirituality framework. *Journal of Marriage and Family*, 72, pp. 805–827.
Malan, D. (1979) *Individual psychotherapy and the science of psychodynamics*. Butterworth-Heinemann.
Manning, J.C. (2006) The impact of internet pornography on marriage and the family: A review of the research. *Sexual Addiction & Compulsivity*, 13(2–3), pp. 131–165.

Marriage Foundation. (2019) *Average length of marriage*. Available at: https://marriagefoundation.org.uk/wp-content/uploads/2019/12/MF-note-Average-length-of-marriage.pdf
Marx, K. (1959) *Economic and Philosophic Manuscripts of 1844*. Moscow: Progress Publishers.
Marx, K. (1867) *Das Kapital: Kritik der politischen Ökonomie* [Capital: A critique of political economy], Volume 1. Otto Meissner.
May, J. (2013) *Clean language*. Clean Publishing.
Metz, M.E. and McCarthy, B.W. (2007) The "Good-Enough Sex" model for couple sexual satisfaction. *Sexual and Relationship Therapy*, 22(3), pp. 351–362.
Ministry of Justice. (2022) *Youth justice statistics: 2021 to 2022*. Ministry of Justice.
Moitessier, B. (2019) *The Long Way*. Translated by W. Rodarmor. Dobbs Ferry: Sheridan House.
Montemurro, B., Bartasavich, J. and Wintermute, L. (2015) Let's (not) talk about sex: The gender of sexual discourse. *Sexuality & Culture*, 19, pp. 139–156.
Morison, S.E. (1942) *Admiral of the Ocean Sea: A Life of Christopher Columbus*. Boston: Little, Brown and Company.
Newstrom, N.P. and Harris, S.M. (2016) Pornography and couples: What does the research tell us? *Contemporary Family Therapy*, 38, pp. 412–423.
NHS. (2023) *Infertility*. Available at: https://www.nhs.uk/conditions/infertility/
NHS Digital. (2023) *Mental health of children and young people in England 2023*. NHS Digital.
Nicolescu, B. (2016) *The hidden third*. Quantum Prose.
O'Connor, J. (1990) *Introducing NLP*. Thorsons.
O'Connor, J. (2000) *NLP workbook*. Thorsons.
O'Connor, J. (2001) *The NLP coach*. Piatkus.
Ofcom. (2023) *Children's media lives: Year 9 findings*. Ofcom.
Olson, J.R., Marshall, J.P., Goddard, H.W. and Schramm, D.G. (2015) Shared religious beliefs, prayer, and forgiveness as predictors of marital satisfaction. *Family Relations*, 64, pp. 519–533.
ONS. (2013) *Marriage and cohabitation* (General Lifestyle Survey Overview - A report on the 2011 General Lifestyle Survey). Office for National Statistics.
ONS. (2022) *Loneliness - What characteristics and circumstances are associated with feeling lonely?* Office for National Statistics.
ONS. (2023a) *Families and households in the UK: 2023*. Office for National Statistics.
ONS. (2023b) *Marriage and civil partnership status in England and Wales: Census 2021*. Office for National Statistics.
ONS. (2024a) *Divorces in England and Wales: 2022*. Office for National Statistics.
ONS. (2024b) *Marriages in England and Wales: 2021 and 2022*. Office for National Statistics.
Owen, N. (2004) *More magic of metaphor*. Crown House Publishing.
Passmore, J. (2010) *Excellence in coaching*. Kogan Page.
Payne, J. (2005) *The healing of individuals, families and nations*. Findhorn Press.
Perelli-Harris, B., Hoherz, S., Lappegård, T. and Evans, A. (2019) Mind the "happiness" gap: The relationship between cohabitation, marriage, and subjective well-being in the United Kingdom, Australia, Germany, and Norway. *Demography*, 56(4), pp. 1219–1246.
Perls, F., Hefferline, R. and Goodman, P. (1951) *Gestalt therapy: Excitement and growth in the human personality*. Julian Press.
Perls, M., Goodman, P. and Hefferline, R. (1994) *Gestalt therapy*. Souvenir Press Ltd.

Peterson, C. and Seligman, M.E. (2004) *Character strengths and virtues: A handbook and classification.* Oxford University Press.

Petch, J., Lee, J., Huntingdon, B. and Murray, J. (2014) Couple counselling outcomes in an Australian not for profit: Evidence for the effectiveness of couple counselling conducted within routine practice. *Australian and New Zealand Journal of Family Therapy*, 35, pp. 445–461.

Pew Research Center. (2019) *Key findings on marriage and cohabitation in the U.S.*

Pietromonaco, P.R. and Collins, N.L. (2017) Interpersonal mechanisms linking close relationships to health. *American Psychologist*, 72(6), pp. 531–542.

Pigafetta, A. (1969) *Magellan's Voyage: A Narrative Account of the First Circumnavigation.* Translated and edited by R.A. Skelton. New Haven: Yale University Press.

Procentese, F., Gatti, F. and Di Napoli, I. (2019) Families and social media use: The role of parents' perceptions about social media impact on family systems in the relationship between family collective efficacy and open communication. *International Journal of Environmental Research and Public Health*, 16, p. 5006.

Prochaska, J.O. and Norcross, J.C. (2001) Stages of change. *Psychotherapy: Theory, Research, Practice, Training*, 38(4), p. 443.

Public Health England. (2023) *Health behaviours in school-aged children: England national report.* Public Health England.

Rees, J. (2008) *Clean language.* Crown House Publishing.

Rivera, J.L. (1992) The stages of psychotherapy. *European Journal of Psychiatry*, 6(1), pp. 51–58.

Rogers, C.R. (1951) *Client-centered therapy: Its current practice, implications, and theory.* Houghton Mifflin.

Rogers, C.R. (1961) *On becoming a person: A therapist's view of psychotherapy.* Houghton Mifflin.

Roller, B. and Nelson, M. (1991) *The art of co-therapy - How therapists work together.* Guildford Press.

Rose, A. (1968) *My Lively Lady.* London: Nautical Publishing Company.

Rust, J., Bennun, I., Crowe, M. and Golombok, S. (2010) The Golombok Rust Inventory of Marital State (GRIMS). *Sexual and Relationship Therapy*, 25(1), pp. 48–53.

Sandbakken, E.M., Skrautvol, A. and Madsen, O.J. (2022) 'It's my definition of a relationship, even though it doesn't fit yours': Living in polyamorous relationships in a mononormative culture. *Psychology & Sexuality*, 13(4), pp. 1054–1067.

Satir, V. (1988) *The new peoplemaking.* Science and Behavior Books.

Schofield, M.J., Mumford, N., Jurkovic, D., Jurkovic, I. and Bickerdike, A. (2012) Short and long-term effectiveness of couple counselling: A study protocol. *BMC Public Health*, 12(1), p. 735.

Scott, R.F. (1913) *Scott's Last Expedition: The Journals.* London: Smith, Elder & Co

Scott, R.F. (2005) *Journals: Captain Scott's Last Expedition.* Edited by M. Jones. Oxford: Oxford University Press.

Scott, S. (2004) *Fierce conversations.* Berkley Books.

Seligman, M.E.P. and Peterson, C. (2004) *Character strengths and virtues.* Oxford University Press.

Senge, P.M. (1990) *The fifth discipline: The art and practice of the learning organization.* Doubleday.

Seymour, J. (1990) *Introducing NLP.* Thorsons.

Shackleton, E.H. (1998) *South: A Memoir of the Endurance Voyage.* New York: Carroll & Graf.

Shackleton, E. (2015) *South: The Endurance Expedition*. London: Penguin Classics
Skellern, S.K., Sanri, C., Iqbal, S., Ayub, N., Jarukasemthawee, S., Pisitsungkagarn, K. and Halford, W.K. (2022) Assessment of the perceived importance of religion in couple relationships in Christians, Muslims, Buddhists, and the Nonreligious. *Family Process*, 61, pp. 326–341.
Slochower, J.A. (2013) *Holding and psychoanalysis: A relational perspective*. Routledge.
Slocum, J. (1978) *Sailing Alone Around the World and Voyage of the Liberdade*. London: Rupert Hart-Davis
Spanier, G.B. (1989) *Dyadic adjustment scale*. Toronto: Multi-Health Systems.
Starr, S. (1993) Heart and soul and communication: An interview with Virginia Satir-Part III. *Journal of Couples Therapy*, 3(1), pp. 1–8.
Stewart, I. (2012) *Transactional analysis counselling in action*. Sage.
Subrahmanyam, S. (1997) *The Career and Legend of Vasco da Gama*. Cambridge: Cambridge University Press
Sullivan, W. (2008) *Symbolic modelling*. Crown House Publishing.
Turner, P.R., Valtierra, M., Talken, T.R., Miller, V.I. and DeAnda, J.R. (1996) Effect of session length on treatment outcome for college students in brief therapy. *Journal of Counseling Psychology*, 43(2), pp. 228–232.
UK Government. (2023) *Children looked after in England including adoptions*. Available at: https://explore-education-statistics.service.gov.uk/find-statistics/children-looked-after-in-england-including-adoptions/2023
Uswitch. (2022) *Gen Z communication preferences: Digital natives survey*. Uswitch.
Wallerstein, J.S. and Lewis, J.M. (2004) The unexpected legacy of divorce: Report of a 25-year study. *Psychoanalytic Psychology*, 21(3), pp. 353–370.
Whitfield, C.L. (1991) *Co-dependence: Healing the human condition*. Health Communications.
Whitmore, J. (2017) *Coaching for performance*. Nicholas Brealey.
Whittington, A. (2016) *Systemic family constellations*. Karnac Books.
Wilcox, W.B., Dew, J. and ElHage, A. (2019) *Cohabitation doesn't compare: Marriage, cohabitation, and relationship quality*. Institute for Family Studies.
Will, H. (2018) The concept of the 50-minute hour. Time forming a frame for the unconscious. *International Forum of Psychoanalysis*, 27(1), pp. 1–10.
Wilkie, N. (1994) *The adoption process in the UK*. MBA Thesis. Cranfield University.
Wilkie, G. S. (2025) *Responsiveness in the Evolving Landscape of Work: An Edgewalker's Tale*. Doctoral Thesis, Middlesex University.
Wolfinger, N.H. and Wilcox, W.B. (2008) Happily ever after? Religion, marital status, gender and relationship quality in urban families. *Social Forces*, 86(3), pp. 1311–1337.
Whyte, D. (2009) *The Three Marriages: Reimagining Work, Self and Relationship*. New York: Riverhead Books.
Yacoub, C., Spoede, J., Cutting, R. and Hawley, D. (2018) The impact of social media on romantic relationships. *Journal of Education and Social Development*, 2(2), pp. 53–58.
Yapko, M.D. (2012) *Trancework: An introduction to the practice of clinical hypnosis*. Routledge.
Yehuda, R. and Lehrner, A. (2018) Intergenerational transmission of trauma effects: Putative role of epigenetic mechanisms. *World Psychiatry*, 17(3), pp. 243–25.
Yoo, H., Bartle-Haring, S., Day, R.D. and Gangamma, R. (2014) Couple communication, emotional and sexual intimacy, and relationship satisfaction. *Journal of Sex & Marital Therapy*, 40(4), pp. 275–293.
Young-Bruehl, E. (1996) *The anatomy of prejudices*. Harvard University Press.

Index

Note: **Bold** page numbers refer to tables.

Allen, M. 87
Amundsen, Roald 95
Andreas, S. 87
Aravind, K.K. 87
artificial intelligence (AI): current applications 59; fundamental limitations 60; promise 59
attachment theory 27, 100, 139, 162, 163

Bandler, R. 87
Bateson, G. 67
Bateson, N. 13, 21, 93, 94, 99, 101
Berne, E. 33, 34, 87
betrayal: financial 130; impact of social media 18; intimacy after 5; Michael and Olivia (case study) 8, 199–203; physical or emotional affair 84; trust 90, 127
Bettelheim, B. 100
bids for connection 98, 126
Bourdieu, P. 53
Bowlby, J. 86, 87, 100

Campbell, J. 95
Carey, T.A. 50, 150
Carrie and Keith (case study): civilised coexistence 196; "good enough" relationships 199; grief and disconnection 197; long-term relationships 5, 8, 199; portrait of successful marriage 196–197; return of desire 197–198; ripple effects 198–199; skills 198; transformation 197–199
Cathy 79, 83
Chichester, F. 95
classical psychoanalysis: archaeological deep-sea divers of therapy 28; excavation challenge 29; excel at 28–29; foundational discovery 28; geological surveys 29; individual focus 28, 160; lasting relationship transformation 30; in practice 29; for relationship work 30; structural limitations 29; unconscious patterns 69
client responsibility: commitment 114; investment and clarity 114; openness and perspective-taking 114, 117; physical presence 112
coaches, guidance for 7, 132, 133, 176–177, 187; advantages 136–137; artificial divide 136; balance attention and alliance 139; boundaries and building network 138; clear contracts 139; courage to explore 142–143; ethical dimension 139–140; experiments 138; interaction patterns 139; Mark and Joanna's (case example) 140–142; pattern recognition 137; relationship systems thinking 138; session 139; traditional coaching 135–136; working with couples 138–139; work with person 137
co-creation 189
cognitive behavioural therapy (CBT): destructive thought patterns **120**, 163; elements 163; engine room vs. navigation bridge 39; evidence base 39, **120**; individual cognitive patterns 146; marine engineers 38; in practice 40; practitioners 38–39; for relationship work 40–41, **120**; relief from destructive patterns 39; session 38; symptom vs. source dilemma 39; systematic approach 38; thoughts and behaviours 40; tools

for relationship repair 40, 70, 145; unexplored 39
Cohen, D.B. 87
Columbus, Christopher 95
commitment (as paradigm element) 7, 12, 13, 16, 92, 125, 126, 128, 129, 131
communication (as paradigm element) 7, 12, 13, 16, 92, 125, 128–131
connection (as paradigm element) 7, 12, 13, 16, 92, 125–126, 128, 129, 131
constellation work 84, 118, 173
conversational styles 98
Cook, Captain James 95
co-therapy/co-therapist: anticipation and discovery 171; benefits 47; challenge 172; with colleagues 123; eight years of transformation 172–173; extended sessions 173; future of work 174; gender balance and preventing triangulation 80, 118, **121**, 151; guidance for coaches, counsellors, and psychoanalysts 176–177; key factors 47; message to future 175; message to readers 175; multiple modalities 173; Neil's perspective 175–176; own practice 174; partnership 48, 118, 151–152; practitioner's perspective on transformation 171; principles and practices 8; problems and vulnerability 47–48; in relationships 48; shared navigation 175–176; six sessions and 24/7 support 173–174; two therapists 172; value of 151–152
counsellors, guidance for 7, 132, 133, 176–177, 187; avoiding triangulation 151; Claire's discovery 153–155; competence boundaries 150; comprehensive assessment process 152–153; coordinated navigation 144; co-therapy, value of 151–152; courage to integrate 156; cultural and value considerations 151; Duo Coaching framework 151–153; ethical considerations 150–151; from individual to systemic perspective 146; integrative practice 145–146; managing multiple relationships 151; 50-minute sessions 149–150; from neutral to strategic balance 148–149; outcome focus 150; from past/present to multi-temporal perspective 147; pattern recognition, value of 152; power of "Me," "You," and "Us" framework 152; practical support between sessions 152; self-care and support 151; single-modality approaches 145; from single-tool to multi-method approach 148; from verbal to multi-channel communication 147; working with relationship issues 149
Crowhurst, Donald 95

Darwin, Charles 95
Day, A. 87
destination 3, 9, 10, 35, 43, 46, 72, 78, 81, 88, 143, 148, 150
Dilts, R. 87
diversity and universality 92–93
Drake, Francis, Sir 95
Dunbar, M. 87
Duo Coaching framework: 24/7 between-session support 5, 11, 121, **121**, 173–174; comparison 121–122; co-therapy partnership 48, 118, 151–152; creation of 6, 77–89; evolution of practice 122–123; extended sessions (3.5-hour initial/2.5-hour follow-up) 5, 11, 83, 118, **121**, 132, 173; finite timeline (typically six sessions) 5, 11, 83, 118, **121**, 132; integrative approach 5, 11, 83–84, 118, **121**, 145–146; "Me, You, Us" focus 5, 11, 121, **121**, 192; outcome focus 44, 84, 117, **120**, **121**, 150, 169; for relationship therapy 7, 60–62, 112–123; trilogy 10–11; two therapists 5, 11, 83, **121**

eclectic therapy: adaptive precision 44; artificial constraints 45–46; challenges 45; eclecticism 45; freedom from theoretical constraints 44–45; key distinction 44; outcome-focused **120**; philosophy 43–44; pragmatic captains 43; pure responsiveness 44; for relationship work 46
effective relationship therapy: client responsibility 112, 114–117; essential conditions for 112, **113–114**; essential elements of 112; therapist responsibility 117
Emma and James (case example) 118
emotionally focused therapy (EFT) 27, 163
Erickson, M.H. 87
extended sessions (3.5-hour initial/2.5-hour follow-up) 5, 11, 83, 118, **121**, 132, 173

Faulkner, C. 87
finite timeline (typically six sessions) 5, 11, 83, 118, **121**, 132
Franke, U. 87
Freud, S. 24, 26, 28, 49, 52, 86
fun (as paradigm element) 7, 12, 13, 16, 92, 125–129, 131

Gafner, G. 87
Gama, Vasco da 95
gender dynamics 53, 65, 85, 167
Gestalt therapy: awareness of contact 36; challenge 36; enhanced relationship work 37–38; lasting relationship transformation 37; in practice 37; practitioners 36; present-moment navigators 35; relationship satisfaction or distress 36; revolutionary insight 35–36
ghosts from the past 97–98
ghost ship (metaphor) 4–5, 97–98
Gottman, J.M. 98, 125
Gottman, John 79
Gottman, Julie 79
Grinder, J. 87
growth (as paradigm element) 7, 12, 13, 17, 92, 125, 127, 128, 131
guidance for extending practice: for coaches 7, 132, 133, 135–143, 176–177, 187; for counsellors 7, 132, 133, 144–156, 176–177, 187; for psychoanalysts 7, 132, 133, 157–170, 176–177, 187

Hall, L. 87
Hall, M. 87
Hammond, D.C. 87
Hellinger, B. 87
Hero's journey 95–96
Heyerdahl, T. 95
Hodgson, P. 87
Hudson, Maria 7, 83, 86, 92, 96–98, 107–111, 133, 170, 171, 175–177
Hudson, P. 87

Ingold, T. 13, 66, 68
inspiration 79, 87–89
integrative approach/integration 5, 11, 83–84, 118, **121**, 145–146
integrative therapy: adaptive flexibility 42; art 42; challenge 42; master mariners 41, 43; philosophy 41; principled integration *vs.* random eclecticism 42–43; for relationship work 43, **120**; session 41; whole-person healing 41
inter-generational trauma 99–100

Jacobs, M. 86
James, T. 87
John and Sarah (case study): conflicts 193, 195; crisis management 195; individual growth 194–195; invisible erosion 192–193; partnership 196; passionate lovers 8, 196; rediscovering intimacy 193–194; relationship as co-management 8, 192; ripple effects 195; transformation 193, 194
Johnson, Sue 163
Jung, C.G. 24

Kahler, T. 87
Klein, M. 86
Knox-Johnston, Robin, Sir 95

Lacan, J. 49, 102
Lawley, J. 87
lighthouse effect 181–182
liminal space **113**, 117, **121**, 176
loneliness pandemic 182
long-term relationships: Carrie and Keith (case study) 5, 8, 196–199; conjoint therapy 60

Machiavelli, N. 53
Magellan, Ferdinand 95
Malan, D. 86
Mark and Joanna (case example) 140–142
Marx, K. 53, 100
May, J. 87
"Me, You, Us" framework 5, 11, 121, **121**, 192
Michael and Olivia (case study): challenges 202, 203; courage required 203; decision point 200–201; double betrayal 200; emotional disconnection 201; individual growth 202; moment of truth 200; new marriage 201–202; rebuilding after betrayal 8, 199–200; reconstruction 201; renewal 203; ripple effects 202–203
Michael and Rebecca (case example) 118
Michael and Sarah (case example) 167–168
Mill, J. S. 53
Moitessier, B. 95

navigators 9, 35–38, 111, 124–125
Nelson, M. 47
Neuro Linguistic Programming (NLP) 82, 87, 148
newly appointed experts 81
Nicolescu, B. 67

object relations approaches 27
O'Connor, J. 87
organic evolution 83–84
outcome focus/outcome-focused therapy 44, 84, 117, **120**, **121**, 150, 169
Owen, N. 87

parental relationships 99
partnership approaches: co-therapy 48, 118, 151–152; John and Sarah (case study) 196; online programs 58; professional therapy 58; reading books together 58; relationship therapy 58–59; structural challenges 59; therapeutic framework 59; traditional couples therapy 58
Passmore, J. 87
pattern recognition 28, 31, 32, 34, 45, 46, 67, 69, 71, 117, 137, 152
Payne, J. 87
Perls, F. 35, 87
person-centred counselling: authenticity 24; empathy and acceptance 25, 68, 73, 82, **119**, 145, 146, 173; non-directive listening 25; reality with couples 25; for relationship work 25–26; for self-discovery 25, **119**; therapeutic space 153, 155; unconditional positive regard 24
phenomenology of relationships 10
practical transdisciplinarity 65–66
practitioners, challenge to 188
Prochaska Model of Change 56
psychoanalysts, guidance for 7, 132, 133, 157–170, 176–177, 187; accessibility between sessions 169–170; active structuring 165; with ancient maps 157–158; attachment theory 162; balancing depth 166–167; between-session work, integration of 166; bringing deep-sea discoveries to shared waters 157; cognitive-behavioural techniques 163; confidentiality and secrets 166; conscious use of self 165; countertransference complexities 166; depth and pragmatism, integration of 170; developmental perspective 158–159; Duo Coaching framework 169–170; emotionally focused therapy (EFT) 163; emphasis on past over present 161; ethical considerations 166–167; extended timeframe 162; individual focus 160, 169; in integrative couple work (case example) 167–168; mindfulness-based approaches 163; multiple approaches, integration of 169; multiple relationships 166; neutral stance 160–161; outcome focus 169; physical setting 165; power dynamics 167; primarily verbal process 161–162; projective processes 164; relationship focus 169; to relationship understanding 158; session length and frequency 165; shared defensive structures 164; symbolic processes 159; systems theory 162–163; time structure 169; tracking parallel processes 163–164; transference and countertransference 159–160; transference in multiple dimensions 164; unconscious dimension 158; unconscious in couple therapy 163–164; using dreams and fantasies 164
psychodynamic couple therapy 27
psychodynamic therapy **119**; challenge 27; counselling 86–87, 144, 146, 148; evolution 27; family-of-origin patterns 64; individual journey 27, 68–69; past experiences 59, 147; in practice 27; present-moment intervention 72; relational excavation 68–69; to relationship work 26–28; sessions 26; unconscious patterns in childhood 26, 145
psychotherapy: CBT 38–41; classical psychoanalysis 28–30; co-therapy 46–48; eclectic therapy 43–46; exploration of delivery 46; family therapy 48–49; Gestalt therapy 35–38; group therapy 46; historical foundation 24; integrative therapy 41–43; person-centred counselling 24–26; psychodynamic therapy 26–28; systemic counselling 30–32; therapeutic relationship 51–53; therapeutic session 49–51; transactional analysis 33–35; types of 23

Rees, J. 87
reflection 8, 17, 68, 73, 87–89, 98, 103, 111, 132, 153, 154, 191, 201
relationship education 179, 184, 188–189, 191; reimagining 188–189

relationship paradigm (six-element assessment framework): commitment (as paradigm element) 7, 12, 13, 16, 92, 125, 126, 128, 129, 131; communication (as paradigm element) 7, 12, 13, 16, 92, 125, 128–131; connection (as paradigm element) 7, 12, 13, 16, 92, 125–126, 128, 129, 131; fun (as paradigm element) 7, 12, 13, 16, 92, 125–129, 131; growth (as paradigm element) 7, 12, 13, 17, 92, 125, 127, 128, 131; trust (as paradigm element) 7, 12, 13, 17, 92, 125, 127–131
relationships: challenges 18–19; context and structure of 17; counselling 77–78; failure of 20–21; future of 22; life cycle of 19; love 21–22; need for 16; normal 16–17; problem 84–86; purpose of 15–16; and religion 17; satisfaction and wellbeing 19–20; symmathesy 21
relationships, importance of: good relationships 182–183; implementation strategy 183–184; lighthouse effect 181–182; mission 184–185; practitioner's role 184; societal crisis 182; systemic approach to transformation 183
relationship therapy: from both partners 61; forms of 61; limited research 60; measurement challenge 61; partnership approaches 58–59; pragmatic perspective 61; from the process 62; relationship help for couples 55–56; research challenge 60; solo journey options 56–58; from therapists 62
revolutionary framework 79–80
Rogers, C.R. 24, 25, 49, 87
Roller, B. 47
Rose, A. 95

sailing (case study) 8
sailing metaphor(s) 3–4, 10
Sarah and James (case study) 63–64
Satir, V. 48, 87
schooling 100–101
Scott, R.F. 95
Scott, S. 87
Seligman, M.E. 87
sexuality 188
Seymour, J. 87
Shackleton, Ernest, Sir 95
Slochower, J.A. 53
Slocum, J. 95

societal importance of relationships: inter-generational trauma 99–100; lighthouse effect 181–182; loneliness pandemic 182; relationship education 179, 184, 188–189, 191
solo journey options: change process reality 57; in childhood experiences and previous relationships 56–57; fundamental challenge 57; individual self-help 57, 58; Prochaska Model of Change 56; for relationship issues 58
spirals, positive and negative 128
Stewart, I. 87
Sullivan, W. 87
systemic counselling: changing patterns 32, **119**; individual depth work 32; power 31; in practice 32; practitioners 31; reading currents between people 30–31, **119**; for relationship work 32; revolutionary insight 31

therapeutic modalities: CBT 38–41; classical psychoanalysts 28–30; Clean Language 82; clinical hypnotherapy 82; coaching 82; constellations 82; eclectic therapy 43–54; emotionally focused therapy (EFT) 27; gestalt therapy 35–38; integrative therapy 41–43; person-centred counselling 24–26, 82; psychodynamic therapy 26–28, 82; systemic counselling 30–32; transactional analysis 33–35
therapeutic relationship: bureaucratic power 52; conscious and subconscious levels 51; countertransference 159–160; family-of-origin triangles 151; managing multiple relationships 166; professional power 51; relevance of power 51; socio-political power 52; stages of 51–52; therapist's role 117; transferential power 51–52, 159–160, 168
therapist responsibility 117
together loneliness 126
transactional analysis (TA): ego states transactions 33–35, 69–70, **77**; games 34, **120**; moment-to-moment transaction 34–35; navigation challenge 34; pattern recognition 34; players in conversation 33; of relationship dynamics 33, 35; for relationship work 35; revelation 33
transcontextuality 94
transdisciplinarity 6, 13, 136, 145; CBT practitioners 70; classical

psychoanalysts 69; eclectic therapists 71; Gestalt therapists 70; "the Hidden Third," 67; innovation 72–73; integration challenge 66; integration imperative 67; integrative therapists 71; minor key of relationships 66; missing dimensions 64; multiple ways of knowing 65, 66, 68; pattern recognition 67; person-centred counsellors 68; practical transdisciplinarity 65–66; practitioner's journey 67–68; from problem-focused to pattern-focused 65; psychodynamic therapists 68–69; recognition 64–65; Sarah and James (case study) 63–64; from single-focus to multiple-focus 65; steps towards 72; systemic counsellors 69; transactional analysis practitioners 69–70; transdisciplinary shift 71–72; understanding 72; wayfaring therapist 68

transformative space: art of rhythm 103; awareness, conscious/unconscious 105–106; childlessness 102; children 101–102; competence, conscious/unconscious 106; conversation 98, 103–104; deception dilemma 90; diversity and universality 92–93; embarrassment 92; emotional departure 91; emotional overhang 110–111; face to face and online 104; future goals 103; ghost ship (metaphor) 97–98; hard work, relationships 93–94; Hero's journey 95–96; integration challenge 108–109; intergenerational trauma 99–100; invisible work 109–110; lacking 102–103; male and female client 96–97; morals and ethics 105; multidimensional field of awareness 107; observing language patterns 107–108; parental relationships 99; post-session decompression 111; previous relationships 101; psychotherapeutic approaches 104–105; and reflection 103–104; schooling 100–101; secondary gain of staying stuck 91–92; sex 99; shadows of the past 99; upbringing 100; values 102; warm data 13, 60, 86, 94, 104, 110, 111, 147

triangulation 5, 11, 48, 80, 118, 151
trust (as paradigm element) 7, 12, 13, 17, 92, 125, 127–131
Turner, P.R. 50
24/7 between-session support 5, 11, 121, **121**, 173–174

upbringing 64, 80, 85, 100

values: commitment 131; exploration of 102; interventions 42; psychoanalysis 163; relationship desires 137, 151, 188; shared 17, 183
Vespucci, Amerigo 95

warm data 13, 60, 86, 94, 104, 110, 111, 147
Whitfield, C.L. 87
Whitmore, J. 87
Whyte, D. 93, 95
Wilkie, Neil 3, 5, 9, 10, 12, 13, 20–22, 24, 25, 44, 48–51, 54, 56, 57, 64, 72, 77–79, 81, 83, 85–88, 90–92, 94–97, 99, 100, 102, 105–112, 120, 122–123, 125–129, 142, 143, 145, 170–176, 184, 189, 190
Will, H. 49

Yapko, M.D. 87
Young-Bruehl, E. 52

For Product Safety Concerns and Information please contact our EU
representative GPSR@taylorandfrancis.com
Taylor & Francis Verlag GmbH, Kaufingerstraße 24, 80331 München, Germany

www.ingramcontent.com/pod-product-compliance
Ingram Content Group UK Ltd.
Pitfield, Milton Keynes, MK11 3LW, UK
UKHW021925220426
470282UK00019B/571